Charles Seale-Hayne Library
University of Plymouth
(01752) 588 588
LibraryandITenquiries@plymouth.ac.uk

Reforming French Protestantism

Habent sua fata libelli

REFORMING FRENCH

The Development of Huguenot Ecclesiastical Institutions, 1557–1572

PROTESTANTISM

GLENN S. SUNSHINE

SIXTEENTH CENTURY ESSAYS & STUDIES
VOLUME 66

TRUMAN STATE UNIVERSITY
PRESS

Cover art: Genève, Bibliothèque publique et universitaire, Collections iconographiques

Cover design by Teresa Wheeler
Printed by Sheridan Books, Ann Arbor, Michigan, USA
Text set in Adobe Minion 10/13, display in Adobe Minion and P22 Morris-Troy

LIBRARY OF CONGRESS CATALOGING-IN-PUBLICATION DATA

Sunshine, Glenn S., 1958–
    Reforming French protestantism : the development of Huguenot
ecclesiastical institutions, 1557–1572 / Glenn S. Sunshine.
    p. cm. — (Sixteenth century essays & studies ; v. 66)
Includes bibliographical references and index.
    ISBN 1-931112-28-2 (casebound : alk. paper)
    1. Eglises réformées de France—Government—History—16th century.
2. France—Church history—16th century. I. Title. II. Series.
    BX9454.3 .S86 2003
    284'.5'09031—dc21   2003001141

This book is lovingly dedicated to my wife, Lynn,
whose worth is more than rubies.

Contents

Abbreviations

ANS	Acts of the National Synods, taken from MSS, are designated by synod number, location, and year. E.g., ANS, 1–Paris–1559.
Auzière	Provincial synods, *classes*, and colloquies of Bas Languedoc. Société de l'Histoire du Protestantisme français MS 566, vol. 1 (Auzière collection 68).
Articles polytiques	MS located in the Bibliothèque Publique de Grenoble; published in *Documents protestants inédits du XVIe siècle* (1872), and *Bulletin d'information de l'Eglise Réformée de France* 18 (October 1956): 2–4. All references are to the 1872 edition.
Aymon	*Tous les synodes nationaux des Eglises Reformées de France* (1710). Page numbers refer to vol. 1, second pagination.
BN	Bibliothèque Nationale de France, Paris.
BSHPF	*Bulletin de la Société de l'Histoire du Protestantisme français*
CO	*Ioannis Calvini Opera Quae Supersunt Omnia*. Edited by G. Baum, Ed. Cunitz and E. Reuss. Brunswick: Schwetzke & Sons, 1863–1900.
DE	*Discipline ecclésiastique*, followed by date of issue.
Geneva BPU	Bibliothèque Publique et Universitaire, Geneva.
Histoire ecclésiastique	*Histoire ecclésiastique des Eglises Réformées au royaume de France*. Edited by G. Baum and Ed. Cunitz. Les Classiques du Protestantisme français XVIe, XVIIe et XVIIIe siècles, 2 vols. Paris: Fischbacher, 1883.
Le Mans	"Papier et registre du Consistoire de l'eglise du Mans," in *Recueil de pièces inédites pour servir à l'histoire de la Réforme et de la Ligue dans le Maine*. Le Mans: Monnoyer, 1867.

Abbreviations

OS	*Joannis Calvini Opera Selecta.* 5 vols. Edited by Petrus Barth and Guilelmus Niesel. Munich: Chr. Kaiser, 1928–36.
Pithou	Nicholas Pithou, *L'Histoire ecclésiastique de l'Eglise réformée de la ville de Troyes,* taken from Bibliothèque de la Société de l'Histoire du Protestantisme français, Paris, MS 440.
Quick	*Synodicon in Gallia reformata* (1692). References include synod number, location, and date. Page numbers refer to vol. 1, second pagination.
Rb	Bodleian Library, Oxford, Rawlinson MS D638; second series of acts of the national synods.
RCP	*Registres de la Compagnie des Pasteurs de Genève au temps de Calvin.* Vol. 1: 1546–1553. Edited by R. M. Kingdon and J.-F. Bergier. Geneva: Droz, 1964.
Roussel, "Discipline"	Text of DE 1559 reconstructed by Bernard Roussel in "La *Discipline* des Eglises réformées de France en 1559: Un royaume sans clergé?" in *De l'Humanisme aux Lumières, Bayle et le protestantisme* (1996).
RSV	Revised Standard Version of the Bible.
Wa	Bibliothèque Wallonne, The Hague, MS 2324; first copy of DE 1559.
Wb	Bibliothèque Wallonne, The Hague, MS 2324; second copy of DE 1559.

The National Synods

1. Paris   1559
2. Poitiers   1561
3. Orléans   1562
4. Lyon   1563
5. Paris   1565
6. Vertueil   1567
7. La Rochelle   1571
8. Nîmes   1572
9. St. Foy   1578
10. Figeac   1579
11. La Rochelle   1581
12. Vitré   1583
13. Montauban   1594
14. Saumur   1596
15. Montpellier   1598
16. Gergeau   1601
17. Gap   1603
18. La Rochelle   1607
19. St. Maixant   1609
20. Privas   1612
21. Tonneins   1614
22. Vitré   1617
23. Alais   1620
24. Charenton   1623
25. Castres   1626
26. Charenton   1631
27. Alençon   1637
28. Charenton   1645
29. Loudun   1660

Acknowledgments

As I look back at the long process of producing this book from the initial research for my doctoral dissertation through revising and editing the manuscript, I am struck by just how very many people and institutions gave me help, support, and encouragement along the way. Though I cannot possibly thank each individual who contributed to the book, it would be the ultimate in ingratitude if I did not acknowledge the contributions of a number of those who made this work possible.

Pride of place must go to Robert M. Kingdon, doctoral advisor extraordinaire, who shaped my scholarship in ways great and small. From his nearly legendary seminars, to tutorials in paleography, to obtaining project assistantships for me so I could pay the bills, to ongoing support and encouragement after graduation, Professor Kingdon has been a tremendous inspiration and a real friend to me for the past eighteen years.

My initial research in Paris was made possible by a Fulbright-Hays grant, which enabled me to spend a year there collecting sources and doing basic research. While in Paris, I participated in a very valuable orientation program sponsored by Columbia University's Graduate Research Institute at Reid Hall. The staff at Reid Hall and the Franco-American Commission for Educational Exchange also helped me to understand and work through the French bureaucratic system, a rather intimidating prospect for an American. My thanks to all in both programs.

The Graduate School of the University of Wisconsin provided me with an Alumni Research Grant, which enabled me to work on my dissertation full-time. I was also assisted at this time by the wonderful staff of the University of Wisconsin–Madison Memorial Library Rare Book Room. Upon completion of my degree, I taught for two years at Calvin College and enjoyed a great deal of support from my colleagues in the history department, especially Doug Howard and his family, and from Richard Muller in the seminary. The staff at the H. Henry Meeter Center for Calvin Studies and the Hekman Library, especially Paul Field, have been remarkably helpful on more occasions than I can mention before, during, and after my stint at Calvin.

I have since received considerable support from Central Connecticut State University, which has enabled me to return to France twice for additional research, courtesy of a number of CSU–AAUP Research Grants and additional funding provided by Karen Beyard, then vice president of academic affairs. My colleagues in the history department have without exception given me their support and encouragement in the midst of the struggle to complete the book while teaching a full course load. Heather Prescott—who put up with me while we shared an office for my first few years at Central—Jay Bergman, and Norton Mezvinski have been particularly supportive of my work.

In Europe, I benefited from the assistance of a number of individuals. The staff at the Bibliothèque de la Société de l'Histoire du Protestantisme français have been very helpful on many occasions over the last decade. Olivier Fatio and his family extended their hospitality to my family so I could pursue research in Geneva. Michel Reulos was extraordinarily generous with his time and insights into the development of the Discipline. Above all else, however, I must here acknowledge my profound debt to Bernard Roussel. Not only did he and his wife make my family welcome in France, not only did he guide my work while in Paris and provide crucial assistance at many points along the way, but his work in preparing a critical edition of the *Acts of the National Synods* and of the various editions of the Discipline and his invitation to contribute to the work in whatever ways I could provided the linchpin for my entire analysis. His generosity in giving me access to his transcriptions and microfilms has more than anything else enabled me to work out the details of the development of the Discipline and the institutional structures of the French Reformed Church. Of course, any inaccuracies or errors in this book remain my own.

And last but far from least, there is my family: my mother, Adele Sunshine, and my father, Nathan Sunshine, who passed away just four months before this book made it into print; my mother-in-law, Kathleen Elsner, and my late father-in-law, Ed Elsner, who is sorely missed; my brother-in-law, David Elsner, who lived with us during graduate school and who has supplied laughter, friendship, and tea over the years; my son, Brendan, who waited until the dissertation was completed to arrive; my daughter, Elizabeth, whose first year of life was spent in Paris and who has been waiting to move back ever since; and especially my lovely wife, Lynn, who believed in me when I didn't and without whose unending patience, love, and encouragement I would never have even entered graduate school, much less completed this book. My most profound thanks and love to you all.

Chapter 1

The Problem
of the French Reformation

The first Reformed church in France was founded because of a baby. The year was 1555. Le Sieur de la Ferrière, a Protestant gentleman, left his home in Le Mans with his pregnant wife for his townhouse in the Pré-aux-Clercs just outside the walls of Paris. He was concerned that if the baby was born in Le Mans, the family would be pressured into having the child baptized in the local Catholic church.

Once in Paris, he began to meet regularly with other Protestants for prayer and Scripture readings led by Jean Le Maçon de Launay, also called La Rivière, a young man who had traveled to Switzerland and was familiar with the churches of Lausanne and Geneva. De Launay was careful not to preach or to celebrate the sacraments, since he knew that Reformed churches only permitted legitimately called pastors to do these things. Yet in view of the imminent birth of the child, some provision needed to be made for baptism. De Launay thus led the group through the steps necessary to organize itself formally as a congregation. First, they elected de Launay as pastor; then, after prayer and fasting, they elected a group of elders and deacons to join him in the consistory. The church at Paris was thus established, and the child could be baptized.

This, at least, is the story given in the *Histoire ecclésiastique*,[1] a story which has had a profound impact on the historiography of sixteenth-century French Protestantism and which also reflects the general image of Reformed churches as little

---

[1] *Histoire ecclésiastique*, 1:117–21. This work, traditionally ascribed to Theodore Beza (incorrectly, according to most current thought), was originally published in Antwerp in 1580.

more than "colonies" of Geneva.[2] As an account of the founding of the *first* church in the kingdom of France, however, this rather charming story has its problems. Protestantism had been developing as an underground movement in France since about 1520, and though the Protestants had not begun to organize themselves collectively, some of the cells had grown into full churches: Samuel Mours identified fifty-one churches which were in existence before the Paris church was founded in 1555.[3] Because of the unorganized state of French Protestantism in these early decades and the relatively scant documentation that has survived from the period, our knowledge of the movement prior to the 1550s is sketchy at best. The *Histoire ecclésiastique* itself contributes to the impression that there is not much to say about Protestantism before the founding of the church in Paris. In the Baum and Cunitz edition of the work, the period from Reuchlin and Erasmus to 1555—approximately fifty years—is covered in 115 pages, whereas the next twenty-five years comprise 1,867 pages. It is thus small wonder that the Genevocentric interpretation of French Protestant history has largely won the day.

The biases of the author of the *Histoire ecclésiastique* have not gone unnoticed by historians, particularly in France. For example, Emile Léonard has this to say about the *Histoire*:

> [The *Histoire ecclésiastique*,] reflecting as it does the ecclesiastical views and prejudices of Calvin and his emulators…has played its part in distorting the historiography of the French Reformation, making the period of unorganised Protestantism (roughly 1520–1550) appear comparatively unimportant, whereas it was precisely a time when the religious revolution seemed on the verge of rallying the whole of France; and it enhances the next period, when the Reformed Churches were established with Party and Reformed State, a period marked in fact by a definite shrinking of scope. We have here a purely confessional viewpoint, the one responsible for cluttering the general history of the times with those unreal problems denounced by Lucien Febvre, and causing conditions and stresses to be reflected back on to the early French Reformation which in fact only came to the fore later.[4]

---

[2]The term is that of Theodore Beza; see Theodore Beza, *Correspondance* 3 (1561), no. 165, 80–81.

[3]Samuel Mours, *Les Eglises réformées en France: Tableaux et cartes* (Paris: Librairie Protestante; Strasbourg: Oberlin, 1958), 56–107.

[4]Emile Léonard, *A History of Protestantism*, vol. 2, *The Establishment*, ed. H. H. Rowley, trans. R. M. Bethell (London: Thomas Nelson & Sons, 1967), 95; cf. the original text in *Histoire générale du Protestantisme*, vol. 2, *L'Etablissement (1564–1700)* (Paris: PUF, 1961), 82.

Léonard then argues that in the 1540s the emerging churches looked to Strasbourg for leadership, not to Geneva. His most important evidence for this comes from the *Histoire ecclésiastique* itself. Despite its claims for the primacy of the Paris church, the *Histoire* notes that by 1546, the Protestants of Meaux had formed a church following the model of the French refugee church in Strasbourg, where Calvin had served as pastor during his exile from Geneva (1538–41).[5]

Although Léonard is quite correct in pointing out the vitality of French Protestantism prior to the 1550s, the *Histoire ecclésiastique* does make an important point. Not only did the founding of the Paris church in 1555 inspire a host of imitators across the kingdom of France, as Léonard himself acknowledges, but by the time of *Histoire*'s terminal date of 1580, the dominant force within French Protestantism was clearly Calvinism. With Strasbourg becoming Lutheran and thus less tolerant of Reformed Protestantism, the churches of France looked increasingly to Geneva for direction; the kingdom's most prominent pastors had been trained in Geneva, and Genevan theologians such as Theodore Beza—an expatriate French nobleman, to be sure, but at this point very firmly in place in Geneva—were playing an active role in the affairs of the churches of France.

This chronological division between an early phase of Protestantism looking to Strasbourg for leadership and an institutionalized and politicized Protestantism looking toward Geneva should not be pushed too far. First, religious reform in France was alive and well long before the 1540s when Strasbourg became an important influence. French Protestantism had its origins in French humanism, whose distinctive feature had always been harnessing humanistic studies to reform society and hence the church. Throughout the early modern period, Protestantism in France maintained this essentially humanistic focus, Antoine de la Roche Chandieu's forays into Protestant scholasticism notwithstanding. The influence of Strasbourg became significant in the 1540s largely because the rather diffuse Protestant movement in France needed to become organized doctrinally and institutionally; this process culminated in the growth of French Calvinism, and thus the influences of both Strasbourg and Geneva can be seen as part of a single trend within the French Protestant community.

Strasbourg and Geneva may have been the most important foreign influences on French Protestantism, but other areas, such as the Pays de Vaud in the canton of Berne, also contributed directly to the emerging Huguenot church. Pierre Viret, one of the leading Vaudois ministers until his exile by the Bernese

---

[5] *Histoire générale*, 2:83, 1:67, cf. 1:117 n. 3; the *Histoire ecclésiastique* incorrectly states that Calvin founded the Strasbourg church. It is worth noting that Calvin learned much of his ecclesiology from Bucer during this period in Strasbourg.

authorities in 1558/59, was very highly regarded in France and spent his last years ministering in the kingdom, including acting as moderator of the fourth national synod held in Lyon in 1563. Viret prepared a church order based on the model of the Pays de Vaud, which had a significant impact on ecclesiastical structures in such provinces as Languedoc and Dauphiné throughout the 1560s.

Despite these foreign influences, the French Reformed Church was not simply an import; it built on the base of earlier French Protestantism and French culture. A number of scholars have highlighted these domestic elements in their discussion of the French Reformed Church; for this study, Bernard Roussel and Michel Reulos are particularly important. Roussel has worked extensively on the acts of the National Synods of the French Reformed churches and on the Discipline and has published a number of important articles on them that highlight distinctively French characteristics of the *Eglises réformées*.[6] Michel Reulos, retired vice president of the Tribunal de la Seine, has contributed a number of important articles focusing on the institutional development of the French Reformed churches. Not surprisingly, as a doctor of law he approaches the material using methodologies largely derived from legal history, including internal studies of the Discipline over time, based on the annotations in Isaac d'Huisseau's edition of the Discipline of 1659 (Geneva, 1666), and comparative studies of the legislation of the national synods and French civil law.[7]

Because of this combination of foreign and domestic elements, an adequate history of French Protestantism must take into account the ways in which indigenous reform programs, expatriate thinkers such as Calvin and Beza, and foreign influences interacted to produce the French Reformed churches of the late sixteenth and early seventeenth centuries. At the same time, the study must also examine the contributions of the French Reformed churches to the emerging international Calvinist movement.[8] It is the project of this book to contribute to

---

[6]See, for example, Bernard Roussel, "'Colonies' de Genève? Les premières années de vie commune des églises réformées du royaume de France (ca.1559–ca.1571)," *Bulletin de la Société de l'Histoire et d'Archéologie de Genève* 1996–97: 1–13; "La *Discipline* des Eglises réformées de France en 1559: Un royaume sans clergé?" in *De l'Humanisme aux Lumières, Bayle et le protestantisme*, mélanges en l'honneur d'Elisabeth Labrousse, textes recueillis par Michelle Magdelaine, Maria-Cristina Pitassi, Ruth Whelan et Antony McKenna (Paris: Universitas; Oxford: Voltaire Foundation, 1996), 169–91.

[7]Michel Reulo's methodology, though essential for identifying the institutional and legal matrix in which the French Reformed churches developed, is not sufficient for examining the development of the church structure. For example, it cannot trace articles that were completely dropped from the Discipline prior to 1659. Further, it does not take into account undeniable foreign influences on the French Reformed churches, focusing instead almost entirely on the domestic context.

[8]The only scholarly work which attempted to place the development of synodical government in

constructing such a history. This work focuses particularly on the more limited topic of the institutional development of the *Eglises Réformées de France*, that is, how the churches organized themselves as specifically religious (as opposed to political) bodies in response to the challenges they faced in sixteenth-century France.

The process of institutionalization has several advantages for exploring the varied influences on French Protestantism. A close examination of the details of the development of ecclesiastical structures can reveal lines of influence and elements of practice within French Protestant churches that are not reflected in other surviving sources, either because these elements are relatively obscure or because of a desire to propagandize for a particular theological and ecclesiastical position. More generally, institutionalization was an essential element in the life cycle of the Reformation, and one that has not received as much attention as it deserves.[9] Just as it was necessary to write confessions and to elaborate theological formulas and systems in order to consolidate the insights of the first generation of Reformers and to articulate them in a way that could be taught and defended against attack, so too it was necessary to create institutions to provide a framework for preserving, defending, and spreading the faith of the Protestant communities. Yet beyond a vague notion that the form of church government used in the Western European Reformed churches—the Scotskirk, the Dutch Reformed Church, and the French Reformed Church—had its origin in Calvinism, few studies have examined how and why this unique form of polity developed. Much of it owed far less to Geneva than to the conditions in France where it first arose.

Studies of the institutional development of the French Reformed churches have been hampered by the lack of reliable texts of the primary sources. The principal source for the overall institutional organization of the *Eglises Réformées* is the *Discipline ecclésiastique*, the church order for the French Reformed churches. The Discipline was released in its initial version by the first national synod of the French

its broadest international context is G. V. Lechler's useful but dated work, *Geschichte der Presbyterial und Synodalverfassung seit der Reformation* (Leiden: D. Noothoven Van Goor, 1854).

[9]A major exception is Heinz Schilling, whose work on what he somewhat misleadingly calls "confessionalization" deals with the creation of institutional structures in the churches of Germany and the Netherlands during the so-called Second Reformation. See, for example, his *Civic Calvinism in Northwestern Germany and the Netherlands: Sixteenth to Nineteenth Centuries*, Sixteenth Century Essays & Studies 17, (Kirksville, Mo.: Sixteenth Century Journal Publishers, 1991).

Reformed churches in 1559. It was then expanded and elaborated by each subsequent national synod, but these modifications were unsystematic and the Discipline itself unorganized. To try to remedy this, the fourth national synod (Lyon, 1563) called for the Discipline to be rewritten and organized into chapters. At least two radically different versions of the 1563 Discipline survive.[10] The Genevan version of this text was adopted as the base for the fifth national synod's edition of the Discipline (Paris, 1565), which was then sent to provincial synods for ratification. This version of the Discipline seems to have been unsatisfactory, since after the provinces had considered it, the sixth national synod called on the churches of Paris, Orléans, and Meaux to prepare yet another edition of the text.[11] This version was presented at the next national synod, held in La Rochelle in 1571.

The synod of La Rochelle was in many ways the most important of the national synods. Its moderator was Theodore Beza, come from Geneva specifically to attend the synod; in addition to the delegates of the churches, Jeanne d'Albret (the queen of Navarre), Henri de Navarre (the future Henri IV), Henri de Bourbon (the Prince de Condé), Count Louis of Nassau, and Admiral Coligny were also present. The esteem in which this synod was held is perhaps best illustrated by the fact that even the Gallican Confession, although not extensively modified at the synod, became widely known as the Confession of La Rochelle. The redaction of the Discipline adopted by this synod was likewise viewed as the new base text of the document.[12] As modified by the next national synod (Nîmes, 1572), this edition gave the Discipline the basic structure it would retain with only minor modifications until the revocation of the Edict of Nantes in 1685.[13]

The actual texts of the various editions of the Discipline have been very difficult to establish. The main versions of the first edition of the Discipline (1559) available to scholars have been those found in the *Histoire ecclésiastique* and in Jean Aymon's, *Tous les synodes nationaux des Eglises Réformées de France;*[14] still another version may be found in English translation in John Quick's, *Synodicon*

---

[10]Geneva BPU Archives Tronchin 10, 28ff.; BN FF 13953.

[11]Quick, 6–Vertueil–1567, chap. 8, art. 1(74).

[12]For example, BN FF 1926 includes a copy of the Discipline as corrected and expanded by the eighth national synod (Nîmes, 1572), but which is labeled the Discipline of La Rochelle and lists the moderator and secretary of 1571, not 1572, as signatories. On the other hand, Geneva BPU MS Fr. 405 contains a copy of the 1572 Discipline as well, but labels it the Discipline of 1559.

[13]See Glenn S. Sunshine, "French Protestantism on the Eve of St. Bartholomew: The Ecclesiastical Discipline of the French Reformed Churches, 1571–1572," *French History* 4 (1990): 343–46.

[14]*Histoire ecclésiastique* 1:215–20; Aymon, 1–7. These may also be found in François Méjan, *Discipline de l'Eglise réformée de France* (Paris: Editions "Je Sers," 1947), 300–7; this book also includes an annotated copy of the 1659 edition of the Discipline.

in Gallia Reformata.[15] None of these are particularly reliable: each has been corrupted by modifications to the Discipline introduced by later national synods, as have the vast majority of manuscripts labeled as the Discipline of 1559. Further, it is not entirely clear that there was in fact a single, definitive text for the earlier editions of the Discipline.[16] The variations in the manuscripts suggest that the Discipline circulated in a variety of forms, with different numbers of articles, different organization, even different wording and content in the articles. Along with the 1559 Discipline, perhaps the most glaring example of the enormous variation in the manuscripts is the 1563 Discipline, which survives in two manuscripts that without close examination would appear to be two completely different documents. There are similar variations, though less extreme, in the two surviving copies of the 1561 Discipline. Given the scarcity of manuscripts from other early editions of the Discipline, such textual confusion may have been common. Recognizing these problems, Bernard Roussel has recently published a hypothetical reconstruction of a version of the 1559 Discipline.[17] This rather austere text of thirty-eight articles was based principally on the text in Pierre La Place's *Commentaires de l'Estat de la religion et republique soubs les rois Henry et François seconds et Charles neufviesme* supplemented by a variety of other manuscripts.[18] This is the most reliable starting point for studies of the 1559 Discipline published to date, though a good case can be made for adding certain other articles to the text. Besides the different versions of the 1559 Discipline (and reprints of the texts of Aymon and the *Histoire ecclésiastique*), the only other sixteenth-century version of the Discipline which has been published is that of 1571 and 1572.[19] In order to trace institutional development of the French Reformed churches with any degree of precision, however, a reliable text of each edition of the Discipline is necessary. From the seventh national synod (La Rochelle, 1571) on, most of the Disciplines exist in multiple copies and thus establishing the text is not a serious problem. Finding reliable manuscripts of the earlier Disciplines is much more difficult, however. Fortunately, reliable copies of most of these have

---

[15]Quick, 2–7.

[16]The suggestion comes from Michel Reulos, "L'organisation des Eglises réformées françaises et le synode national de 1559," *BSHPF* 104 (1959): 9–24, esp. 20. The counterargument is that the acts of the national synods refer to specific articles by number, suggesting that there was a definitive text. Whether that was the text that made it to the provinces and local churches is a different matter, as the surviving manuscripts themselves demonstrate.

[17]Roussel, "Discipline."

[18]Pierre La Place, *Commentaires de l'Estat de la religion et republique soubs les rois Henry et François seconds et Charles neufviesme* (1565); ed. J. A. C. Buchon (Paris, 1836).

[19]Sunshine, "French Protestantism," 340–77.

been identified, and it is now possible to track the evolution of the Discipline with some precision.

The bare texts of the Disciplines show us the changes that were made in the organizational structure and legislation for the churches; they do not explain why these changes were made, nor do they give any indication of whether these provisions were actually followed in the churches. Other sources can help fill the gap here, notably the acts of the national synods.[20] These acts record the issues discussed at the synod and the decisions reached, not all of which are incorporated into the Discipline. The acts also include objections raised to the national synod's decisions, requests for clarification, and a great deal of other information that helps reconstruct how and why the Discipline evolved.

The acts of the national synods have been published twice, in English translation by Quick, and in French by Aymon. Despite being in English, Quick's edition is the more reliable of the two, having been prepared from some of the best manuscripts that have been identified to date. Unfortunately, we face the same situation with the acts of the national synods as with the Discipline: neither published edition is completely reliable, and there may in fact not be a single definitive version of the acts, particularly for the earlier synods.[21] The published editions thus must be supplemented by manuscript sources, the most important of which is Rawlinson manuscript D638 in the Bodleian Library. This manuscript, which Bernard Roussel believes to be Quick's principal source, contains two copies of the acts of the national synods, the second of which provides the base text for references to the acts in this work.[22]

Another set of sources includes the minutes of provincial synods, *classes*, colloquies and consistories. The most extensive collection of these is found in BN FF 8669, which includes a copy of the records prepared by M. George as scribe for most of the provincial synods held in Languedoc through 1595.[23] The acts of a

---

[20]Guillaume de Félice, *Histoire des synodes nationaux des Eglises Réformées de France* (Paris: Grassart, 1864), remains the best history of the national synods, though it suffers from the lack of a critical apparatus.

[21]Along with the first national synod, the problem is again particularly acute for the fourth, where Quick seems to have incorporated two versions of the acts into a single text: there is a great deal of repetition in the articles that does not appear in his probable base manuscript.

[22]In addition to a microfilm of Rawlinson D638, I have used an unpublished transcription of the acts of the first six national synods graciously provided to me by Bernard Roussel.

[23]Auzière, a nineteenth-century pastor, prepared a copy of this manuscript (together with a wide range of others related to the history of French Protestantism). Auzière was an excellent paleographer; when his manuscripts are checked against the originals, they prove to be very reliable. I used Auzière's copy of the Languedoc synods, Bibliothèque de la Société de l'Histoire du Protestantisme français MS 566, vol. 1 (Auzière collection 68), in preparing this work.

number of these synods plus some from Dauphiné were published by E. Arnaud in the late nineteenth century.[24] The provincial synods were responsible for bringing issues before the national synod and for ratifying its decisions. As discussed in chapter 4, it is sometimes possible to trace the back-and-forth interaction between the national synod and the provincial synods to develop a picture of legislative processes within the French Reformed churches. This picture challenges the notion that French Reformed Church government was a hierarchy with the national synod on top; it suggests that the real balance of power lay with the provincial synods. Further, since the local churches brought issues they could not resolve themselves directly to the colloquies, *classes,* and provincial synods, the records from these bodies provide an important window into the life of the local churches, including in some cases hints about internal structure and organization.

In addition to the texts of the *Discipline ecclésiastique* and the acts of various synodical assemblies, a number of local Disciplines and church orders of various types survive. The oldest of these is the *Articles polytiques,* a proposed church order for the kingdom of France drafted in 1557, two years before the Discipline, but never actually implemented. The origins of this text and its significance are discussed in chapter 2. Along with national church orders such as the Discipline and the *Articles polytiques,* several more localized church orders were produced. All known surviving copies of these church orders date from the period after the formal adoption of the Discipline, and provide interesting illustrations of the degree of acceptance of the structures mandated by the national synod in specific geographic areas. The only surviving provincial church order was prepared by Pierre Viret for Bas Languedoc and was put into effect there and in Dauphiné. This order survives in the acts of the provincial synod of Bas Languedoc held at Nîmes in February 1562.[25] Two formal local Disciplines have been identified, both from Normandy.[26] It is unclear, however, whether these were examples of prescriptive legislation or whether they actually described the order and functioning of the churches. On the other hand, we can evaluate the effectiveness of another

---

[24]*Documents protestants inédits du XVIe siècle: Synode général de Poitiers 1557, synodes provinciaux de Lyon, Die, Peyraud Montélimar et Nîmes en 1561 et 1562, assemblée des etats du Dauphiné de 1563, etc.,* ed. E. Arnaud (Paris: Grassart, 1872).

[25]Auzière, fols. 2v–3v; cf. *Documents protestants inédits,* 42. The manuscript is dated February 1561 [1562 n.s.]. This church order was misidentified by Arnauld; see the discussion in chap. 5 below.

[26]"Police et Discipline de l'Eglise de Saint-Lô (1563)," annexe to Michel Reulos, "Les débuts de Communautés réformées dans l'actuel département de la Manche (Cotentin et Avranchin)," in "Réforme et Contre Réforme en Normandie," *Revue du Département de la Manche* 24 (1982), *Numéro spécial,* fascs. 93, 94, 95, 31–57; Raymond Mentzer, Robert M. Kingdon, and Michel Reulos, "Police de l'Eglise réformée de Bayeux, 1563," *BSHPF* 130 (1984): 72–81.

local church order through the consistory records of Le Mans in 1561.[27] These records are particularly interesting because when the church was founded in January 1561 by a pastor sent from Poitiers, it adopted a decidedly non-Calvinistic church structure. About three months later, the church closed because of persecution, but then reopened later that year under the leadership of Pierre Merlin, a missionary pastor from Geneva. Merlin completely revamped the church's structure along the lines of Genevan orthodoxy and the Discipline. To explain the new church organization to the consistory, Merlin produced what amounts to a local Discipline for the church. Since we can compare the pre- and post-Merlin church orders, we have an effective gauge of the impact of Genevan pastors on their congregations and a clear example of the practice of an individual church following a de facto local Discipline.

From these sources it is possible to build a nuanced, chronologically precise analysis of the institutional development of the Huguenot churches. To place this analysis in context, chapter 2 discusses several key themes in the development of French Protestantism and provides a narrative of the events that led up to the first national synod of the French Reformed churches, held in Paris in May 1559. Chapters 3 through 8 analyze the institutional structures in the churches. This discussion begins with the provisions for collective government: chapter 3 focuses on national and provincial synods, the highest level organs of collective government; chapter 4 deals with the colloquy, congregational and pastoral oversight, and the Morély controversy. Next, the discussion turns to the local church, with chapter 5 examining the development of the diaconate, and chapter 6, local church government. Each of these chapters begins with a summary of the background and precedents for the ecclesiastical structures being discussed and then traces their development through a close reading of the Discipline, the acts of the national synods, and supplementary sources. Chapter 7 broadens the discussion by placing the ecclesiastical institutions into the context of relations with the French nobility, various local and provincial political authorities, and the royal court. It also looks at some of the international activities of the French Reformed churches. Chapter 8 summarizes the entire discussion and points out implications for the history of both French Protestantism and the spread of Reformed Christianity generally.

This study demonstrates that the French Reformed churches were influenced by a much wider range of ecclesiastical models and displayed a much greater

---

[27]"Papier et registre du Consistoire de l'église du Mans réformée selon l'Evangile 1560–1561 (1561–1562 *nouveau style*)," in *Recueil de pièces inédites pour servir à l'histoire de la Réforme et de la Ligue dans le Maine*, publiées par M. M. Anjubault et H. Chardon (Le Mans: Imprimerie Ed. Monnoyer, 1867).

degree of originality in synthesizing these traditions than has often been recognized. This suggests that even in Calvin's native country and during his lifetime there was hardly a monolithic "Calvinism" marching in lockstep with Geneva: the Reformed world, even the Calvinist world, was far more open to other influences and innovations than is generally recognized. Specifically, this study highlights some important ways in which the *Eglises Réformées* introduced their own elements into Reformed ecclesiastical structures, notably by establishing the first system of synodical government in which no pastor or church was permitted to have de facto or de jure authority over another (that is, the first example of presbyterial polity) in church history. This in turn set a precedent for most other national Reformed churches in Western Europe. The French Reformed churches thus played an important—though largely overlooked—role in the development of Reformed ecclesiology, a fact which highlights the cross-fertilization that occurred between the various Protestant regions and traditions in the second half of the sixteenth century.

Chapter 2

The Nature
of Early French Protestantism

The institutional structure of the *Eglises Réformées de France* did not develop in a vacuum; it was rooted in earlier traditions of French Protestantism as adapted to Calvinist theological principles. It is important to understand both the nature of early French Protestantism and Reformed theories of church government in order to make sense of the institutional development of the French Reformed

Church. This chapter examines several elements that shaped French Protestantism in the years through the first national synod (1559). First, it discusses Protestantism's place as a minority religion in France which led both to extreme diversity within the movement and to persecution by the crown. Second, it surveys briefly some of the explanations that have been suggested for the growth in the number of French Protestants during these persecutions. Next, it examines the issues of the nobility and their growing adherence to Protestantism and the growth of Calvinism in France. It then outlines the events that led up to the first national synod (Paris, 1559), Calvinist ecclesiology, and the challenges that faced the newly formed *Eglises Réformées de France*.

PROTESTANTISM AS A MINORITY RELIGION
In many ways, the key factor which shaped French Protestantism was its status as an unsanctioned religion within the kingdom. Whereas magisterial churches could rely on state support to set doctrinal standards and to establish an institutional structure for the church, early French Protestantism was forced to develop its own systems of belief and organization while being a persecuted minority

religion. In the 1520s and 1530s, Protestantism in the kingdom took a wide range of forms as individuals and small groups across the kingdom adopted a variety of heterodox ideas, which included "prophecy and millenarianism; anti-nomianism; anti-intellectualism, stressing the claims of emotion over rational theology; pacifism; rejection of the world and all its works; women finding self-expression through preaching; and a refusal of pragmatism, with the only justifications for belief and behaviour being the ultimate authorities of scripture and revelation."[1] To this list can be added humanist reformers influenced by Erasmus or Jacques Lefèvre d'Étaples,[2] and in the long run, anti-Trinitarians as well. Some of these groups, particularly the antinomians (Calvin's "libertines" and "Epicureans"), attracted converts from the more well off segments of the urban population and from the well-educated; others drew from segments of the population that were more insecure socially and economically but still had some degree of education.[3] Although some groups formed around itinerant preachers, few of these leaders developed more than a local following. The effect of all of this was the organic growth of small cells of Protestants within the kingdom, influenced by both indigenous local movements and foreign ideas, with a tremendous variety of organizational structures, and with beliefs ranging from humanistic Catholicism to outright heresy by the standards of both Catholics and magisterial Protestants.

Given this "long period of magnificent religious anarchy,"[4] it is no surprise that religious reform movements attracted the attention of Catholic authorities. More surprising is how long it took for this to happen. As long as reforming ideas were discussed only by the educated elite, there was little reaction to them; indeed, the very latitude of medieval French Catholicism made it unclear whether or not some of the ideas were in fact heretical. But when individuals became more public in their criticism of the church, Catholic authorities such as the Sorbonne

---

[1]David Nicholls, "Sectarianism and the French Reformation," *Bulletin of the John Rylands Library* 70 (1988): 36.

[2]E.g., Nicholas Cop's inaugural address as rector of the University of Paris, which combined an Erasmian-influenced exegesis of the Sermon on the Mount with a contrast between the "old" and "new" religion. Whether this speech was truly Protestant is debatable; what is indisputable is that the authorities viewed it as Protestant, forcing Cop and his friend (and the possible ghostwriter of the speech) John Calvin to flee Paris.

[3]Nicholls, "Sectarianism and the French Reformation," 38. For a discussion of the "Nicodemites" who fell between the extremes of Rome and Geneva, particularly those with more Catholic sympathies, see Thierry Wanegffelen, *Ni Rome ni Genève: Des fidèles entre deux chaires en France au XVIe siècle*, Bibliothèque Littéraire de la Renaissance, ser. 3, vol. 36 (Paris: Champion, 1997).

[4]The phrase is from Lucien Febvre, *Au coeur religieux du XVIe siècle*, 2d ed. (Paris: SEVPEN, 1968), 66.

and the Parlement of Paris tried to suppress them. Even in these cases, jurisdictional conflicts made clear and decisive action difficult. In the late 1520s, reforming ideas passed beyond the elites and began drawing converts from the common people and the lower classes. At this point, religious reform began to look considerably more dangerous, even seditious, and more systematic efforts were taken by French authorities to combat it.

The history of anti-Protestant persecution in France is summarized in most Reformation surveys as well as in histories of sixteenth-century France. A few points are worth stressing, particularly with respect to the reaction of the monarchy to Protestantism. Within French Catholicism, the king was viewed as a quasi-sacred person. He was the successor to Clovis, the first barbarian king to convert to orthodox Christianity, and was anointed on his coronation with holy oil that legend said came down from heaven on a dove at Clovis's baptism. One of the king's first acts on being crowned was to celebrate Mass in both kinds, pointedly demonstrating that he was more than a mere layman. The king himself was the immediate embodiment of a permanent, sacred office, which continued unchanging and unchanged throughout the generations. This concept of the king as a sacred figure, as "the most Christian king," had important practical consequences for French Catholicism since it reinforced the notion that the French church occupied a special position within Christianity. The king's fidelity to Catholicism was therefore an essential support for the privileges of the Gallican church so vital to French Catholicism's sense of self. Most ominously for Protestants, his coronation oaths required him to fight heresy.

This vision of the king as a sacred figure was heightened by the nearly messianic expectations surrounding Francis I's reign (1515–47). Fed by the mystical piety of his mother, Louise of Savoy, who on the basis of her astrological and biblical studies believed her son was destined to come to the throne, Francis and those around him saw him as a new Constantine, one who would bring about the renovation of both church *(renovatio ecclesiae)* and "empire" *(renovatio imperii),* as well as a revival of learning *(restitutio litterarum).*[5] Francis's early religious policies need to be seen in the context of this vision of his role in the church and in society. The negotiations leading to the Concordat of Bologna (1516), conducted through Guillaume Briçonnet, were seen as part of the process of renovating the church and, in the context of Gallicanism, the empire as well. This concordat guaranteed the French king the right to appoint his own candidates to all key ecclesiastical positions within the kingdom (subject to papal veto of canonically unqualified

---

[5]Denis Crouzet, *La Genèse de la Réforme française 1520–1562,* Regards sur l'Histoire 109 (Paris: Sedes, 1996), 114, 117–24.

candidates), and it was greeted in France as a recognition of the privileges of the Gallican church. Unfortunately, some of Francis's religious policies were not so welcome by conservative Catholics. In keeping with the theme of the *restitutio litterarum,* Francis sponsored Renaissance humanist scholarship within the kingdom; with the encouragement of his sister, Marguerite of Angoulême, he also supported humanistically inspired reform programs in the church, notably that undertaken by Briçonnet and Lefèvre d'Étaples at Meaux. Much to the annoyance of more conservative elements within the French Catholic Church, Francis even went so far as to shield Lefèvre and his associates from prosecution by the Parlement of Paris and the Sorbonne.

The climate changed radically for religious reformers, with the *Affaire des Placards* (October, 1534). Some of the people associated with Briçonnet at Meaux had gone well beyond the biblical humanism of Lefèvre and had moved into Lutheranism; some, such as Guillaume Farel, had passed beyond Luther into a radical rejection of the ability of material objects to convey spiritual grace. In other words, they became "sacramentarians," taking an essentially Zwinglian view of the Lord's Supper. Farel, in turn, had an important influence on Antoine Marcourt, a Protestant pastor from Picardy who had moved to Neuchâtel in response to Farel's ministry there. Marcourt rather unwisely decided to write a broadside attacking transubstantiation as sheer idolatry and the Catholic concept of the sacrifice of the Mass as blasphemous since it denigrated the work of Christ on the Cross. These placards were then posted simultaneously in Paris, Orléans, Tours, Noyon, Rouen, Blois—even on the door of the king's bedchamber. The placards were more than Francis could tolerate: not only was it an affront to his dignity, but attacking the Mass had political implications that went far beyond sacramental doctrine. As Christopher Elwood argues in his stimulating book, *The Body Broken,* Eucharistic theology provided an essential metaphor explaining the embodiment of power on all levels of society. In this period, the distinction between natural and supernatural was not clearly drawn; the natural world was part of God's creation and thus was sacred, as was society. Further, power was viewed as "simple and undifferentiated"; it could be deployed for different purposes in the natural world, in the political world, and in the church, but essentially these were all expressions of a single concept of power.[6] Thus the Eucharist, in which divine power is embodied in a physical object, became the critical picture used to reinforce the entire social structure, from the elites on

---

[6]Christopher Elwood, *The Body Broken: The Calvinist Doctrine of the Eucharist and the Symbolization of Power in Sixteenth-Century France,* Oxford Studies in Historical Theology (Oxford and New York: Oxford University Press, 1999), 17, 21–22.

down, and particularly to support the authority of the king. The Protestant attack on transubstantiation was thus seen as literally anarchistic by Catholics, and as an attack on the monarchy. Within a month of the posting of the placards, suspects had been arrested and six burned. Nonetheless, Francis's initial reaction appears to have been relatively moderate.[7] But after some "infamous books" attacking Catholic doctrine, and particularly transubstantiation, were discovered at the Louvre and in Paris (13 January 1535), Francis evidently realized that he was dealing with a group of Protestants that was sufficiently widespread and well organized to coordinate the posting of the placards and which he hadn't succeeded in destroying in his initial crackdown. This group was far more radical than the Lutherans, to whom he had always been hostile in any event. He thus sponsored and participated in a procession in Paris honoring the consecrated host, and began a systematic attack on Protestants across the kingdom (even while he continued to shield Marguerite and those under her protection). Although this round of trials and burnings was relatively short-lived—it ended in 1535, largely because Francis was courting the support of German Lutheran princes—other bouts of persecution followed, especially toward the end of Francis's reign in the mid-1540s. One particularly vivid example is Francis's attack on the so-called Meaux Lutherans in 1546, which resulted in sixty-four arrests and fourteen executions.[8] William Monter describes this as "the only time when the kingdom of France punished Protestants more intensively and severely than any other part of Latin Christendom." Contrary to the common view of Francis's religious policies, these last years of his reign marked the zenith of anti-Protestant persecutions in the kingdom (as measured by the number of executions for heresy) and the last time that king and the parlements would work together effectively in a policy of religious repression. Although Henri II (r. 1547–1559) would issue numerous decrees against Protestantism, even establishing the infamous *chambre ardente*, executions for heresy actually declined during his reign.[9]

THE GROWTH OF FRENCH PROTESTANTISM

Curiously enough, despite the hostility of the monarchy and ongoing persecutions by lower authorities within the French secular and ecclesiastical hierarchies, French Protestantism began a period of rapid expansion in the 1540s that accelerated still further in the 1550s. There is little consensus among historians about the

[7]Crouzet, *La Genèse de la Réforme française*, 231.

[8]Frederick J. Baumgartner, *France in the Sixteenth Century* (New York: St. Martin's Press, 1995), 143, cf. *Histoire ecclésiastique* 1:67.

[9]William Monter, *Judging the French Reformation: Heresy Trials by Sixteenth-Century Parlements* (Cambridge, Mass., and London: Harvard University Press, 1999), 109–10.

nature of and reasons for this growth. One important perspective argues for an economic explanation rooted in class tensions and the price revolution of the six-teenth century. The late-nineteenth-century historian Henri Hauser was one of the early advocates of this position, arguing that the French Reformation drew primarily from the ranks of the urban proletariat. This view has largely been replaced by Lucien Febvre's, which sees the bourgeoisie as the logical clientele of Protestantism. More recently, Henry Heller has argued that French Protestantism was a religious response to the extreme economic uncertainty of the 1540s, and that it became popular among the urban middle classes as a means of coping with the fear of poverty and of controlling the poor.[10]

This economic interpretation has been challenged by historians attempting to create a "social geography" of French Protestantism. Through detailed local and regional studies, scholars such as Natalie Zemon Davis and David Nicholls have shown that there is little or no correlation between economic crises and conver-sions to Protestantism.[11] Indeed, far from promoting Protestantism, economic insecurity in the Vaucluse region led to its repression.[12] Instead of focusing on the "why" of conversions to Protestantism, the social geography approach examines "who" and "where": what groups in which regions were more likely to convert to Protestantism? The basic geographical distribution of Protestantism in France is well established. Protestant churches were concentrated in a crescent extending from Lyon through the Midi to La Rochelle, and in Normandy, with a scattering of churches in the other provinces. Detailed studies of specific cities or provinces in the areas of greatest concentration provide a profile of the groups most likely to convert to Protestantism while still recognizing regional variations. The results of these studies sound remarkably like Lucien Febvre's or Max Weber's interpretation of Protestantism: French Protestants initially tended to come from cities, and were drawn from the professional classes, especially lawyers, and from merchants, fin-anciers, and artisans whose trades either required a fairly high level of literacy or were relatively new and thus less tied to traditional social and political power structures.[13] The petty nobility were also well represented, especially from the mid-1550s. Peasants and unskilled or illiterate workers, on the other hand, were less

[10]This argument is most fully developed in Henry Heller, *The Conquest of Poverty: The Calvinist Revolt in Sixteenth Century France*, Studies in Late Medieval and Reformation Thought, vol. 35, ed. Heiko A. Obermann (Leiden: E. J. Brill, 1986).

[11]Natalie Zemon Davis, *Society and Culture in Early Modern France* (Stanford: Stanford University Press, 1975); David Nicholls, "Social Change and Early Protestantism in France: Normandy," *European Studies Review* 10 (1980): 288.

[12]David Potter, *A History of France, 1460–1560: The Emergence of a Nation State* (New York: St. Martin's Press, 1995), 233.

[13]Nicholls, "France," 131–33.

likely to become Protestants. For example, Barbara Diefendorf notes that in the records of the *Conciergerie* in Paris, of those accused of Protestantism in the years 1564 to 1572, 31 percent were artisans, 22 percent held "lower offices" in government, 15 percent were merchants, and 9 percent were nobles; of the artisans, 5 percent came from trades with very high rates of literacy, 42 percent from trades with high rates of literacy, 34 percent from trades with average rates of literacy, and only 19 percent from trades with low rates of literacy. Diefendorf notes that these results are compatible with the analyses of Natalie Zemon Davis for Lyon, Philip Benedict for Rouen, and Joan Davies for Toulouse.[14]

Useful as these generalizations are, they do not apply in all cases. The studies of areas from Lyon to Rouen to Paris to the Midi show that all groups in society, from the peasantry to the nobility, were deeply divided over religion. In no case is there a clear, unambiguous connection between social class or occupation and adherence to either Protestantism or Catholicism. In fact, Nicholls makes the point that the groups that were more likely to adhere to Protestantism were for the most part the very same groups that formed the backbone of militant Catholicism: the issue was more that they took an active interest in religion than that they were particularly predisposed to Protestant ideas.[15] Further, for every element in this generalized picture, there are significant exceptions and regional and local variations: Protestantism was an urban phenomenon, though one of its staunchest bastions was in the rural Cévennes; Protestantism attracted the more affluent sections of society, but not in Amiens where it was adopted primarily by poor textile workers; Protestantism was most popular among the well educated or at least literate classes, but again, not in Amiens, where these classes remained more Catholic than did the less literate.[16] The examples can be multiplied. As David Potter summarizes the problem, "every town and region seems to have had different determinants for its religious destiny."[17] Although some of these paradoxical examples can be explained by shifting the terms of the argument, given the extent of regional and local variations, a broad socioeconomic model may not be the best approach for trying to explain the growth of French Protestantism.[18]

---

[14]Barbara Diefendorf, *Beneath the Cross: Catholics and Huguenots in Sixteenth-Century Paris* (New York and Oxford: Oxford University Press, 1991), 109–10.

[15]Nicholls, "France," 131.

[16]Potter, *A History of France*, 234–36, citing D. Rosenberg, *Social Experience and Religion Choice, a Case Study: The Protestant Weavers and Woolcombers of Amiens in the Sixteenth Century* (Ph.D. Dissertation, Yale, 1979). Emmanuel LeRoy Ladurie makes a similar point about the textile workers in Montpellier, though in his case the contrast is between the poor urban workers who convert to Protestantism and the peasants who do not (*Les paysans du Languedoc* [Paris: SEVPEN, 1966], 1:348).

[17]Potter, *A History of France*, 235.

[18]For example, the Amiens textile workers can be explained in part because they were a part of a

Denis Crouzet, in his monumental *Les Guerriers de Dieu,* looks at the problem from the opposite direction.[19] In this exploration of the problem of religious violence in sixteenth-century France, he examines the root causes of the intensity of support for French Catholicism and then interprets the more limited appeal of Protestantism in terms of a rejection of the elements that gave Catholicism its nearly fanatical backing among the broader population. According to Crouzet, popular Catholicism in France was steeped in mysticism and apocalypticism and fed by almanacs filled with reports of "signs and portents" and with astrological predictions of disasters and the end of the world. No amount of failed predictions weakened the appetite for such fare any more than it has in modern America. The spread of Protestantism in Europe raised these eschatalogical fears to a fever pitch, ultimately leading to extreme religious violence and the Wars of Religion. Barbara Diefendorf independently identified many of the same elements in her study of the St. Bartholomew's Day massacres in Paris.[20] In contrast, Calvinism can best be understood as a rejection of this mystical view of the world; its appeal lay in a replacement of the "prophetic anguish" of Catholicism with a serene assurance of salvation on the part of the elect. In this context, Calvin's treatise against judicial astrology and Beza's condemnation of almanacs as promoters of Catholic violence become more than simply sidebars in their religious programs; they are fundamental elements in the attack on Catholic "superstition" that permeates their work.

Crouzet's study provides an exceedingly interesting and provocative perspective on religion in sixteenth-century France; it is particularly important for placing religion instead of socioeconomic tension at the center of confessional conflict during the Reformation. It also takes into account a fundamental difference in the nature of religious allegiance in the sixteenth century versus the twentieth century. In early modern Europe, religion was more than just a matter of personal belief: as John Bossy points out, religious identity was centered on being a member of a community rather than subscribing to a set of doctrinal norms.[21] This community focus was one of the roots of religious violence: for each group, those with different religious beliefs—indeed, different worldviews—polluted the society and thus had to be purged.

---

new and potentially exploited industry who already saw themselves as separate from the traditional social structures of the city; see Nicholls, "France," 132; Mack P. Holt, *The French Wars of Religion, 1562–1629,* New Approaches to European History (Cambridge: Cambridge University Press, 1995), 37.

[19]Denis Crouzet, *Les Guerriers de Dieu: La Violence au Temps des Troubles de Religions vers 1525– vers 1610,* 2 vols. (Seyssel: Champ Vallon, 1990).

[20]Diefendorf, *Beneath the Cross,* 182 n. 10.

[21]John Bossy, *Christianity in the West, 1400–1700* (Oxford: Oxford University Press, 1985), 152–87.

The 1540s and 1550s saw the beginnings of other important trends among French Protestants. Due, perhaps, to the combination of numerical growth and the impetus of the persecutions conducted by Francis I and Henri II, French Protestantism began to move out of its unorganized phase to embrace a distinctly Reformed theology. One influence for this shift may have been refugee churches, including those in London under John à Lasco and in Strasbourg under the general direction of Martin Bucer. Strasbourg became a particularly important model for French Protestants, partly because of its proximity to the kingdom and the presence of the French church in the city, partly because Bucer was one of the first major Protestant leaders to take an active interest in religious developments in France.[22] Although it is widely assumed that French Protestantism was moving toward Geneva and Calvin during this period, it had not yet done so: again, the Protestants in Meaux had looked to Strasbourg for direction on church structure in the mid-1540s, not to Geneva. Calvin himself had been the pastor of the refugee church in Strasbourg from 1538 to 1541 and did not draft the Genevan *Ecclesiastical Ordinances* until 1541; through the 1540s and early 1550s, his position in Geneva had not yet been consolidated. The older, better-established church in Strasbourg was thus quite logically viewed as a more viable model for organizing Protestant churches in France than the as-yet-untested Genevan church.

This is not to say that Calvin was ignored in France in the 1540s. As Francis Higman demonstrates, so many of Calvin's writings were pouring into the French market during this period that the Sorbonne found it necessary to censure more of his books than those of any other author, including Luther. In fact, by 1545 approximately two-thirds of the books banned by the Sorbonne came from Geneva.[23] Calvin's vernacular writings were particularly influential: for the first time, well-argued sophisticated theological works were available in French, and these had an enormous impact in shaping the direction of Protestant thought in the kingdom. This influence grew during the 1550s. With Strasbourg's forcible conversion to Lutheranism and Bucer's exile from the city, Geneva increasingly became the major inspiration for French Protestants and the principal city of refuge for those fleeing persecution. With Calvin's victory over the *Perrinistes* (1555)—whose objection to Calvin centered primarily on the growing influence of wealthy French refugees in Geneva—still more refugees flooded into the city, especially from France.[24] And even before the official founding of the Academy

---

[22]Léonard, *Histoire générale*, 2:83.

[23]Francis Higman, *Censorship and the Sorbonne: A Bibliographical Study of Books in French Censured by the Faculty of Theology of the University of Paris, 1520–1551*, Travaux d'Humanisme et Renaissance 172 (Geneva: Droz, 1979), 62; see also "Index of Authors and Titles of Works in French," 181–89.

[24]See William G. Naphy, *Calvin and the Consolidation of the Genevan Reformation* (Manchester: Manchester University Press, 1994).

(1559), Geneva had become the main training center for missionary pastors who would be sent back to France to establish Calvinist churches within the kingdom, thereby further enhancing Calvin's influence in his native land.[25]

Perhaps the most important consequence of the turn to Calvinism in France was a growing emphasis on church discipline, understood in the narrow sense of enforcing morality. Increasingly, "being Protestant" in France involved adherence to a strict moral code that emphasized obedience to God and the magistrate and was enforced within the community via consistories, church courts patterned on the model of the Genevan Consistory instituted by Calvin. Close examination of the work of the French consistories would take us too far afield; its evolution as an institution is discussed in more detail in chapter 6. Suffice it to say that French Protestants were increasingly adopting Calvinist theology and practice, including setting up consistories to enforce their definition of Christian standards of behavior within the community.

THE CONVERSION OF THE NOBILITY

It was in this context of congregationalism, Calvinism, and church discipline that another important phenomenon began to transform the face of French Protestantism: the conversion of increasing numbers of the nobility to the Protestant cause. Although some members of the nobility had been involved in Protestantism from its earliest days in France, in the mid-1550s their numbers began to skyrocket. The reason for individual conversions were quite varied: "greed [to get control of church lands and benefices], anticlericalism, political ambition, a traditional warrior mentality and, in some cases, genuine religious conviction governed noble actions."[26] Yet the reasons for the trend as a whole are less clear. A century ago, some scholars such as Henri Hauser argued that these conversions were triggered by an economic crisis in the 1540s; most recent studies suggest that the nobility did not in fact suffer across the board from such a crisis at any time in the sixteenth century.[27] A more promising interpretation focuses on the role of

---

[25]This process has been discussed most thoroughly in Robert M. Kingdon, *Geneva and the Coming of the Wars of Religion in France 1555–1563* (Geneva: E. Droz, 1956). This shift toward Geneva may explain the claim in the *Histoire ecclésiastique* that the first church in France was established in 1555: it may refer to the first explicitly Calvinist church in the kingdom; alternately, it may reflect the author's view of the church of Paris as a "mother church" for French Protestantism. Either interpretation is consistent with the author's biases.

[26]Nicholls, "France," 136.

[27]The classic statement of the argument for economic causality is Henri Hauser, *Etudes sur la Réforme française,* Bibliothèque d'Histoire Religieuse (Paris: Alphonse Picard et Fils, 1909). The economic evidence is most conveniently summarized in Potter, *A History of France,* 176–87.

kinship and patronage networks. These networks were an important element of the life of the French nobility, particularly among the petty nobility in rural areas. Many of these nobles could only provide an education for their sons by sending them to wealthy neighbors as pages. As an adult, the former page would look to his patron for help in obtaining positions in the military, civil administration, or the church, and in return the page's family would be expected to support the patron's interests.[28] These patronage networks were crucial to the spread of Protestantism among the French nobility. For example, Janine Garrisson demonstrated that a significant percentage of the five hundred people condemned for heresy by the Parlement of Bordeaux in 1569 were the clients of a single Protestant nobleman, Pons de Polignac.[29]

Many of the key people within these patronage networks were women. We have already seen the importance of Marguerite d'Angoulême in sponsoring and protecting religious reformers. Many members of her circle were also active in promoting Protestantism. R. J. Knecht lists some of these:

> They included Louise de Montmorency, the sister of the Constable and the mother of Gaspard de Coligny, the future Admiral and leader of the Huguenot movement; Jacqueline de Longwy, Duchess of Montpensier, who defended Huguenots at the court of Catherine de Medici; and Michelle de Saubonne, ancestress of the Rohans, who led the Huguenots in the later civil wars.... Other important Protestant ladies were Madeleine de Mailly, Countess of Roye, whose daughter married and converted the Prince of Condé; Charlotte de Laval, the wife of Admiral Coligny; Françoise de Seninghen, mother of the Prince of Porcien; and Françoise du Bec-Crespin, mother of Philippe Du Plessis-Mornay, one of the leading spokesmen of the Huguenot cause.[30]

One of the most important women influenced by Marguerite was her daughter Jeanne d'Albret, who was instrumental in converting her husband, Antoine de Bourbon, to sympathy to the Protestant cause.[31]

---

[28]R. J. Knecht, *The French Wars of Religion 1559–1598*, Seminar Studies in History (London and New York: Longman, 1989), 14.

[29]Janine Garrisson, *Protestants du Midi 1559–1598* (Toulouse: Edouard Privat, Editeur, 1980), 22–28.

[30]Knecht, *The French Wars of Religion 1559–1598*, 15.

[31]Holt, *French Wars of Religion*, 39. For a complete discussion of Jeanne d'Albret, see Nancy Lyman Roelker, *Queen of Navarre: Jeanne d'Albret, 1528–1572* (Cambridge, Mass.: Harvard University Press, 1968); Roelker's article, "The Role of Noblewomen in the French Reformation," *Archiv für*

The significance of the nobility, including the leading role of noblewomen, was not lost on the leaders of the Genevan reform. Calvin in particular engaged in an active correspondence with several of these noblewomen,[32] and both he and Beza focused their missionary strategy on the conversion of nobles as a means of effecting chains of conversions down (and occasionally up) patronage lines.

Whatever the motivation of these conversions, by the 1560s a significant percentage of the nobility of France—some of them Princes of the Blood—had become Protestant. In some ways, this added to the divisions within the Protestant movement. Whereas the hallmark of the earlier urban Protestantism had been living by a strict moral code focused on obeying not only God, but also the magistrate, this was less true for the nobility. Conversion to Protestantism did not change this group's fundamental ethos: they continued to view themselves as a privileged class with special rights vis-à-vis the monarchy. This attitude would cause serious problems for the Huguenot cause; it had disastrous consequences in the Conjuration d'Amboise, for example. Yet the conversion of the nobility did offer some immediate advantages. Unlike the artisans and bourgeois that had been the backbone of French Protestantism from the 1520s through the 1540s, the nobles brought with them enough status and power to create a Protestant party whose interests were represented at court and whose military muscle forced the crown to take them seriously. On a more local level, the nobility provided a degree of protection for Protestants worshiping under their care. Protestant *prêches* were protected by patrols of armed and mounted nobles, and Psalm-singing assemblies gathered publicly outside the gates of Paris led by Princes of the Blood. But even more important than protecting *prêches*, the nobles also sponsored churches. Some of these, such as the church of Rennes in Brittany, were established by a noble with ties to the area, and then developed into local churches that continued to be sponsored and protected by the noble without being formally dependent on their founder. Many others were part of noble households. In fact, by some estimates, half of the Protestant churches of the kingdom were located in the homes of the nobility. These house churches were thus a central element of French Protestantism in the 1550s and 1560s, although they only rarely participated in the other important development within the Huguenot movement in this period: the drive for greater organizational unity.

Reformationsgeschichte 63 (1972): 168–94, identifies a number of other noblewomen who influenced the growth of French Protestantism.

[32]For an examination of Calvin's correspondence with Renée of France, sister-in-law of Francis I and duchess of Ferrara, see F. Whitfield Barton, *Calvin and the Duchess* (Louisville: Westminster/John Knox Press, 1989).

Chapter 2

The Drive toward Unity

During the early phase of French Protestantism, churches were congregational in polity, that is, they were independent and self-governing. Institutional structure was thus not an important issue in this period; in fact, the first indication of a concern for church order among French Protestants was the group of Protestants from Meaux mentioned in chapter 1 which went to Strasbourg to study church organization. On this group's return, they established a church at Meaux on the Strasbourg model, which was subsequently scattered by the persecution of 1546.[33] The church order of Strasbourg (or of Geneva, for that matter) was perfectly compatible with congregational polity since it served a city-state; there were no layers of civil government above the city and no need to establish ecclesiastical structures for overseeing churches in broader territorial units. The church order could thus be adapted to the conditions under which early French Protestantism developed. By the late 1550s, French Protestant leaders began to view some form of collective government for the churches as a desideratum: it would enable increased cooperation among the churches; it would provide for a measure of internal discipline (a point which was particularly important to Reformed thinkers such as Bucer and Calvin); and perhaps most importantly, it would permit the Protestants of the kingdom to adopt a unified doctrinal statement and system of church government to demonstrate to the monarchy that they were neither heretics, nor schismatics, nor sectarians.

The earliest known attempt to establish a collective government for the churches was a "synod" that met in Poitiers in 1557 and drafted a church order for French Protestantism, the *Articles polytiques*. The church at Poitiers was very important in this period. Founded in either 1554 or 1555, Poitiers was essentially the "metropolitan" church for the Protestants of the middle Loire valley.[34] The synod that met there in 1557 and the nature of the Articles it produced are something of a mystery, since except for the Articles themselves, the "synod" left almost no trace in the historical record. The provincial synod of Dauphiné (Montélimar, 1562) listed the synod of Poitiers, 1557, as a general synod and as the source of the later *Discipline ecclésiastique*,[35] but there is little reason to consider it such. As Arnauld points out, it could not have been a general or national synod in the strict sense of the term, since it seems not to have included representatives from a wide range of the provinces of the kingdom.[36] Given that there was no attempt to

[33]See the brief summary in Léonard, *Histoire générale*, 2:83–84.

[34]Arnaud, *Documents protestants inédits*, 83, has 1554; Mours, *Le Protestantisme en France au XVIe siècle* (Paris: Librairie Protestante, 1959), 56–107, has 1555; *Documents protestants inédits*, 83.

[35]Arnaud, *Documents protestants inédits*, 36.

[36]Arnaud, *Documents protestants inédits*, 82.

put the Articles into effect, the document may have been intended simply as a working draft of a church order for the kingdom.[37] Even at this level, the connection between the Discipline and the Articles is tenuous at best. Though the Articles may have influenced the content of some of the provisions in the earliest versions of the Discipline, the basic principles underlying the two systems are significantly different. The ecclesiastical structure outlined in the Articles, which was presumably based on the structure of the church at Poitiers,[38] is decidedly non-Calvinistic and thus provides important evidence for the vitality of non-Genevan theological traditions even within an essentially Reformed church as late as 1557.

The *Articles polytiques* would have been little more than a stillborn attempt at establishing a church order for French Protestantism were it not for its role in a meeting held in Poitiers and attended by Antoine de la Roche Chandieu. Chandieu, who had spent some time in Geneva, joined Le Maçon in 1557 as the second pastor of the church in Paris. In December 1558, Chandieu visited Poitiers to help settle a long-running controversy stirred up by LaVau, described by A. Bernus as "an old friend of Servetus and then under the influence of Castellio."[39] LaVau was part of a group of "Nicodemites" at Poitiers who opposed the growing influence of Calvin on French Protestantism, viewing him as power-hungry and less concerned about holiness than he was about fighting Catholicism. While Chandieu was at Poitiers to help settle this controversy, ministers of nearby churches met with him to celebrate the Lord's Supper and to discuss the doctrine and discipline of the Protestant churches in the kingdom.[40] According to Bernus, the churches expressed a desire to establish a common doctrinal statement and church order to replace *règlements particuliers* such as those of Poitiers—almost certainly the *Articles polytiques*[41]—and *confessions spéciales* such as those of Paris. Chandieu would thus have been familiar with the Articles, though given his role in drafting and defending the Discipline, it is highly unlikely that he approved of them. In any event, Chandieu returned to Paris and at the inspiration of the

---

[37]Arnaud, *Documents protestants inédits*, 83, suggests that it was a "first attempt" at a Discipline proposed by the province of Poitou in conjunction with representatives of the provinces adjacent to the southern Loire valley.

[38]This suggestion comes from Arnaud, *Documents protestants inédits*, 83.

[39]A. Bernus, "Le ministre Antoine de Chandieu d'après son Journal autographe inédit," *BSHPF* 37 (1888): 126.

[40]See Léonard, *Histoire générale*, 2:92–93; *Histoire ecclésiastique*, 1:199–200. LaVau would later be condemned by the first national synod.

[41]Léonard, *Histoire générale*, 2:93n., comments that it is "tempting" to view this meeting as the "synod" which produced the Articles, even though the year is wrong; on the whole, this seems unlikely: with Chandieu as the principal architect of the Discipline, it is difficult to see how he could have agreed to the Articles, given its broad incompatibility with the system outlined in the Discipline.

meeting at Poitiers, a national synod was called to create a unified system of doctrine and discipline of the French Protestant churches.

This first national synod met in Paris in May 1559, under the nose of a monarchy actively engaged in persecuting Protestants.[42] The number of churches represented is unclear; the manuscripts of the acts of the national synod suggest ten or eleven, nearly all from the northwestern quarter of France.[43] The synod is thus open to the same charge Arnauld leveled at the "synod" of Poitiers in 1557: it was not representative of the entire country and thus cannot be considered to be a true national synod. On the other hand, unlike Poitiers, the later national synods clearly accepted the work of the 1559 Paris synod and ratified its decisions. Whether the synod was truly representative of the range of Protestant churches throughout the kingdom, its acceptance by the *Eglises Réformées* as its founding synod provides ex post facto justification for viewing it as the first national synod.

François Morel, a missionary pastor from Geneva assigned to the church in Paris, was elected to preside over the actions of the synod and, with Chandieu, shaped much of its work. In keeping with the desires expressed five months earlier at Poitiers, the synod's main goal was to adopt a confession of faith, known as the Gallican Confession,[44] and a church order, the *Discipline ecclésiastique*. The purpose of the Confession was to summarize the teachings of Scripture on what the churches considered to be the fundamental points of the Christian religion. Interestingly enough, Calvin seems to have initially opposed the writing of this Confession:[45] he apparently believed that the available confessions were adequate, and that for ecumenical reasons the French churches should subscribe to one of them. The realities of the situation in France made this unworkable, however. One of the essential goals of French Protestantism was to convince the monarchy

---

[42]Jacques Pannier follows the traditional interpretation, since challenged by Monter, *Judging the French Reformation*, 109–10, that this was the period of the most severe persecutions of Protestants to date in France. See idem, *Les Origines de la Confession de Foi et la Discipline des Églises Réformées de France*, Études d'histoire et de Philosophie Religieuses publiées par la Faculté de Théologie protestante de l'Université de Strasbourg fasc. 32 (Paris: Félix Alcan, 1936), 95.

[43]Pannier, *Les Origines*, 99–100.

[44]The best historical discussion of the Confession remains Pannier, *Les Origines*. See Hannelore Jahr, *Studien zur Überlieferungsgeschichte der Confession de foi von 1559*, Beiträge zur Geschichte und Lehre der Reformierten Kirche 16 (Neukirchen-Vluyn: Neukirchener Verlag des Erziehungsvereins, 1964) for a list of the printings of this Confession.

[45]Brian G. Armstrong, "*Semper Reformanda:* The Case of the French Reformed Church, 1559–1620," in *Later Calvinism: International Perspectives*, Sixteenth Century Essays & Studies, vol. 22, ed. Fred Graham (Kirksville, Mo.: Sixteenth Century Journal Publishers, 1994), 125, cf. Brian G. Armstrong, *Calvinism and the Amyraut Heresy: Protestant Scholasticism and Humanism in Seventeenth-Century France* (Madison: University of Wisconsin Press, 1969), 25–30.

that it was possible to be a loyal subject to the crown without being loyal to Rome; the national synod could not make this case convincingly if it adopted the creed of a foreign church. At the same time, a confession of faith was needed: given the diversity within French Protestantism, the national synod had to establish a uniform system of doctrine both for the sake of theological purity and to refute the charges of sectarianism leveled against the Huguenots by their Catholic opponents. The only way to reconcile these conflicting needs was to adopt a distinctively French confession of faith. Calvin reluctantly acquiesced, and sent Morel a draft confession. Morel claimed in a letter to Calvin that the synod added a few articles but adopted the rest "with few changes."[46] There are good reasons to suspect Morel was being diplomatic here: not only does the Confession seem to have incorporated much of the 1557 Confession of the church of Paris, but differences in theological methodology and detail in a number of important articles make it unclear how much (if any) of the final text Calvin actually wrote.[47] Calvin's authorship of the Gallican Confession is thus open to serious question, though he certainly influenced its contents.

For present purposes, the Confession is particularly important because of what it says about ecclesiastical government. As a statement of the essentials of the faith, the Confession did not go into a great deal of detail about church government; it left the specifics of the church order to the Discipline. Nonetheless, the Confession does include a number of articles which spell out the nonnegotiable aspects of church organization, that is, those aspects which the first national synod believed were articulated in Scripture. In most respects, the Confession followed Calvin and Beza on these points.[48] On a local level, the Confession argues that there are three basic offices in the church: pastors (or "ministers of the Word," frequently shortened to "ministers"), "overseers" (that is, elders),[49] and deacons (art. 29). This follows Calvin's basic analysis of church officers, but omits doctors.

---

[46] *[P]erpauca vero commutare*, CO 17:540.

[47] See Pannier, *Les Origines*, 120–21. See also Armstrong, *Calvinism and the Amyraut Heresy*, 25–30, for a summary of the arguments for a greater degree of independence from Calvin than has commonly been recognized.

[48] For a more thorough discussion of the relationship of Calvin's and Beza's ideas on church polity in 1559 with those of the Gallican Confession, see Glenn S. Sunshine, "Reformed Theology and the Origins of Synodical Polity: Calvin, Beza and the Gallican Confession," in *Later Calvinism: International Perspectives*, ed. Fred Graham, Sixteenth Century Essays & Studies 22 (Kirksville, Mo.: Sixteenth Century Journal Publishers, 1994), 141–58.

[49] The term *"surveillants,"* translated as "overseers," is itself a French translation of the Greek *"episcopos,"* or bishop. It is here identified with elders since the task of overseeing the congregation is placed in the hands of the elders by the Discipline; further, since pastors and deacons are both local offices, it seems unlikely that a term which appears between the two in the list could refer to any

This omission was not particularly significant from the perspective of either theory or practice among the Reformed churches of France. Calvin himself on occasion groups pastors and doctors together as ministers of the Word,[50] and Beza does so even more systematically. Further, the French churches followed Calvin in practice by distinguishing between pastors and doctors: as early as the second national synod (Poitiers, 1561), the Discipline indicated that doctors who were *also* pastors could celebrate the sacraments, but those who were only doctors could not.[51] The difference in the number of offices has little real significance.

The Gallican Confession next articulated the most fundamental principle of French Reformed polity: the absolute prohibition of hierarchy among churches and ministers (art. 30). This was a commonplace among many Protestant theologians, but the French church would apply the principle in a new way. Although, for example, Calvin and Beza both insisted on the equality of and colleagiality of ministers, they also argued that a single minister needed to preside over the ministerial assembly as a *primus inter pares* to maintain order and see that the assembly's business was conducted in an appropriate manner. The early church labeled these officers "bishops"; though Calvin and Beza disliked the term, they clearly saw this office as a necessary part of the church structure. They also argued that the early church's bishops had a role in overseeing clerical discipline through visitations and regular synods. At need, higher-level synods could also be called, with archbishops or patriarchs overseeing their work. To put it differently, Calvin and Beza both argued that the early church governed itself via a system of synods over which bishops, archbishops, and patriarchs presided; both approved of this system and advocated its restoration, at least up to 1559. Alexandre Ganoczy notes that in a letter to the king of Poland written in December 1554, Calvin recommended the establishment of a purified episcopate operating within a synodical system, including an archbishop over the entire Polish church.[52]

As it turns out, however, the French church would take the notion of ministerial equality in a radically different direction. The principle would quickly be translated into an insistence on a relatively high degree of autonomy for local churches and on a nonhierarchical approach to the ministry. In this form it would

---

supervisory office above the local church. In short, it is clear that the term in question is to be identified with the elders.

[50]Cf. Calvin's commentary on Eph. 4:11, in which he acknowledged that it was legitimate to group pastors and teachers into a single office, though he preferred to distinguish between them.

[51]DE 1562, 48; cf. Quick, 3–Orléans–1562, chap. 4, art. 13 (15).

[52]Alexandre Ganoczy, *Calvin, théologien de l'église et du ministère,* Unam Sanctam 48 (Paris: Les Editions du Cerf, 1964), 389–90, cf. *CO* 15:383.

be enshrined in a number of articles in the Discipline and would lead to the development of a new approach to polity as a replacement for episcopacy, even of the limited sort advocated by Calvin and Beza. The Confession was not the place to work out the details of this new system; such issues were not matters of faith per se, and thus they were left to the Discipline, which according to the Confession was to be written by those who governed the churches (art. 32). The rules of government established by church leaders were not to be arbitrary, however; they had to conform to scriptural principles by promoting unity and by not commanding more than God did (art. 33). In practice, this permitted disciplinary canons that were considerably broader in scope than might be expected. For example, from 1571 on, an entire chapter of the Discipline was devoted to regulations governing the behavior of specific classes of individuals, such as lawyers, judges, notaries, and booksellers. At several points, the national synods even felt compelled to address the vexing moral problem of dancing(!). These regulations were not blocked by the Confession, presumably because they were viewed not simply as human inventions but as applications of God's Law to the conditions faced by the Huguenots in the sixteenth century. To put it differently, the regulations involved "subjection to the Word of God" —one of the marks of the church according to article 28 of the Confession—and thus were permissible.[53] Further, in the face of persecution and civil war, the Protestant communities needed to preserve their doctrinal and moral purity; in this context, as Roussel notes, almost nothing is *adiaphora*.[54] In any event, the Confession also insisted on the right of the church government to censure those found guilty of sin, following procedures outlined by Christ himself (Matt. 18:15–17); the church must even have the right to excommunicate sinners who refuse to repent (art. 33).[55]

The Confession thus followed Calvin and Beza in defining specific offices for local churches, but did not claim there was any scripturally mandated model for collective ecclesiastical government. In fact, it only offered two basic principles in this area: first, there must not be any hierarchy of ministers or churches, thus eliminating episcopacy; second, those entrusted with the government of local churches were to be free to develop their own collective form of government as long as it was neither too restrictive of the believer's freedom (narrowly understood) nor too weak to enforce biblical ethical and moral standards following scriptural models.

[53]Art. 27, 28; see Glenn S. Sunshine, "Discipline as a Third Mark of the Church: Three Views," *Calvin Theological Journal* 32 (1998): 471–72.

[54]Roussel, "'Colonies' de Genève?" 9.

[55]Bucer, Calvin, Viret, and Beza all fought for the church's right to excommunicate unrepentant sinners without the interference of the civil government; excommunication was opposed by the more Zwinglian Reformers in Zurich, Berne, and other cities.

The Discipline was designed to apply the ecclesiastical principles articulated in the Confession to the historical and cultural circumstances facing French Protestants. It outlined local church structure, a system of collective government for the churches, and disciplinary practices. Unlike the Confession, which was considered normative and, as a summary of Scripture, was not changed often or lightly,[56] the Discipline was designed to respond to the changing needs of the church and was thus updated to a greater or lesser extent by each national synod. As with the Confession, Calvin was once again an important influence on the Discipline. Guillaume de Félice goes so far as to claim, "This constitution was dictated by Calvin."[57] This is clearly an exaggeration. Samuel Mours is more judicious in his statements, but nevertheless argues that Calvin's clarity of thought and organizational genius were the inspiration for the authors of the Discipline.[58] That may be the case, but it misses an important point. By turning the focus on Calvin and Geneva, Mours fails to recognize that it was the internal dynamics within French Protestantism itself that gave the Discipline much of its originality. Although on a local level, the church structure outlined in the Discipline largely followed Calvin's model, it did not do so in all details; further, as we shall see in later chapters, the Discipline's provisions for collective government showed a great deal of ingenuity and innovation on the part of the French churches. If anyone should be given credit for these innovations, it should not be Calvin but Chandieu, who prepared the first version of the Discipline in consultation with Morel,[59] though in reality, the system of church government laid out in the Discipline is more the legacy of the national synods than of any individual.

The first national synod marked the official birth of the *Eglises Réformées de France* as at least theoretically a unifying organization for French Protestantism. Much work remained to be done: churches needed to be informed of the Confession and Discipline and invited to join; ministers needed to be recruited, and promising candidates for the ministry needed to be trained; doctrine and discipline needed to be regularized in practice, not just in theory; and the Discipline and to a lesser

---

[56]This is particularly true for the years 1559–1571; see Brian Armstrong, *"Semper Reformanda,"* for a summary of changes introduced in the Confession the following five decades.

[57]Guillaume de Félice, *History of the Protestants of France from the Commencement of the Reformation to the Present Time,* translated with an introduction by Henry Lobdell (New York: Edward Walker, 1851), 89.

[58]Samuel Mours, *Le Protestantisme en France au XVIe siècle,* 103.

[59]Bernus, "Le ministre Antoine de Chandieu," 125.

extent, the Confession needed to be fine-tuned. This process was further complicated by the emergence of the Huguenot Party and the beginning of the Wars of Religion in 1562, just three short years after the first national synod. At this point the center of gravity of French Protestantism shifted away from the primarily urban churches which had founded the *Eglises Réformées* to the party's political and military leadership and the rural nobility who supported them. At the same time, the leaders of the French Reformed churches were nothing if not pragmatic: they knew they needed the help of the nobility if they were to succeed in making France a Protestant kingdom. The churches thus supported the claims of the high nobility and worked with them in trying to enforce Calvinist faith and piety in the areas controlled by Protestants.

For their part, the Protestant nobility and magistracy were happy to receive the support of the *Eglises Réformées* and to support their program in turn. Particularly in northern France, Protestant nobles often worked to establish and protect churches in towns which they controlled. These churches often met in noble residences, but rapidly evolved into independent local churches not tied directly to noble households. The Protestant nobility also took on Calvinist pastors as chaplains for the churches attached to their households and looked to the Gallican Confession to set doctrinal standards. On the other hand, these house churches—which made up as many as half the Protestant churches in the kingdom—were never integrated into the institutional structures of the French Reformed churches: there is virtually no evidence of consistories in the house churches, and these churches are likewise conspicuously absent in the surviving synodical records. As we examine the institutional structures of the "official" French Reformed Church, it is important to remember the "other half" of French Protestantism connected to the nobility who were the effective leaders of the Huguenots but not integrated into the ecclesiastical structures examined in this work.

Perhaps the greatest challenge in the Discipline was to develop a system of collective church government that would unite the disparate Protestant churches in the kingdom without the support of the magistrate and in the totally unprecedented absence of any form of hierarchical relationships between the churches. Accordingly, we turn first to this issue, focusing on the national and provincial synods.

The National
and Provincial Synods

The system of collective government adopted by the French Reformed churches combined elements of Reformed ecclesiology with indigenous structural innovations to produce a novel and influential form of synodical polity. This chapter examines the higher-level units in this system, the national and provincial synods. The first section outlines the history of Reformed synods in other parts of Europe and in pre-1559 French Protestantism. The next section focuses on the national and provincial synods as they evolved in France from 1559 to 1572 and beyond. The final section addresses the question of the origins of the system, focusing particularly on indigenous factors that shaped the collective government of the French Reformed Churches.

REFORMED SYNODS

Many Reformed churches had held synods prior to 1559, though in the majority of cases the synods functioned differently from those of the French Reformed churches. In Strasbourg and Geneva, the principal influences on French Protestantism, synods played little role in the church structure. Part of the reason for this was that both were city-states in which almost any ecclesiastical issue which needed to be addressed could be handled through the normal, day-to-day structures in the church. Geneva did not hold any synods, and Strasbourg had only two (1533 and 1539) which dealt with basic doctrinal issues (that is, the nature of the reform in the city) and with sacramental, liturgical, and pastoral activities.[1] Other Protestant cities held similar synods to lay the foundation for their churches, including Zurich (1528), Basel (1530), and Berne (1532).

In addition to their founding synods, Zurich and Berne established systems of regularly scheduled synods to discuss matters of general concern for the churches within their cantons and to maintain clerical discipline following the example of the early church. Although the Zurich synods functioned more regularly than did those of Berne, the Bernese ecclesiastical government, particularly in the Pays de Vaud, had a more direct influence on the churches in the kingdom of France via the ministry of Pierre Viret; accordingly, Berne will serve here as the model for an early Reformed synodical polity.[2]

In theory, general synods of all of the ministers in each linguistic community in the canton of Berne were to meet annually; in practice, although they met more often in the German-speaking areas than in the French, neither group met very regularly. The German synods began meeting in 1532; the first French synod was 1536. The French synods met annually for three years before being suspended out of fear that they would acquire a degree of authority over the Vaudois churches and weaken the dominance of the church of Berne in the region.[3] The next synod was not held until 1549, in Berne rather than in the Pays de Vaud itself. In what can only be described as a cultural clash, the meeting which Viret interpreted as going extremely well seemed so disorderly to the Bernese authorities that the synod was cut short after four days of "fraternal admonitions"; no more general synods of the Vaudois ministers were held.

Other assemblies did continue to meet, however. Berne divided the canton into ecclesiastical districts called "chapters" in the German-speaking areas and *classes* in the French areas. The "chapters" were established in 1530; the *classes* were set up at the Synod of Lausanne in 1537. The ministers of the *classe* were intended to meet weekly. Each elected a *doyen* and four *jurés;* the specific electoral procedures and term of office varied from *classe* to *classe,* but usually lasted two to three years. The *doyen* was the chair of the weekly meeting and was responsible for overseeing the doctrine preached in his district, the qualifications of new ministers, and the liturgical forms used in the churches; he also ensured that ministers did not involve themselves in the affairs of churches other than their own. The

---

[1]Gottfried Hammann, *Entre la secte et la cité: Le projet d'Eglise du Réformateur Martin Bucer* (Geneva: Labor et Fides, 1984), 51, 67.

[2]The following discussion of synods and "general chapters" is abridged from Henri Vuilleumier, *L'Eglise réformée du Pays de Vaud sous le régime Bernois,* vol. 1, *L'Age de la Réforme* (Lausanne: Editions la Concorde, 1927), 290–97; the discussion of classes and *colloques* is abridged from 1:278–89 of this work.

[3]Vuilleumier, *L'Eglise réformée du Pays de Vaud,* 1:291.

jurés and the *doyen* together monitored the conduct of the ministers in their area, with the *jurés* conducting regular visitations of the churches. If a minister censured by one of these officers did not correct his life or doctrine, he was referred to the *Chorgericht*, or morals court, in the capital city.

The sessions of the *classe* began with a Scripture reading and exposition by one of the pastors; the others added their comments after the expositor had finished. Next, other business was conducted, including examination of candidates for the ministry (and in the *classe* of Lausanne, for professorships at the Academy), administrative matters, and any issues brought before them by the civil government, the ministers of Berne, or another *classe*. In particular, the *classe* was permitted by law to decide whether or not a candidate for ministry was qualified before the Bernese Senate confirmed him in office. In practice, however, the *classe* was not always consulted about ministerial candidates, particularly when the church of Berne was directed by Kunz, a man with decidedly hierarchical views of ecclesiastical government.[4] At any rate, at regular intervals the meetings of the *classe* also included time for "fraternal" mutual censure. The meetings ended with a common meal.

With the suspension of general synods, the Bernese government needed to reestablish some point of contact with the churches in the Pays de Vaud; they thus established the "general chapter," a meeting of all of the *classes* of the region. At the general chapter, the pastors and civil officials of each *classe* in turn were examined by delegates of the Bernese civil and ecclesiastical government. The pastors were required to evaluate the civil officials in their districts, and vice versa. After the meetings, the delegation returned to Berne and presented a report to the government, which then took whatever action it deemed appropriate with regard to any pastors or officials who were found wanting. Although these general chapters were intended to be held annually, in practice they became less and less frequent over time.

Given the size of the *classes,* it was not practical for the ministers to meet weekly; by 1539—two years after their establishment—their weekly meetings were converted to quarterly sessions which opened with a public sermon. At the same time, the *classes* were subdivided into smaller units called *colloques.* Each *colloque* held a meeting at least monthly which began with a public exposition of Scripture followed by a question and answer session similar to that of the *congrégations* of Geneva. Afterwards, the ministers retired to continue the discussion and to handle censures and administrative matters. The Bernese authorities, fearing that heretical ideas might arise as a result of public participation in the Bible

---

[4]Vuilleumier, *L'Eglise réformée du Pays de Vaud*, 1:282–83.

studies, suppressed the *colloques* in 1549. The Lausanne *classe*, led by Pierre Viret, protested this vigorously. The Bernese responded by permitting weekly meetings to continue in Lausanne alone, and with stringent restrictions: only one minister could present a scriptural exposition; he was not permitted to teach anything contrary to the theses approved at the Dispute of Berne (1528); the laity could attend but could not speak; the meetings were to conclude with prayer and a collection for the poor. Lausanne objected to these restrictions, quite justifiably accusing the Bernese theologians of taking on quasi-episcopal authority over the Vaudois churches. The protest was to no avail, however; not until 1561 were meetings other than the quarterly *classes* again permitted in the Pays de Vaud outside of Lausanne, and even then, they were seriously restricted: they could only meet four times per year, they could only discuss Scripture, they had to invite the local bailiff to attend, and they could only deal with local administrative matters assigned to them by the *classe*.

A few general points should be made here about the Bernese synodical system. First, magisterial interference in ecclesiastical affairs, particularly in the francophone areas, made it impossible for the churches to govern their internal affairs in any meaningful way. General synods were banned outright; even within the *classes*, practices designed to make the system more workable were restricted or abolished by the government. Second, in each of these examples, the magisterium worked in concert with the church of the city of Berne itself. While it would be stretching the point to call the *doyen* of the *Convent* (the assembly of the pastors and professors of the capital) a bishop, the *Convent* and *Chorgericht* of Berne did exercise a considerable amount of control over the churches of the canton; Viret's (and Calvin's) accusations were well founded on this point. The Bernese church may not have been an episcopacy in the strict sense of the term, but it was in essence hierarchical, albeit centering authority in a "central place" rather than a "central person." This was not much better from the point of view of the Vaudois. The linguistic, cultural, and theological gaps between the German-speaking Bernese and the French-speaking Vaudois led inevitably to conflict, and the "central place" structure of the church meant that the French party invariably lost. This in turn meant that many of the greatest leaders of the Vaudois church were dismissed from their positions in 1558; many of them went into exile in Geneva, most notably Viret and Beza.

Of course, magisterial interference was the norm rather than the exception in Protestant communities; even Beza—a victim of Bernese domination of Lausanne—argued that the magistrates were the church's principal members.[5] This

---

[5]Theodore Beza, *Confession de la Foy Chrestienne, faite par Theodore de Besze, contenant la confirmation d'icelle, et la refutation des superstitions contraires: Reveue et augmentee de nouveau par luy,*

was in keeping with the common assumption that church and state could not and should not be separated; religion was seen as far too important a matter not to be regulated by the government. And since both civil and ecclesiastical governments were ordained by God, it was only logical to assume that they would mirror each other. Thus Protestant principalities tended to adopt episcopal structures, whether the Church of England and the refugee church in London, where John à Lasco functioned as a bishop for the Protestant refugees, the Lutheran churches in the empire, or the Reformed Church of Hungary. This may also help explain Calvin's advice to the king of Poland: not only did the archiepiscopal arrangement he advocated follow the model of the early church, but it mirrored the structure of the kingdom to a fair extent. Conversely, Protestants in city-states and other Renaissance republics tended to adopt a conciliar style of ecclesiastical government, avoiding any hint of a traditional episcopacy. For these states, sole rule, whether by a prince or a bishop, smacked of tyranny.[6] But opposition to episcopacy did not necessarily translate to opposition to hierarchy any more than opposition to monarchy did. In the case of Berne, no matter how republican its constitution, the capital city dominated the canton politically; why should it not do so ecclesiastically, even without a bishop? For the Bernese, the problem with episcopacy was its centering of authority in a single person; centering it in a church run collegially thus eliminated the problem. Of course, the francophone ministers objected to this, arguing that the Bernese system amounted to a functional episcopacy. For them, the issue was hierarchy: traditional bishops violated the Reformed (or, more generally, the Protestant) principle of equality of ministers, as did the church of Berne, whose ministers had authority over those in the Pays de Vaud.

This conflict highlights a key dilemma facing Reformed ecclesiology in the 1550s. It emphasized the equality and collegiality of ministers and yet had found no clear way to reconcile this with the hierarchical nature of sixteenth-century society. For Berne, the solution was to emphasize collegiality while giving the city church extra authority in keeping with the canton's political structures; for the Hungarian Reformed Church, in parallel with other Hungarian Protestant groups,[7] the solution was an episcopate with senior pastors, archdeacons, and

---

avec un abregé d'icelle ([Geneva]: Conrad Badius, 1559), 175.

[6]There were some exceptions, such as the *Antistes* of Zurich or Bucer in Strasbourg, but the Erastian nature of the church in these areas limited the effective authority of these quasi-episcopal leaders.

[7]Sources for the history of Hungarian Protestantism are very difficult to come by in English. The most accessible secondary studies include David P. Daniel, "Hungary," in *The Early Reformation in Europe*, ed. Andrew Pettegree (Cambridge: Cambridge University Press, 1992); idem; "Calvinism in

"superintendents" (that is, bishops) who operated in conjunction with synods while effectively giving the higher clergy extra authority.[8] In all cases, the principle of collegiality was maintained even while emphasizing a central place like the city of Berne or a central person like a Hungarian bishop: local churches were typically governed by councils—the *Convent* or consistory—and larger areas by some form of synod. In all cases, the synods interlocked with a hierarchical structure which to a greater or lesser extent paralleled the structure of the civil government.

The first Reformed polity to apply systematically the principle of ministerial and ecclesiastical equality was the *Eglises Réformées,* starting with the first edition of the Discipline in 1559; in other words, the first Reformed church to eliminate all forms of hierarchy from its ecclesiastical structure emerged in a hostile, predominantly Roman Catholic kingdom. To understand how and why this happened, we must examine the development of the Protestant churches in the kingdom prior to 1559.

FRENCH PROTESTANTISM PRIOR TO 1559: THE *ARTICLES POLYTIQUES*
In the decades preceding the first national synod, French Protestantism had developed along essentially congregationalist lines. Local Protestant churches in the kingdom worked together reasonably well to promote their mutual interests without devising any formal mechanisms for interchurch relations. In fact, the local church continued to be the fundamental unit within the ecclesiastical system long after the adoption of the Discipline: even the very name *Eglises Réformées de France* pointed to the individual churches which subscribed to the Discipline rather than to the synods that oversaw them. By the late 1550s, however, influential leaders within French Protestantism began to work toward developing a more systematic church order on the local, provincial, and national levels out of a perceived need to reconcile the conflicting institutions and practices that had developed in different regions of France, or indeed in individual churches. The first attempt to set up such a church order was the *Articles polytiques* of 1557;

Hungary: The Theological and Ecclesiastical Transition to the Reformed Faith," in *Calvinism in Europe: 1540–1620,* ed. Andrew W. Pettegree, Alastair Duke, and Gillian Lewis (Cambridge: Cambridge University Press, 1994); idem, "Hungary" and "Synods: Synods in Eastern Europe," in *Oxford Encyclopedia of the Reformation* (1996); Winfried Eberhard, "East Central Europe," in *Handbook of European History, 1400–1600,* ed. Thomas A. Brady, Jr., Heiko A. Obermann, and James D. Tracy, vol. 2, *Visions, Programs, and Outcomes* (Leiden: Brill, 1995).

[8]This functionally occurred in Geneva as well: Calvin was the permanent moderator of the Company of Pastors, and it is hard to argue that he did not possess greater de facto authority even without extra de jure authority.

accordingly, this document should be seen as an essential element of the background to the Discipline of 1559.

The *Articles polytiques* did not explicitly call for synods as a regular element of church government, but it did allow for them to decide issues of mutual concern between churches. The first article of the chapter, *Articles politiques,* reads: "Since all primacy is dangerous and aspires to tyranny, as is seen in the example of the papacy, [churches] must guard against resolving any matter which affects other churches without their consent and without requesting such consent. This is to be done in a legitimately assembled synod where those who are deputed from each church are able to attend." [9] Such synods were to be held in a location convenient to the churches involved and presumably were limited to those churches. Despite the recognition that synods were necessary, the Articles did not attempt to establish a true synodical system of ecclesiastical government; in fact, the Articles do not set up any system of collective government for the churches. Instead, their focus is almost entirely on the local church in keeping with the nature of French Protestantism.

This essentially local focus was supported indirectly by the justification for calling synods: if a church was allowed to make decisions that affected other churches unilaterally, it would hold de facto primacy over the others, which in turn would lead almost inevitably to tyranny. The argument is not couched in terms of the familiar *Quod tanget omnes* principle of medieval law. Instead, the focus of the argument is entirely negative (to prevent tyranny) rather than positive (to preserve the church's right to a say in decisions that touched it). Of course, the problem with tyranny was that it illegally usurped another's legitimate rights and prerogatives, and thus the justification for holding synods hinged somewhat paradoxically on preserving the independence of the local church from outside authority. This radically egalitarian (by sixteenth-century standards), antihierarchical approach to church government grew as much out of the de facto congregationalist structure of French Protestantism as from theological principles, and it amounted to a rejection not only of episcopacy but of a Bernese-style "central place" system.

At the same time that they affirm the independence of local churches, the Articles also stress the need for cooperation between churches, particularly in disciplinary matters. This was designed in part to protect ministers who might

[9]"Pour autant que toute primauté est dangereuse et aspire a une tyrannie comme en voit l'exemple en la papauté, a cette cause on se donnera garde de resoudre chose qui touche les autres eglises sans le consentement d'icelles et en estre requis; ce qui se pourra faire en synode legitimement assemblé, la ou pourront assister ceux qui seront deputez d'une chacune eglise." *Articles polytiques,* "Articles politiques," 1 (11).

become unpopular as a result of carrying out their proper tasks in the church. Pastors were not to be deposed from the ministry lightly, at the whim of the congregation, but only by the "good and just judgment" of the ministers, elders, and deacons; if needed, ministers from neighboring churches could be called in as well.[10] Another area of interchurch cooperation involved maintaining the purity of the Lord's Supper: no one from another church was to be admitted to the sacrament in "our" church without an attestation from her or his home church's consistory; similarly, no one from "our" church should be accepted for Communion in another church without an attestation from "our" consistory, so that those who were excommunicated from one church might not simply go to a nearby church for the Lord's Supper.[11]

While the *Articles polytiques* provided for coordination of discipline and matters of mutual interest among churches, it did not propose any formal or regular structures for collective government among the churches. The document essentially preserved the congregationalist polity of the pre-1559 churches. Even the article dealing with synods supports this observation, since it was designed to prevent domination of one church by another. It did provide for ad hoc regional and even national synods to coordinate policy among the churches of the kingdom as a whole vis-à-vis the monarchy as well as in other areas of general concern. Although not a regular element of the church government outlined in the Articles, such synods would be a prominent feature of the Discipline adopted two years later at the first national synod in Paris.

The Synodical System of the Discipline

In the two years between the *Articles polytiques* and the first national synod, Chandieu worked out a system that combined the concerns for the independence of local churches that characterized French Protestantism with the synodically based polity that Bucer, Calvin, and other humanist-inspired theologians saw in the early church. Remarkably enough, many of the essentials of the system were set in place in the first edition of the Discipline in 1559, though other aspects evolved over time through clarification or change of the original provisions, addition of new elements, and judicial decisions and supplementary legislation. The discussion here summarizes the provisions for provincial and national synods in the 1559 Discipline, then traces the development of these levels of the ecclesiastical

---

[10] *Articles polytiques*, "Des ministres," 4 (6–7).

[11] *Articles polytiques*, "Articles politiques," 12, 13 (14); cf. *Articles polytiques*, "Charge commune," 3 (11). The last two articles, with their references to "our" consistory, tend to support the idea that the *Articles polytiques* was originally a local church order, probably from Poitiers, that was proposed as a model for a standardized church government for French Protestants.

government up to the eighth national synod (Nîmes, 1572), and continues with a brief summary of the continuing evolution of rules for appeals of disciplinary cases to the national synod. To help clarify the respective roles of the provincial and national synods, the section concludes by tracing some examples of the interaction of the synods in developing and fine-tuning legislation.

The Discipline of 1559

The 1559 Discipline begins with three articles dealing with the general characteristics of collective church government and synods. The first article asserts the equality of churches: "No church is to pretend to have primacy or dominion over another."[12] This repeats the last clause of article 30 of the Gallican Confession, which states that since all ministers are equal, no church can claim authority over another. The two together effectively followed the lead of the *Articles polytiques* by prohibiting episcopacy either in the form of a "central person" or of a Bernese-style "central place." Beyond the concern about tyranny expressed in the *Articles polytiques,* a practical consideration may have been at work here as well: independent churches were unlikely to submit themselves voluntarily to the authority of another church; thus, if the Discipline was to unite the churches and establish a system of collective government, it needed to preserve congregational independence. The article may also have been aimed specifically at the real or imagined ambitions of certain churches to ecclesiastical primacy.[13]

The second article addressed the question of the moderatorship of the synods, the historical origin of the episcopal office, according to Calvin. The Discipline took the radical step of having the moderator elected at each synod and only holding office for the duration of the synod. His responsibilities and the selection procedure were described as follows: "Each synod is to elect by common accord a president to preside over the colloquium and to handle affairs related to it, and this charge ends with [the closing of] each synod and council."[14] Another well-attested version of the article specified the duties in more detail:

[12]Nulle eglise ne pourra pretendre primauté ne domination sur l'autre. The third national synod (Orléans, 1562) expanded this article by adding, "ne pareillement les ministres d'une eglise, les uns sur les autres, et notamment ceux d'une mesme eglise"; it also added immediately after this article another: "Les anciens et les diacres ne pourront pretendre primauté ni domination les uns sur les autres"; cf. Quick, 3–Orléans–1562, chap. 2, art. 6 (23). By 1571, this had become three articles ("Des ministres," 20, "Des anciens et diacres," 6, and "Des consistoires," 1). The prohibition of hierarchy also was the basis for a number of specific decisions related to provincial synods.

[13]I owe this last idea to Bernard Roussel, who suggested Paris, Poitiers, or even Geneva as possible targets of the article.

[14]Un president en chacun synode sera esleu d'un commun accord pour presider au colloque et faire ce que y appartient, et finira ladicte charge avec chacun synode et concile. I have translated *colloque*

Each synod is to elect by common accord a president to send word of the days and places where the sessions of the colloquium are to meet, to collect votes, to declare the largest number, and to announce the conclusion. *Item:* to see that each speaks in turn and without confusion, to impose silence on those who are too sharp or contentious, and if they are unwilling to obey him, to send them out in order to decide how to censure them. And he is to preside over all censures, to make remonstrations, and to respond to those who ask counsel or send letters during the synod, following in all things its decision; and he himself is subject to censure. The charge of the presidency expires at the end of the colloquium, and the following council is free to reelect him or to elect another.[15]

Although the *classes* of the Pays de Vaud provided a precedent for a nonpermanent presiding officer in a synod (that is, the *doyen,* who was reelected periodically following the traditions of the specific *classe*), there is no precedent for the office expiring at the end of the synod, except in the case of ad hoc synodical meetings. Further, the specific responsibilities of the moderator were limited to keeping the synod running smoothly; again unlike the *doyens* of the Pays de Vaud, the moderator had no responsibilities outside of the synod. In many ways, this definition of the role of the moderator is one of the most original aspects of the polity developed by the churches of France. This limited moderatorship had a profound influence on the structure of the Reformed churches of France and

---

as "colloquium" here and in the next quotation to avoid confusing it with the colloquy, an assembly that had not yet been defined in the Discipline.

[15]En chascun synode sera esleu d'un commun accord un president pour faire advertir des jours et lieux auxquels on s'assemblera aux sessions du colloque, recueillir les voix, en declarer le plus grand nombre, et prononcer la conclusion. Item de faire que chascun parle d'ordre et sans confusion, imposer silence a ceux qui sont trop aspres en contentieux et s'ils n'y voulaient obeir les fayre sortir pour adviser sur la censure qui y appartiendra. Et presidera a toutes censures, fera des resmonstrances et fera la responce a ceux qui demanderont conseil ou envoyeront lettres pendant le synode, suivant en tout l'advis d'icelluy et sera lui-mesme subject aux censures. La charge du president expirera à la fin du colloque et sera en la liberté du concile suivant d'eslire cestuy là ou un autre. This text (with minor variations in wording) is attested by MSS Wb and Rb, Pithou, and the acts of the first national synod; it was included in the 1561 Discipline but leaves no trace in the acts of the second national synod (Poitiers, 1561). This version of the article thus can reasonably be dated to 1559, though Roussel remains unconvinced that it should be included in the 1559 Discipline and thus omitted it from Roussel, "Discipline." A similar text was adopted by the provincial synod of Languedoc meeting in Nîmes in February 1561. The short version of the article appears in *Histoire ecclésiastique* and Wa.

provided a crucial precedent for synodical polities introduced later in the Low Countries and Scotland.[16]

Article 3 turns to the issue of representation at national synods.[17] The article states that pastors are to bring one or more elders and deacons with them to synods, all of whom are to have a vote. Subsequent editions of the Discipline would modify this greatly, and these changes would affect the very nature of the synodical system, making it far more workable.[18]

Article 4 of the 1559 Discipline discusses procedural issues for national (or general) synods. It specifies simply that they are to meet "as needed" *(selon la necessité des eglises)* and include a time of fraternal and friendly admonition,[19] to be followed by the celebration of the Lord's Supper.[20] Two other articles deal with the role of national synods, albeit in relatively vague terms. Article 31 concerns

[16]The acts of the national synods starting with the second (Poitiers, 1561) indicate that one or more scribes were appointed at the national synod in addition to the moderator prescribed by the Discipline; the first probably had a scribe as well. Starting with the tenth synod (Figeac, 1579), they also appointed "assessors." The twelfth national synod (Vitré, 1583) decreed that provincial synods should also appoint at least one scribe in addition to the moderator; see Quick, 2–Poitiers–1561, chap. 10 (12), 10–Figeac–1579, chap. 1 (128–29), 12–Vitré–1583, chap. 3, art. 8, par. 6 (148).

[17]The article itself does not specify national synods except in its less reliable versions in Quick and Aymon. But since article 5 deals with representation in provincial synods, this article presumably deals with national synods. The earlier general articles on synods cover material that is not repeated in other articles dealing with provincial synods, and so may be taken to refer to all synods and not just the national.

[18]There are two principal versions of this article in the manuscripts and published sources. The reading adopted here is that of Roussel, "Discipline," supported by the *Histoire ecclésiastique*, Pithou, and MS Rb. Quick, Aymon, and MS Wb read "one or two at most" elders or deacons are to attend synods; Aymon and Wb add that all the elders and deacons in the host church can vote. Since all these variations can be traced to the second national synod (Poitiers, 1561), it seems likely that Roussel's is the original text, and that the later texts were corrupted by the decisions of the second national synod.

[19]The thirteenth national synod (Montauban, 1594) explained that the *censure* was only to deal with matters arising during the synod; Quick, 13–Montauban–1594, chap. 3, art. 13 (160). The motivation for this late "clarification" is unclear, though it presumably was caused by problems that arose in the course of the synod.

[20]The third national synod (Orléans, 1562) declared this celebration to be open to the entire church, while the twelfth national synod (Vitré, 1583) called on churches holding the national synod to schedule one of their regular celebrations of the Lord's Supper to coincide with the synod and to prepare the congregation accordingly. This is somewhat curious, since the national synods of Paris (1565) and La Rochelle (1571) had both "encouraged" the churches to celebrate the Lord's Supper more frequently; combining the Lord's Supper at the end of the national synod with one of the quarterly celebrations in the church hardly seems to be encouraging more frequent celebration of the Sacrament. See Quick, 3–Orléans–1562, chap. 2, art. 3 (23), 12–Vitré–1583, chap. 2, art. 16, cf. chap. 3, art. 9, par. 11 (145, 148), 5–Paris–1565, chap. 11, art. 19 (66), 7–La Rochelle–1571, chap. 8, art. 7 (97).

church discipline: "As for those who have been excommunicated for lesser causes [than those mentioned in the previous article], it is left to the prudence of the church [that is, the consistory] to decide if the reason should be revealed to the people or not, until it is decided otherwise by the ensuing general council."[21] The national synod thus reserved the right to decide potentially controversial or divisive disciplinary cases in local churches, though leaving the immediate decision in the hands of the consistory. The last reference to the national synod in the 1559 Discipline occurs in the final article, dealing with the nature of the church order itself: "These articles which are contained herein concerning discipline are not enacted among us such that if the need of the Church should require it, they cannot be changed, but it is not in the power of an individual [church] to do this without the advice and consent of the general council."[22] Thus the national synod again reserved for itself the right to deal with matters which affected the French Reformed churches generally, following the principle set forth in the *Articles polytiques* that no church has the right to make decisions which affect other churches without their consent.

Given the decentralized focus of French Protestant ecclesiology, it is not surprising that the 1559 Discipline had considerably more to say about provincial synods than it did about national synods. The fifth article outlines the basic structure of provincial synods: "The ministers and at least one elder or deacon from each church of each province are to meet together twice per year."[23] In this edition of the Discipline, the provincial synod is the basic unit of the collective government of the churches: unlike the national synod, which only was to meet on an ad hoc basis, the provincial synod was to meet regularly. In addition to frequency

[21]DE, art. 31; Roussel, "Discipline," art. 27; Quant à ceux qui auroyent esté excommuniez pour plus legeres causes, ce sera en la prudence de l'eglise d'adviser si elle les devra manifester au peuple ou non, jusques à ce qu'autrement en soit diffini par le concile general ensuyvant.

[22]Ces articles qui sont ici contenus touchant la discipline ne sont tellement arrestez entre nous, que si l'utilité de l'eglise le requiert, ils ne puissent estre changez, mais ce ne sera en la puissance d'un particulier de ce faire sans l'advis et consentement du concile general.

[23]Les ministres et un ancien ou diacre pour le moins de chacune eglise de chacune province s'assembleront deux fois l'annee. The best manuscripts all read "chacune eglise *ou* chacune province" (emphasis added), which suggests that this is a description of the national synod, with representation either from churches or provinces. But art. 4 specifies that national synods are to meet "selon la necessité des eglises," and not twice per year as this article specifies; the text has been amended from *ou* to *de* following the later manuscripts. MSS Wb and Rb, influenced by the second national synod (Poitiers, 1561), add "et choisiront le temps et le lieu qui leur sera plus commode pour le faire." This addition harks back to the *Articles polytiques*. The first provincial synod of Brittany (held in Chateaubriand, 1561) evidently included delegates who were either elders or heads of families; Philippe Le Noir, *Histoire ecclésiastique de Bretagne depuis la Réformation jusqu'à l'Édit de Nantes*, edited by B. Vaurigaud (Paris: Grassart; Nantes: Guéraud, 1851), 70.

and composition, the 1559 Discipline also identifies numerous roles for the provincial synod. In terms of general principles, the Discipline stresses the familiar theme that churches must act together in matters of mutual interest: "No church can do anything of great consequence or which could involve the interest or injury of other churches without the advice of the provincial council if it is possible to assemble it, and if the affair is pressing, the church is to communicate with the other churches of the province by letter at least for their advice and consent."[24] In addition to regulating areas of common concern among its churches, the provincial synod was given a great deal of responsibility for overseeing local churches and especially their officers. It was to mediate conflicts over elections of church officers and the legitimacy of calls to a pastorate;[25] it was also to mediate between a pastor and his consistory in situations where the consistory sent him to minister in another church, whether temporarily or permanently, but he refused to go;[26] and to oversee the transfer of pastors between churches.[27] In terms of disciplinary action, the provincial synod was to decide whether any church officer found guilty of a lesser vice or crime, or a pastor who claimed that he was unjustly convicted of a serious crime, should be deposed.[28] In a specific case, the 1559 national synod also authorized the relevant provincial synod to investigate and take action with regard to the "notorious heresies" of LaVau that had prompted Chandieu's visit to Poitiers in 1558, implying that the provincial synod had authority to deal with doctrinal issues as well.[29]

At this stage, the disciplinary responsibilities of the synods were limited to church officers: the national synod had no specified disciplinary duties beyond mutual admonitions among the deputies; the provincial synods were responsible for pastoral oversight and discipline of church officers, but not of ordinary church

---

[24]Nulle eglise ne pourra rien faire de grande consequence où pourroit estre compris l'interest et dommage des autres eglises sans l'advis du concile provincial, s'il est possible l'assembler, et si l'affaire le pressoit, elle communiquera et aura l'advis et consentement des autres eglises de la province, par lettres pour le moins. DE 1559, art. 41; Roussel, "Discipline," art. 37.

[25]DE 1559, art. 6, 12; MSS Rb and Wb add to art. 8 text that deals with provincial synods as well. Among other things, these additions indicate that the provincial synod was to determine whether churches which refused to subscribe to the Discipline but accepted the Confession were to be declared schismatic. This article is included in the 1561 Discipline released by the second national synod (Poitiers, 1561) but does not seem to have been added by that synod, judging from the acts. It may have been included in some versions of the 1559 Discipline, which then formed the base for the version ratified at Poitiers.

[26]DE 1559, art. 11.

[27] DE 1559, art. 15.

[28] DE 1559, art. 18, 19, 26; Roussel, "Discipline," art. 17, 18, 24.

[29]Quick, chap. 3, art. 4 (7). Cf. Léonard, *Histoire générale*, 2:3n.

members except perhaps in cases of heresy. As we will see, both the national and the provincial synod would later take on the additional role of appellate courts for church discipline cases. In 1559, however, the synods were only called on to perform "clerical" discipline, following the example of the early church and the precedents of Zurich and Berne.

A Counterproposal

Perhaps because of the small number and limited geographic range of the churches that were represented at the first national synod, the Discipline did not meet with immediate support in all segments of French Protestantism. The churches of Brittany are a case in point. There were only two formally established churches in the province, one in Rennes pastored by M. Du Gravier, and the other in Vitré, pastored by M. Du Fossé. Both churches had been founded and continued to be sponsored and protected by nobles, though they were centered in the cities rather than in the noble households. Further, Brittany had not sent any representatives to the national synods.[30] In the beginning of May 1560, Du Gravier traveled to Orléans and Paris to ask their advice concerning church organization.[31] Apparently, he was given copies of the Discipline and Confession during this trip. On May 13 he returned to Brittany and met with "several gentlemen and other persons who had a charge in the church" in a "consistorial council or synodal consistory" *(conseil consistorial ou consistoire synodal)* at la Fonchaye.[32] They accepted the Confession readily enough—it was presented to the seneschal at Rennes a week later[33]—but they seem to have rejected the provisions for collective government in the Discipline, at least initially. They decided instead that each province should choose four gentlemen to handle matters related to the church. They were to hold six-month terms, at the end of which four others were to be elected. The meetings were to be held in "some city under a pretext decided upon by two of the gentlemen," thus setting the stage for "secret political synods."[34] One or more pastors would meet

---

[30]Le Noir, *Histoire ecclésiastique de Bretagne*, 25, cf. 41, believed that Du Fossé attended the first national synod, but not entirely as a representative of the province: his superiors had sent him to Meaux temporarily to work as a pastor there, and while passing through Paris to get to Meaux he may have attended the national synod.

[31]Le Noir, *Histoire ecclésiastique de Bretagne*, 37. Le Noir places this meeting after the second national synod, held in Poitiers in March 1561 (34). This is an error in chronology on Le Noir's part: the manuscript dates of the records for the synod of Poitiers all place the year as 1560, yet since the year officially began at Easter during this period and the synod had met prior to Easter, by modern reckoning (that is, with the year beginning on January 1), the year was 1561.

[32]Le Noir, *Histoire ecclésiastique de Bretagne*, 37.

[33]Le Noir, *Histoire ecclésiastique de Bretagne*, 39.

[34]Le Noir, *Histoire ecclésiastique de Bretagne*, 38.

with them to "conduct the action" (that is, act as moderator) and open and close the meetings with prayer. This council would discuss and decide all ecclesiastical affairs. M. Du Fossé was dispatched to Normandy to try to garner support for this system, but to no avail. Instead of holding a "synodical council of four nobles," Normandy held a provincial synod in Caen a month later, following the terms of the Discipline, and Du Gravier and an elder of the church at Rennes attended as delegates from Brittany.[35] The council of four nobles thus seems to have been abandoned before it ever had a chance to be established.

The differences between the approach to collective government in the Discipline and in the Breton noble council are striking. In the Discipline, leadership is based on the pastors and elders of the local church; in the Breton system, leadership comes from the nobility. In fact, though a pastor may be the moderator of the synod, it is unclear whether he could vote, and even if he could, he would be outnumbered four to one by the nobles. Later in the century, the noble-dominated political assemblies would restrict the pastors' role in the assembly to pronouncing the prayers—essentially the same function they were to perform in the Breton councils. What we see here are two competing visions for leadership in the Huguenot community founded on the fundamental division within French Protestantism between what I term local churches and noble churches. Although the churches such as Rennes and Vitré in Brittany were not part of noble households, they were nonetheless dependent on the nobles who founded them and protected them. It is small wonder that the nobles were looked upon to provide leadership for the churches. The churches that met in the national synod, however, were drawn from the older, nonnoble churches that had formed the core of French Protestantism in the decades prior to the conversion of the nobility. These churches had functioned independently and still sought to preserve their autonomy even as they worked to establish a system of collective government. Naturally, they would look for leadership within the congregations themselves, rather than to noble protectors who had little historical connection to the churches. In the end, these were the churches that participated in the synodical system, and so their priorities won out in the collective government of the churches. Since the Breton churches were not part of noble households, they could freely send representatives to the synods as well; they quickly joined the provincial synods when it became obvious that their proposal did not have sufficient support to go forward. Nonetheless, however ephemeral the council of four nobles was, it serves as a

---

[35]Le Noir, *Histoire ecclésiastique de Bretagne*, 42. Curiously, Le Noir states that in the beginning these councils "served greatly to advance the churches" (38), yet given the timing, it is unclear how or when they would ever have met.

potent reminder of the diversity of experience and organizational structures that existed within French Protestantism in the middle of the century.

THE STRUCTURAL DEVELOPMENT OF THE SYNODICAL SYSTEM

The synodical system outlined in the 1559 Discipline developed considerably over the next decade; in fact, some of the most significant changes were introduced by the second national synod, held in Poitiers in 1561.[36] The fourth article of the Discipline issued by this synod includes legislation which changed the national synod in fundamental ways:

> *Item:* it is decided that at the end of each general synod a specific church will be given authority to assemble another general council within one year, to which all the provinces of the kingdom will convene, that is, a minister and a deacon or elder from each province, other ministers always being at liberty [to attend] if it seems good to them [and] with the permission of their church.
>
> The aforementioned general council is to decide all ecclesiastical matters and differences, reserving the points which it judges to be necessary for a universal council of all the churches of this and other kingdoms which wish to attend, the convocation of which will be left to the discretion of the aforementioned general council, as circumstances require it [that is, the convocation of a universal council].[37]

This article introduced three major changes to the national synod. First, it was no longer to meet simply on an ad hoc basis; rather, it was now to meet annually (at least in theory).[38] This made the national synod a regular part of the church

---

[36]The manuscripts are dated 1560, but this is "old style" dating; the synod met in March prior to Easter, the beginning of the New Year. By modern standards, with January 1 being the beginning of the New Year, the synod met in 1561. The text of the Discipline used here was supplied by Bernard Roussel and is based on manuscript sources in Grenoble and Le Mans.

[37]Item a esté arresté qu'à la fin d'un chascun synode general sera donnee puissance a une certaine église d'assembler dans l'an un autre concile general auquel conviendront toutes les provinces de ce royaume, a sçavoir un ministre et un diacre ou ancien de chascune province, estant toutesfois en la liberté des autres ministres de s'y trouver si bon leur semble avec le congé de leur église.

Lequel concile general poura decider de toutes choses ecclesiastiques et differens, reservant les poincts qu'il jugera estre necessaire au concile universel de toutes les églises de ce royaume et autres qui s'y voudroyent trouver, la convocation duquel sera remise a la discretion dudit concile general, quand la necessite le requerra.

[38]The eighth national synod (Nîmes, 1572), in tacit recognition of the difficulties of annual meetings, added that the national synod was to meet yearly *if possible (tant que faire se pourra).* Quick, 8–Nîmes–1572, chap. 3, art. 10 (106), cf. DE 1572, "Des synodes nationaux," 2.

government in a way that the 1559 Discipline did not. Second, the article changed the system of representation at the synod from pastors and one or more elders and deacons *per church* to one pastor and one elder or deacon *per province*, plus any other pastors who wished to attend and who had permission from their "church" (that is, consistory).[39] This was another extremely important development that transformed the basic structure of the national synod: the change from deputies sent from local churches to deputies sent from the provincial synods weakened the almost democratic focus on the authority of the local church found in the 1559 Discipline and reinforced the authority of the provincial synods.[40] Third, the article gave the national synod final say in all ecclesiastical matters within the kingdom, unless it wished to send a question to a (Reformed) ecumenical council. In practice, however, this authority was severely limited: the very next article in the 1561 Discipline restricts the topics the national synod could discuss to matters of general concern and those approved by the provincial synods, thereby reinforcing the Discipline's emphasis on the more local levels of the ecclesiastical system.[41] This impression is further confirmed by the next national synod, held at Orléans in 1562 as the armies were mobilizing for the first War of Religion. This synod decided that since so many deputies were unable to attend, a full record would be made of the actions of the synod and the reasoning behind them, and that this would be sent to the unrepresented provinces. The actions of the synod would then be reviewed at the next national synod and, if the provinces objected to anything, discussion would be reopened.[42] Despite the Discipline, the authority of the national synod continued to rest on the authority of the provinces.

[39]The fifth national synod, meeting in Paris in 1565, eliminated this last provision, noting that the Wars of Religion made it too dangerous for large numbers of pastors to gather in one place; Quick, 5–Paris–1565, chap. 10, art. 23 (65–66). Even after the Edict of Nantes removed this threat, the rules remained unchanged.

[40]Only two other changes were introduced to the legislation dealing with deputies to the national synods. The eleventh national synod (La Rochelle, 1581) adjusted the number of deputies from the provincial synods to two pastors and two elders; Quick, 11–La Rochelle–1581, chap. 3, art. 32 (139); the thirteenth national synod (Montauban, 1594) added that they must bring an attestation signed by the moderator and scribe of the provincial synod; Quick, 13–Montauban–1594, chap. 3, art. 13 (160).

[41]The only other change to the provincial synods introduced in 1561 involved frequency: According to DE 1561, art. 8, instead of meeting twice per year, they were now to meet "once or twice" annually.

[42]Et neantmoins lesdites provinces seront suffisamment averties des choses decidees et resolues en ce concile, avec les raisons pour lesquelles nonobstant leur absence, on a esté contraint de passer outre, comme aussi elles seront plus amplement discutees au prochain concile general, auquel semblablement les raisons de ceux qui defaillent seront entendues, et ensemble leurs remonstrances, si aucuns en ont affaire sur les decisions du present concile (art. 1).

What are we to make of these changes? The Discipline had been adopted less than two years before, yet here, at the first opportunity, the nature, composition, and role of the national synod was changed in fundamental ways. The deputies evidently thought the 1559 Discipline flawed, particularly with respect to the national synod, and thus came to Poitiers planning to improve it. The basic church structure laid out in 1559 was accepted as sound; there was no move to scrap the whole church structure and start again. But the national synod needed to be made a regular part of the church government, with clearly defined responsibilities and limitations and a more rational composition. The initiative for this almost certainly came from the provincial synods, the center of gravity of the collective government of the churches in 1559 and the doorkeeper to the national synod from 1561 on. Ratifying and correcting the decisions of the national synod would be a continuing role of the provincial synods as the century wore on.

The next major modifications of the synodical system and the Discipline came at the fourth national synod, held in Lyon in 1563 under the moderatorship of Pierre Viret. The first of these developments dealt with ecclesiastical provinces. Although the first edition of the Discipline had provided for provincial synods, their boundaries were not specified in either the Discipline or the acts of the national synod. The register of the consistory of Le Mans in 1561 suggests that the provinces did not correspond directly to those of the kingdom: although each ecclesiastical province was to send a deputy to court, there was to be only one from Anjou, Touraine, and Maine combined.[43] Prior to 1563, the only legislation at the level of the national synods dealing with this issue was an article passed by the third national synod (Orléans, 1562) permitting provinces to divide if they grew too large, subject to the provincial synod's approval. The national synod of Lyon in 1563, in the first clear statement of provincial boundaries in the acts of the national synods, divided the kingdom into eight ecclesiastical provinces, subject to the approval of the provincial synods. Although these provinces would not last more than a few years—the fifth national synod (Paris, 1565) declared that each province of the kingdom should have its own provincial synod, or divide if there were too many churches—the fourth synod's action in defining provincial borders signaled a movement toward a more systematic approach to ecclesiastical government among the Reformed churches of France.[44]

This change was also signaled by this synod's legislation dealing with the organization of the Discipline and preservation of the acts of the national synods.

---

[43]Le Mans, 24.

[44]Quick, 3–Orléans–1562, chap. 2, art. 7 (23–24); 4–Lyon–1563, chap. 18, art. 7 (46); 5–Paris–1565), chap 7, art. 14 (63).

Up to this point, the Discipline existed simply as an unorganized collection of articles; the fourth national synod called for it to be organized into chapters by the church at Lyon, and then updated at the end of each national synod. The up-to-date Discipline was then to be read at the opening of both national and provincial synods.[45] The pastors of Geneva were also asked to comment on the "principal points" of the Discipline and to send their opinions to the church of Lyon; Lyon was then to distribute the comments to the provincial synods for further discussion at the next national synod.[46] The deputies were also to bring copies back to their home province of the acts of the national synod signed by the moderator and scribe.[47]

The trend toward increasingly precise and systematic regulation of the work of synods continued in the fifth national synod (Paris, 1565). Perhaps because the reorganized Discipline uncovered weaknesses in the legislation dealing with the national synod, or because of changing conditions in the kingdom, or because of growing bureaucratization of the churches, the fifth national synod established a clear set of regulations for setting the agendas and preparing delegations for the national synods. In one sweeping article, this synod specified that the church in which the national synod was to be held set the time and place of the meeting and notify the provincial synods; the provincial synods were then to send items for debate to the church hosting the national synod, which was to distribute them to the churches which were planning to attend at least three months before the synod was scheduled to begin; these items were limited to those not already resolved by the national synod and those which needed the decision of the national synod (that is, common concerns and issues the provinces could not resolve themselves).[48] These procedures remained in effect for the rest of the century.

With a clear set of regulations in place for the national synod, the sixth national synod (Vertueil, 1567) turned its attention to the provinces. First of all, it again modified the boundaries of ecclesiastical provinces. Following the example of the fifth national synod,[49] the synod of Vertueil recommended that ecclesiastical provinces follow the kingdom's provinces, though it was a bit more realistic in its assessment of the Reformed churches' position in the kingdom: rather than discuss procedures for dividing overlarge provinces, it allowed for redefinition of provincial boundaries if there were not enough ministers in a particular province

---

[45]Quick, 4–Lyon–1563, chap. 2, art. 1, 2 (31); chap. 12, art. 13 (36); chap. 17, art. 4 (45).

[46]ANS, 4–Lyon–1563, "faits particuliers," 16. Quick, 4–Lyon–1563, chap. 18, art. 8 (46) has a slightly different procedure for informing the provinces.

[47]Quick, 4–Lyon–1563, chap. 2, art. 15 (31).

[48]Quick, 5–Paris–1565, chap. 10, art. 23 (65–66).

[49]Quick, 6–Vertueil–1567, chap. 7, art. 14 (63).

to set up a provincial synod. Under these circumstances, or if any other conflict should arise, an uninvolved province was to mediate between the churches or provinces involved in the redistricting.[50] This provision for mediation would seem to violate the article from the fifth national synod, which specified that matters a province could not handle on its own were to be brought before the national synod. In fact, however, the intent of the fifth synod's article was to limit what could be brought before the national synod, not to mandate what must be brought there; in this case, the desire of the French churches to attempt to settle matters on as local a level as possible and to avoid bringing in uninvolved parties dictated that disputes between or within provinces be mediated by only one additional province, rather than by the deputies of the entire kingdom.[51]

The seventh national synod (La Rochelle, 1571) continued to expand the legislation dealing with provincial synods. It passed two articles which dealt with procedural issues: the first changed the frequency of provincial synods from annually to a minimum of twice per year; the second required deputies to bring an attestation from their consistory indicating that they had been chosen as their church's representatives to the synod. The next national synod (Nîmes, 1572) ordered local churches to pay the expenses of the deputies to provincial synods; the following national synod (St. Foy, 1578) added that the churches must pay expenses of deputies not only to provincial synods but to colloquies as well, and that if a church failed to do so, it would lose its minister. By the same token, however, this same national synod also ordered ministers either to attend the provincial synods and colloquies or to send full "memoires" or face censure themselves; in other words, the national synod insisted that both churches and ministers do their duty by participating in colloquies and provincial synods.[52]

---

[50]Quick, 6–Vertueil–1567, chap. 2, art. 8 (71). This legislation was repeated by the tenth national synod (Figeac, 1579), which further stipulated that the site of the provincial synod be selected for the convenience of the churches attending; Quick, 10–Figeac–1579, chap. 3, art. 28 (132). The provision for mediation in conflicts between provinces would be upgraded from a decision of the national synod to an article in the Discipline by the seventh national synod (La Rochelle, 1571; *Des synodes provinciaux*, 6), presumably after receiving input from the provincial synods.

[51]This national synod also introduced legislation regulating some of the activities of colloquies and *classes*; see chap. 4.

[52]Quick, 7–La Rochelle–1571, chap. 7, art. 13, 14 (96); 8–Nîmes–1572, chap. 5, art. 25 (109); 8–St. Foy–1578, chap. 3, art. 13 (118), cf. 13–Montauban–1594, chap. 3, art. 10, chap. 4, art. 26 (159, 163); 8–St. Foy–1578, chap. 4, art. 28 (120); cf. 11–La Rochelle–1581, chap. 3, art. 31 (139); the responsibilities of both church and minister are linked together and repeated in the thirteenth national synod, Quick, 13–Montauban–1594, chap. 4, art. 26 (163); the thirteenth synod also declared that the "memoires" of deputies attending provincial synods be signed by the minister and an elder of their home church, presumably to guarantee authenticity; Quick, 13–Montauban–1594, chap. 3, art. 11 (159). Other changes

In addition to revising the regulations for deputies, the eighth national synod (Nîmes, 1572) passed regulations dealing with appeals of disciplinary decisions in case of schism. Those stirring up dissensions that break the unity of the churches (note the plural) were to be brought before the consistory; if they did not desist, they were then to be sent to the colloquy, then to the provincial synod, then to the national synod. If at any point they recanted, no further penalty was to be imposed; if they did not, they were to be excommunicated and, if a minister or elder, suspended from ecclesiastical office. This article was presumably a response to Morély and his associates, whose running battle with the leadership of the *Eglises Réformées* (and with Geneva) over the nature of ecclesiastical government came to a head at this synod.[53]

Subsequent national synods continued to refine the rules governing appeals, particularly to the level of the national synod. The most important legislative sequence began with the tenth national synod (Figeac, 1579), which again limited appeals to the national synod to issues involving deposition of church officers, transfers of ministers between provinces, and doctrinal issues; these limitations were specifically intended to prevent the national synod from becoming too tied up with local matters. This apparently did not sit well with the provincial synods, however: the eleventh national synod (La Rochelle, 1581) reversed this decision and generalized the extension of the censure/appeal process to the national synod; that is, appeals to the national synod were no longer limited to schism, doctrinal disputes, and pastoral discipline.[54] This was the final step integrating the appeal system for cases of church discipline across the entire synodical system. It also marked a growing centralization of the government of the French Reformed churches. Prior to this, the decisions of provincial synods were final; now, however,

---

in the system of representation followed. For example, the twelfth national synod (Vitré, 1583) took the interesting step of permitting deputies attending another province's synod on official business to vote on all matters brought before that synod, whether related to their home province or not; Quick, 12–Vitré–1583, chap. 2, art. 25 (146). This may indicate that the Reformed churches of the kingdom had developed a greater sense of unity among themselves, since, properly speaking, matters related to the internal affairs of a province were no concern of the deputies of another province even if they were attending the synod on a matter of mutual interest. On the other hand, however, the same national synod which passed this legislation also accepted deputies from the Dutch churches as full participants in its own sessions, Quick, 12–Vitré–1593, chap. 1; chap. 2, art. 1 (142–43); it could hardly have objected to a parallel practice on the provincial level.

[53]Quick, 8–Nîmes–1572, chap. 4, art. 18 (107); chap. 7, art. 12 (113).

[54]The ninth national synod (St. Foy, 1578) ruled that in all appeals, the appellants must appear in person or send a complete account of the case; should they fail to do so, the colloquy or synod would make its decision without their input, Quick, 9–St. Foy–1578, chap. 4, art. 27 (120); the twelfth national synod (Vitré, 1583), discussing specifically appeals to the national synod, added that they must also have a legitimate reason for their absence should they not appear in person, Quick, 12–

the national synod assumed the right to overturn their decisions as the new court of final appeal in the disciplinary system of the churches.

The Interaction of the National and Provincial Synods

The evolution of the appeals system was almost certainly the result of the provincial synods' reviewing and commenting on the decisions of the national synod. This sort of review was an indispensable part of the legislative process in the French Reformed churches since it permitted them to reach consensus about ecclesiastical policy.[55] It is helpful to examine some examples of this interaction to clarify the relationship between the national and provincial synods in developing legislation for the churches.

The records of the provincial synods of Languedoc provide only three examples of the provincial synod's reviewing and responding to decisions of the national synod, though internal evidence from the acts of the national synods suggests it occurred far more frequently than the Languedoc synods would indicate.[56] The most detailed of these responses comes from the provincial synod of Montpellier (1581), which prepared a list of comments on and protests of decisions made by the tenth national synod (Figeac, 1579).[57] Some of these objections are particularly interesting since they help explain otherwise undocumented actions taken by the eleventh national synod (La Rochelle, 1581). Although this example is slightly later than the period of this study, there is nothing in the records to indicate that this is a new procedure. It can thus serve to illustrate the process of accommodation and change in ecclesiastical policy that had been taking place since the founding of the *Eglises Réformées* in 1559.[58]

Vitré–1583, chap. 3, art. 9, par. 8 (148); 10–Figeac–1579, chap. 3, art. 31 (132); 11–La Rochelle–1581, chap. 3, art. 28 (138).

[55]In a sense, the ratification of the Discipline by the first provincial synods in the provinces represents a form of this sort of review; for example, the provincial synod of Dauphiné and Lyonnois (Lyon, 1561) ratified the Discipline of 1559 as modified by the second national synod (Poitiers, 1561); *Documents protestants inédits*, 18.

[56]The acts of the provincial synods of Dauphiné published by Arnaud, *Documents protestants inédits*, include no examples of this type of review; they do include several examples of calls for all deputies at the synods and/or all pastors to sign either the Discipline or the Confession; e.g., provincial synods of Lyon (1561), 18; Dye (1561), 21; Lyon (1561), 29, 31; and Montélimar (1562), 36.

[57]Auzière, fol. 157r. The provincial synod of Nîmes (1571) reviewed the decisions reached by the seventh national synod (La Rochelle, 1571) and protested at least one of them; Auzière, fols. 44v–45r. Unfortunately, the numbering of the article in question is incorrect, and thus I have been unable to determine the precise issue raised by the province. The provincial synod of Anduze (1595) reviewed the decisions of the thirteenth national synod (Montauban, 1594); Auzière, fol. 305v.

[58]Other articles in the acts of the eleventh national synod reflect provincial reactions to the decisions

The provincial synod of Bas Languedoc protested new rules about the frequency of synodical and colloquial meetings, presumably because the province wanted to set them in accordance with its own needs: the provincial synod had met at least annually for over a decade, and sometimes several times per year, though the response of the eleventh national synod seems to indicate that the provincial synod wished for the freedom to meet less frequently. The eleventh national synod replied to the protest by insisting that provincial synods and colloquies meet as often as the national synod—especially the tenth—had legislated. Bas Languedoc also recommended that the national synod remove reference to "the most eminent members of the church" *(les plus appoinctz de l'eglise)* from the article in the Discipline that dealt with nonpayment of pastors; the eleventh synod agreed with the suggestion and eliminated the phrase. A third article that the province recommended be modified concerned children of Reformed parents who insisted on marrying outside of their faith. The synod called on parents to try to dissuade their children from these marriages, but if the children still insisted, the parents were to protest the marriage openly; after the protest, the parents could still provide a dowry. Presumably in response to the input from Languedoc, the eleventh national synod added that in such a situation, the father was to appear before the consistory to inform them that he had done his best to prevent the marriage.[59]

In two cases, the province observed that the actions of the synod were superfluous, since earlier synods had already enacted legislation on the subjects. An article which bans drama that is based on Scripture, including the Apocrypha, repeats the legislation of the eighth national synod (Nîmes, 1572); another article, which insisted that the ban on prayers or exhortation at graves during funerals be strictly observed, explicitly refers back to the third national synod (Orléans, 1562).[60] The national synod did not take any new action in response to these objections, perhaps because the problems that these redundant decisions addressed were widespread; funeral ceremonies certainly were.[61] The national synod thus believed that additional reinforcement of the ban on these practices was warranted.[62]

The provincial synod also recommended changes to article 15 of the tenth national synod that deals with holders of ecclesiastical benefices (that is, the

---

of the tenth national synod, explicitly mentioning the articles from Figeac that were to be modified. These include Quick, 11–La Rochelle–1581, chap. 2, art. 17 (137); chap. 3, art. 22 and 26 (138).

[59]Quick, 11–La Rochelle–1581, chap. 3, art. 37 (139); 16 (131); 50 (140).

[60]Quick, 8–Nîmes–1572, chap. 5, art. 29 (109); 3–Orléans–162, chap. 2, art. 15 (24).

[61]Garrisson-Estebe, *Protestants du Midi*, 249–52.

[62]In two other cases, art. 13 and 30, there is no indication that the eleventh national synod acted

temporalities), and urged them to clear up any lingering connections to idolatry; the province also suggested that this article and article 24, which censures those who use income from ecclesiastical benefices for personal gain, be combined. The eleventh synod seems to have agreed, decreeing that all who hold benefices unlawfully (for example, by papal bull), and who are involved in idolatry as a result of those benefices, are suspended from the Lord's Supper. Meanwhile, the synod called for a review of benefice legislation at the next national synod, though it permitted Gascony and Languedoc to censure benefice farmers. During the interval between the eleventh and twelfth national synods (the latter being held at Vitré in 1583), the provincial synods seem to have reviewed the legislation dealing with benefices to provide input for the national synod; on the basis of this advice, the twelfth synod further modified the article on benefices in the Discipline.[63]

This reconsideration of the legislation on benefices exemplifies a phenomenon that occurs several times in the acts of the national synods. Final decisions on questions are postponed until the next national synod, presumably to enable the provincial synods to debate the issues and send recommendations to the national synod. The first national synod (Paris, 1559) provided a precedent for this practice. It left undecided the question raised by the pastor of Chastelheraud concerning whether the children of Roman Catholic parents could be baptized in the Reformed church; the decision reached by the next synod (Poitiers, 1561) was that such children could only be baptized if the parents yielded the child's religious education to a Protestant godparent.[64] The third national synod postponed a decision about diaconal catechism until the fourth national synod.[65]

The fourth national synod (Lyon, 1563) sent back to the provinces for discussion a question on the propriety of holding morning and evening prayers. The next national synod (Paris, 1565), presumably with the input of the provincial synods, ruled that these prayer services should be banned to avoid superstition as well as the neglect of the regular preaching services on the Lord's Day, and to

---

on the issues in question. Both of these deal with liturgical matters. Art. 13 permits ministers to use any appropriate words while administering the Lord's Supper; the provincial synod replied: *"Non est recepvable. Et seront advertis par les pasteurs n'introduire* [Aymon: *n'interdire*] *telle costume de parler en recepvant."* Art. 30 calls on ministers, elders, and heads of families to see to it that all involved in public or family prayer show due reverence by uncovering their heads and kneeling unless prevented from doing so by sickness or other infirmity; the provincial synod suggested that this be applied to the Psalms as well as prayer.

[63]Quick, 11–La Rochelle–1581, chap. 3, art. 34, 35 (139); 12–Vitré–1583, chap. 2, art. 15 (145).

[64]Quick, 1–Paris–1559, chap. 3, art. 3 (7); 2–Poitiers–1561, chap. 6, art. 3 (17).

[65]See chap. 5 for a discussion of this incident.

encourage prayer at home.[66] An unstated reason may have been a desire to keep a closer rein on the liturgical activities of deacons and other laypersons to avoid potential problems caused by theologically untrained leadership at the services. Because of questions raised in a number of provinces, the sixth national synod (Vertueil, 1567) decided to discuss "the tenth article" of "Des Particuliers" concerning judges and notaries at the seventh national synod (La Rochelle, 1571); although it neither refers to the synod of Vertueil nor to the input of the provinces, the synod of La Rochelle did, in fact, modify this article.[67]

Probably because of the eleven-year gap between the twelfth and thirteenth national synods, the latter (held at Montauban, 1594) sent more questions back to the provinces for study than any other prior to the Edict of Nantes. These issues included whether a general confession of sin was adequate in public worship, whether it was appropriate to hold theological disputations at colloquies, a question on the content of marriage promises, and whether it was licit to marry one's brother's widow. Each of these was addressed at the fourteenth national synod (Saumur, 1596). This synod, in turn sent two questions to the fifteenth national synod (Montpellier, 1598): whether Beza's metrical setting of "Scripture songs" should be approved for public worship, and whether to require widows to remain as widows for a longer period of time before they remarry.[68]

The range of questions sent back to the provincial synods is striking: the responsibilities of deacons, regulations for "particular orders," marital legislation, and liturgical questions. None of these was a strictly regional issue, of course, and for the sake of uniform practice within the kingdom some consensus needed to be reached. The national synods did not systematically ask for the advice of the provinces in any of these areas. Presumably, the national synods sent questions back to the provincial synods for advice when it could not reach consensus, whether because the provincial deputies had received no instructions or because they simply disagreed too strongly among themselves. Unfortunately, the acts of the national synods in the sixteenth century are not detailed enough to determine precisely why these issues proved to be controversial while other equally broad questions were not.[69]

---

[66]Quick, 4–Lyon–1563, chap. 16, art. 7 (38); 5–Paris–1565, chap. 7, art. 11 (63).

[67]In view of the contents, the actual article under consideration was "Des Particuliers," 3, Quick, 6–Vertueil–1567, chap. 8, art. 7 (75); 7–La Rochelle–1571, chap. 9, art. 5 (99).

[68]Quick, 13–Montauban–1594, chap. 4, art. 17, 25, 37 (162, 163, 164), cf. 14–Saumur–1596, chap. 3, art. 8 (177), chap. 4, art. 3 (179); chap. 3, art. 18 (178); 14–Saumur–1596, chap. 4, art. 10 (180), chap. 3, art. 22, cf. 15–Montpellier–1598, chap. 5, art. 3 (196), chap. 3, art. 18 (193).

[69]As noted earlier in this chapter, internal evidence from the acts of the national synods suggests yet another form of interaction between the national and provincial synods which in a sense combined

One final point should be noted about the interaction of provincial and national synods. Unlike, for example, the United States Congress, which determines its legislative agenda independently of the states, the national synod's program was determined by deputies from the provincial synods who brought with them specific issues to be discussed. In other words, the provincial synods acted as gatekeepers for the national synod and thus controlled its agenda. Even at the end of the sixteenth century, when a more centralized approach to church government was beginning to emerge, the provinces continued to insist on keeping a close watch over the national synod's deliberations. For example, the fifteenth national synod of Montpellier (1598) declares that future modifications of the Discipline are to be initiated by one of the provincial synods, which was to send the proposal to the other provincial synods so they could debate it and bring an opinion to the next national synod; the decision of the national synod was to be binding on the provincial synods.[70] The collective decision thus had more weight than the desires of an individual province, though the provincial synods maintained a great deal of control over the process.

THE QUESTION OF ORIGINS

This outline of the structural development of the synodical system adopted by the French Reformed churches traces some parallels with ecclesiastical governments in other parts of Europe. These earlier Reformed precedents seem to be the most promising place to find the inspiration for at least some of the provisions of the Discipline. But what of more homegrown models of representation, such as Gallicanism, the Provincial Estates and Estates General, or the synods of the (Catholic) clergy of France? To what extent can these be viewed as sources for French Protestant polity?[71]

Although Gallicanism, with its conciliarist approach to church government, might appear to have played a role in shaping the synodical system of government adopted by the French Reformed churches, its influence was very limited. Some

---

elements of both of the two discussed here. On occasion, a national synod reached a decision concerning a specific situation in a church, and then the following national synod generalized the decision reached by adding it to the Discipline. This suggests that the national synods did not wish to make the decision for the specific case a regulation for the church as a whole without provincial input; the provinces thus discussed the decision and brought their advice to the next national synod, which in turn passed the subsequent legislation.

[70]Quick, 15–Montpellier–1598, chap. 5, art. 13 (198).

[71]See, for example, Michel Reulos, "Synodes, assemblées politiques des Réformés français et théories des Etats," *Album E. Lousse,* vol. 2 (Louvain: Nauwelaerts, 1963; Paris: Béatrice-Nauwelaerts, 1963), 97–111.

parallels do exist between Gallicanism and the Discipline, yet these can be explained by developments in Protestant regions that had a clearly identifiable influence on the French Reformed churches. For example, even without Gallicanism, virtually all Protestant territories created independent ecclesiastical governments coterminous with the political state; thus, the establishment of a church government for the kingdom of France followed the model of other Protestant churches, despite the lack of state support for the Huguenots. And although the French Reformed churches would adopt a synodical or conciliar style of polity, there were ample precedents for this in other Reformed regions with direct connections to the French Protestant community, regions whose ecclesiastical structures bear much closer resemblance to that outlined in the Discipline than the hierarchical approach taken by the Gallicans.

Similarly, although the estates and the civil government may have had some influence on the development of the system, they seem unlikely to be a decisive source for the Discipline. The estates were structured very differently from the French Reformed synods. The estates included representatives of the clergy, the nobility, and the commons; the synods only included pastors, elders, and deacons, all of whom were technically ministers of the churches. Although the synods of the Roman Catholic clergy might seem to provide a workable model for the Reformed synods, both the Catholic synods and the estates shared another crucial structural point which set them apart from the Reformed system: they were arranged hierarchically, with the senior bishop (as leader of the First Estate in the case of the provincial estates) or his representative at the head of the assembly.[72] This was, of course, anathema to French Protestants, who insisted that each assembly elect its moderator when it first assembled in order to prevent any sort of hierarchy from developing. The nature of the moderator's office in the synods also points out an important difference from the Provincial Estates: by the sixteenth century the Estates had established permanent bureaucracies, including clerks, archivists, treasurers, and syndics, the last being an essential element in defining a legal corporation.[73] The offices of the Reformed synods expired at the end of the synod.

---

[72] For example, in Languedoc the archbishop of Narbonne was the president of the estates; if he was not present the office devolved to the archbishop of Toulouse; if neither was present, the office passed on to the senior bishop present (that is, the one who had assumed the office of bishop first). J. Russell Major, *Representative Government in Early Modern France* (New Haven: Yale University Press, 1980), 62.

[73] Major, *Representative Government*, 165; Gaines Post, *Studies in Medieval Legal Thought* (Princeton: Princeton University Press, 1964), 39–50.

The synods were in no way intended to take on the functions of the estates; each level of the system was to look after disciplinary and, to some extent, doctrinal issues facing the Reformed churches. In other words, they performed almost strictly ecclesiastical functions. Even when they sent deputies to the royal government, it was to obtain permission for the churches to function as accepted (or at least tolerated) religious communities within the kingdom. Various other Protestant assemblies took care of political and military matters and nonecclesiastical administration. For example, François de Beaumont, baron des Adrets and lieutenant general in Dauphiné in 1562, "held Protestant assemblies at Montélimar in December 1562 and at Valence in January–February 1563 that aped the estates in nearly every respect except that the clergy was not convoked."[74] In Languedoc, representatives of the provincial synod were admitted as deputies to the political assemblies, though somewhat grudgingly, indicating again that the synods were not intended to function as estates. The provincial synods, meanwhile, established ecclesiastical policy and left the political and military decisions to the political assemblies, except when dealing with issues which also concerned the churches. In short, the political assemblies and the synods performed very different functions in the Protestant community.

All of this is not to say that existing governmental structures in the kingdom had no influence on the collective ecclesiastical government adopted by French Protestants. The first clearly defined levels in the Discipline—the national synod, the provincial synod, and the local church—corresponded reasonably well with the basic units of the civil government. The churches self-consciously based their ecclesiastical provinces on the provinces of the kingdom. Although the analogy was not made in the period, the colloquy was roughly the equivalent of the *bailliage* or perhaps the diocese. To continue the parallel a step further, one of the reasons the *classe*—a layer of ecclesiastical government between the colloquy and the provincial synod—was never adopted in most of the kingdom and was soon abandoned altogether may be that there was no parallel structure in the civil government or in the Roman Catholic hierarchy; since it did not correspond to any governmental structure with which the Protestant community was familiar, it was not embraced by the Reformed churches.

It would be foolish to discount altogether the role of the civil and Roman Catholic governments in influencing the shape of French Reformed polity. On the other hand, given the sharp structural differences between the estates and the French Reformed synods, these precedents do not provide an adequate explanation for the form of collective government laid out in the Discipline. Reformed

---

[74]Major, *Representative Government*, 229–30.

ecclesiology combined with a humanistic emphasis on a return to the practices of the early church—which, as Bucer, Calvin, Beza, and others had argued, included a system of regular synods—could very well have led to some form of synodical system structured generally like that of the *Eglises Réformées,* but with one notable exception: the early church's system of synods was tied directly and intimately into an episcopal polity. This combination of synods and bishops was implicit in all forms of Gallicanism;[75] it was even advocated by Bucer and Calvin as long as the bishop was a *primus inter pares* with the other ministers. Yet this approach was rejected categorically and repeatedly by the national synods in a complete break with earlier precedents, whether Catholic or Protestant, ecclesiastical or civil, in theory or in practice. And this change in the role of the moderator, in turn, established the first example of the so-called "presbyterial" polity—a nonepiscopal/nonhierarchical synodical system—in church history. The question, then, is why did the French Reformed churches adopt this form of moderator for their collective assemblies? What was its inspiration?

The most likely answer comes from an attempt to accommodate basic principles of Reformed ecclesiology to the realities facing French Protestants in the late 1550s. Bucer, Calvin, and others stressed the fundamental equality of all presbyters—that is, elders and pastors—within the church; thus the French churches insisted that no pastor may assume any form of primacy within his church. In other words, the pastor, or each pastor in turn if the congregation had several, presided over the meetings of the consistory, though without having any special authority over the other members of that body. This was a break with earlier Reformed precedents on two counts: first, in most Reformed churches the moderatorship of the consistory did not rotate; second, the presiding officer was typically a member of the *civil* government, rather than a pastor. For example, in Geneva the first syndic of the city presided over the consistory. Given the fact that most of France still had Catholic magistrates, the Discipline necessarily kept the consistory independent of the civil government, though it permitted magistrates to serve as elders as long as there was no direct conflict of interest.[76] This approach was far better adapted to the practical realities facing French Protestants than direct imitation of Geneva would have been, and led rather logically

---

[75]The thirteenth national synod (Montauban, 1594) rejected any attempt to make an alliance with the Gallicans, including especially a call for an end to nonurgent synods; Quick, 13–Montauban–1594, chap. 6, art. 4 (169). This reveals another difference between the Gallican attitude toward synods and that of the *Eglises Réformées* beyond the question of the moderatorship: for the Gallicans, synods were to be occasional meetings; for the French Reformed, they were an integral part of church government.

[76]ANS, 4–Lyon–1563, "faits particuliers," 5, cf. Quick, 4–Lyon–1563, chap. 4, art. 7; chap. 8, art. 34 (32, 34).

to the pastor's (or pastors') presiding over the consistory, and in consistency with Reformed theological principles, rotating the office between the pastors if there was more than one in a church.

At the same time, the principle of equality of presbyters applied across churches as well as within them. Since in an individual church the moderatorship of the consistory was not to remain with a single individual if there was more than one pastor available, so by analogy the moderatorship of collective assemblies of churches should not remain with a single pastor or church. Accordingly, to prevent a de facto hierarchy from forming, the moderator would be elected afresh at each meeting. The same moderator could be reelected so that the freedom of the synod would not be impaired; in practice, however, this never occurred at the level of the national synods.[77] Since the role of moderator did not give a pastor greater authority over his peers but was limited to ensuring the smooth functioning of the synodical meetings, the office could not carry over once the meetings ended. This helped prevent the moderator from usurping authority over local churches. This same principle had the additional side effect that visitations, such as those outlined in Viret's church order, could not be carried out either: there were no continuing synodical offices, and visitations would set one minister as a disciplinary authority over his peers.[78]

Although the French Reformed approach to the moderatorship of the synods was a logical application of the principle of equality among ministers and independence of churches, neither Bucer nor Calvin nor any other theologian had yet articulated this approach to church government. So what was its inspiration? The most likely explanation comes from the conditions under which the *Eglises Réformées* emerged. French Protestant churches had developed as independent entities during the preceding decades, following a de facto congregationalist polity that allowed cooperation among churches without establishing hierarchical structures. Since it is very unlikely that previously independent churches would voluntarily place themselves under the authority of another church, it was vitally important for the framers of the Discipline to develop a form of government that systematically excluded any form of hierarchy (coincidentally in keeping with Bucerian/Calvinist ecclesiological principles). The only plausible solution was to prevent any church from becoming the regular meeting place of a synod, any pastor from becoming a permanent moderator of a synod, or any moderator from overseeing churches between synods. This effectively eliminated "central

[77]Viret's church order has rules designed to prevent this as well, presumably following one of the Vaudois models for selecting *doyens* for the *classe* where the office rotated among the churches.

[78]See chap. 4.

place" systems such as Berne used, and episcopal systems, whether traditional or synodical. The extremely limited moderatorship adopted by the French was essentially the easiest solution under the circumstances, and also happened to fit quite well with Reformed ecclesiology. It would also prove quite influential: French Reformed polity was adopted (and adapted) by all of the other national Reformed churches in Western Europe.

The system of collective government established in the Discipline involved considerably more than these "higher-level" structures and regulation of broad issues of concern for all the churches of the kingdom. In fact, the bulk of the work of the national synods, and of the Discipline for that matter, dealt with issues on a provincial or local level, particularly regulations regarding the pastorate.

Chapter 4

Between the Province
and the Local Church

French Protestantism had developed organically as an illegal minority religion in

the decades prior to the creation of the French Reformed churches. This produced a

great deal of diversity in both doctrine and practice, a tendency further reinforced

by the churches' de facto congregationalist polity. It fell to the national synods to try

to bring order out of this chaos, since unlike other magisterial Protestant churches,

the Huguenots could not rely on the civil authorities to impose a satisfactory religious settlement in the kingdom. The Confession and the synodical system discussed in the previous chapters were important parts of the national synod's response to this situation, but in many ways the more difficult issues, perhaps even the most fundamental issues, involved integrating the existing autonomous churches into the *Eglises Réformées* and providing for pastoral and congregational oversight. Thus the national synod had to establish procedures for inviting already established churches and ministers to sign on to the church's program; it had to decide what to do about ministers who refused to sign the Confession and/or the Discipline; it had to establish procedures for selecting new pastors, elders, and deacons; then it had to establish a system for overseeing the ministers and churches that had joined the *Eglises Réformées*. The regulations handling these questions had to be written to balance both the need for doctrinal and organizational unity in the church and the insistence on a high degree of congregational autonomy demanded by both the antihierarchical principle at the heart of French Protestantism and by the practical demands of trying to integrate previously independent churches into a single ecclesiastical organization.

The national synod did not legislate on all of these issues at once; the regulations dealing with pastoral selection and oversight developed largely as ad hoc responses to questions or problems that arose within the churches. Only with the seventh national synod meeting in La Rochelle, 1571, was there an attempt to organize systematically ministerial and congregational oversight, and only with the eighth national synod meeting in Nîmes, 1572, does a lower-level synodical unit, the *colloque,* become part of the structure of the Discipline. This chapter examines the development of the colloquy and its connection to pastoral supervision and discipline in the broad sense described above. It traces the evolution of the colloquy from ad hoc meetings of local ministers called to handle various issues related to pastoral selection and supervision. It then examines the role of the colloquy in overseeing pastors and churches and addresses the specific question of pastoral depositions and vagrancy. It also discusses two issues related to pastoral and congregational oversight which were addressed by the third national synod (Orléans, 1562): the provincial church order which Viret prepared for Bas Languedoc, and the Morély controversy, the most serious conflict within the French Reformed churches prior to the St. Bartholomew's Day massacres.

Evolution of the Colloquy

The first edition of the Discipline makes the provincial synod responsible for preserving good order within the churches. Given the Huguenots' antihierarchical ecclesiology, this meant allowing churches to govern their own affairs except in serious matters or in situations which involved another church. In these cases, no church could be allowed to make a unilateral decision and impose it on the others. Rather, the provincial synod was to be summoned if possible to decide what should be done; if it was not possible to assemble the synod and if a decision was urgent, the church was to send letters about the problem to the other churches of the province for their advice and consent on action to be taken.[1]

Further, the provincial synod was to deal with problems relating to selection of church officers and pastoral discipline, areas which Bucer and Calvin had argued were part of the work of the synods in the early church.[2] Since the whole point of the Confession and the Discipline was to preserve or, more accurately, to create a certain variety of Protestant orthodoxy and to unite the churches into a single ecclesiastical structure, pastoral selection and oversight was considered an

---

[1] DE 1559, art. 41; Roussel, "Discipline," art. 37.

[2] Le Noir reported several examples of this in his *Histoire ecclésiastique de Bretagne.* One notable example which included a variety of conflicts over ministerial assignments, questions of doctrinal orthodoxy, and other similar problems, was the synod of Roche-Bernard, 1563 (103–7).

issue that involved all the other churches. Because of their public role, church officers were in many ways a class apart from ordinary church members; thus clerical discipline was not considered a matter for the congregation, but rather the proper responsibility of the provincial synod. For example, the provincial synod was to handle dissent over selection of members of the consistory[3] and to decide the status of pastors who, despite having the consent of the "people," were challenged by another church;[4] the synod was also to approve temporary transfer of pastors,[5] and to make final determinations in cases of pastors deposed for vice.[6] As we will see when we discuss the Morély affair later in this chapter, this special status accorded to church officers in the *Eglises Réformées* would cause enormous problems over the next decade.

The provincial synod's responsibilities for pastoral oversight were in keeping with its role as the center of collective ecclesiastical government: in the 1559 Discipline it was the only synodical body which met regularly; no business could be brought to the national synod except through a provincial synod. To some extent, the role of the provincial synod paralleled the situation within the kingdom as a whole in this era prior to the effective establishment of central authority. In many ways, provinces were largely self-governing under a monarchy which was unable or unwilling to interfere with provincial rights and privileges. The first edition of the Discipline reflects this in the ecclesiastical structure it devised.

Though it may have been the main organ of collective government, the provincial synod was too large and unwieldy to handle routine matters in individual churches. This was recognized in article 27 of the 1559 Discipline,[7] which prohibits the printing of religious books unless they are approved by two or three pastors who are above suspicion. The use of a small committee to evaluate these books suggests that the national synod recognized that the provincial synod could not handle all areas where pastoral supervision might prove necessary.

Once the Discipline was approved, the deputies returned home, set up provincial synods, and began to apply the Discipline's provisions. When the next national synod met in 1561, practical experience led the deputies to extend and modify the Discipline considerably to make it more workable. One area of expansion involved the role of nearby churches and ministers in pastoral discipline. The synod added two articles relating to this issue: no pastor was permitted to leave (*délaisser*) his church without the permission of his consistory and the approval

---

[3]DE 1559, art. 6.
[4]DE 1559, art. 12.
[5]DE 1559, art. 15.
[6]DE 1559, art. 18, 19, 26; Roussel, "Discipline," art. 17, 18, 26.
[7]Roussel, "Discipline," art. 25.

of the neighboring churches,[8] and two or three nonsuspect pastors were to confirm decisions of the consistory concerning deposition of ministers guilty of serious crimes.[9] In terms of pastoral selection, the 1561 Discipline forbade a single pastor with his consistory to "elect" a new pastor; instead, this was to be done either by two or three pastors with the consistory or by the provincial synod, which then would present the candidate to the congregation for approval.[10] This article assumed that the church had already joined the *Eglises Réformées.* In situations where a church had a pastor but was not in ecclesiastical fellowship with the French Reformed Church (that is, had not signed the Confession and the Discipline, and thus by the definition of the *Eglises Réformées* was not "established" [*dressée*]), neighboring churches also had a role:

> If a people among whom the ministry of the Word of God has not yet been established have chosen a pastor, the nearby churches are to ask him amiably but urgently to confer with them and are to exhort him to sign the Confession of Faith and the order and Discipline agreed upon among us. And if he is unwilling to sign the Confession, three or four ministers of the nearby churches with their elders are to assemble and then to declare [him] schismatic, and the people are to be warned to be wary of and to avoid such a person. But if he is only unwilling to abide by the Discipline, he is not to be labeled schismatic simply for this, until such time as he is so declared by the provincial council.[11]

[8]DE 1561, art. 20.

[9]DE 1561, art. 25.

[10]DE 1561, art. 9; Quick and Aymon both have this article refer explicitly to the *colloque* and suggest that it was to be established everywhere there were consistories. This is not supported by the best manuscripts, however; no reference to the colloquy appears in this context until the acts of the fourth national synod (Lyon 1563). Curiously, surviving manuscripts of the Discipline from 1563 and later do not reflect this change. In any event, relying on the published editions of the acts of the national synods in this case leads to the mistaken conclusion that the French Reformed churches were more highly organized at this early date than they actually were.

[11]Si un peuple entre lequel le ministere de la parolle de Dieu ne seroit point dressé avoit esleu un pasteur, les prochaines eglises le solliciteront amiablement et instamment de conferer avec elles, et l'exhorteront à soy soubsigner à la Confession de foy et à l'ordre et Discipline arrestee entre nous. Et au cas qu'il ne voulut soubsigner a ladite Confession seront assemblez trois ou quatre ministres des prochaines eglises avec leurs anciens, et lors sera declaré schismatique, et sera le peuple adverti de se garder et abstenir d'un tel personnage. Que si seulement il ne se vouloit ranger a la Discipline arrestee entre nous, il ne pourra pas pourtant estre reputé schismatique, jusques a ce qu'il soit ordonné par le Concile provincial. DE 1561, art. 13. The eighth national synod (Nîmes, 1572), which would introduce a chapter on colloquies into the Discipline, changed these regulations to refer specifically to the colloquy rather than simply the neighboring churches; further, it made the minister subject to the

Similarly, those who "intruded" into the ministry (to use Quick's term) even with congregational support were also subject to outside oversight if there was a controversy over their status:

> Whoever insinuates himself [into the ministry], even with the approval of his people, cannot be approved by the neighboring ministers or others if there is some question about his approval by some other church. But before proceeding, the provincial council [i.e., synod] shall be assembled as soon as possible to decide on the matter, except in places where there is a colloquy composed of at least six ministers, in which case the aforementioned colloquy can deal with it.[12]

Thus informal meetings of the leaders of local churches were to be involved in recruiting churches and pastors into the *Eglises Réformées*, but if problems arose, the provincial synod was to step in.

Although the term *colloque* had been used in both the 1559 and 1561 Disciplines as a general term for a synodical meeting, article 17 is the first and only instance in these editions where the word is used for a specific type of assembly, one located between the local church and the provincial synod. This does not mean that the colloquy had become a standard part of the ecclesiastical structure, however: after this article, references to the colloquy disappear from the acts of the national synod for several years, and the next few national synods refer only to neighboring ministers meeting ad hoc to deal with issues related to pastoral supervision, but not to colloquies as a specific unit in the church structure.

The third national synod met at Orléans in 1562, where the Protestants had established a base of operations for the first War of Religion. This synod dealt with two issues related to pastoral discipline and the balance between collective and local church governments: a church order prepared for Bas Languedoc by Pierre Viret, and Jean Morély's *Traicté de la Discipline et Police ecclésiastique*. Since neither would have a long-term effect on shaping the practice of the *Eglises Réformées*, these works are discussed later in this chapter. The synod did add one article to the Discipline which expanded the role of nearby churches in regulating

---

approval of either the colloquy or provincial synod; Quick, 8–Nîmes–1572, chap. 3, art. 7; chap. 5, art. 23 (105, 108).

[12]Celuy qui se seroit ingeré, encore qu'il fut approuvé de son peuple, ne pourra estre approuvé des ministres prochains ou autres, s'il y a quelque different sur son approbation par quelque autre eglise. Mais devant que passer outre, le plustost que fere se pourra, sera assemblé le concile provincial pour en decider, sinon aux lieux ausquels ou il y aura colloque composé de six ministres pour le mois, auquel cas ledit colloque en pourra cognoistre. DE 1561, art.17.

the loan and return of pastors.[13] A pastor was to be assigned to a specific church, but nonetheless could be lent to another church when necessary. If the church to which he was sent refused to receive him, however, he could either return to his home church or await the decision of the provincial synod; if he opted for the latter, he was not to preach without the consent of two or three nearby ministers. This article, which was intended to discourage itinerant preaching, continued the trend begun earlier of assigning the task of immediate pastoral supervision to nearby pastors. It is a good example of the ad hoc way in which the Discipline was being developed: the regulations leave the distinct impression that they were responses to specific situations rather than the result of systematic legislation. The article was also a practical response to conditions facing French Protestants. Since pastoral discipline was primarily the responsibility of the provincial synods, they were to make a final determination in cases such as the one described in this article;[14] but until such time as the synod could meet and consider the case, nearby churches could still permit a pastor to preach whose qualifications might have been called into question by his rejection by the receiving church. In an era with a chronic shortage of pastors, this decision simply made good sense.

In practice, other circumstances could warrant a meeting of deputies from the churches below the level of the province. For example, in September 1562, a "synod" met in Blain in Brittany to encourage pastors to stay with their congregations and to deal with the threats to the churches posed by an edict that ordered all ministers to leave France within two weeks. Philippe Le Noir pointed out that there was a formal provincial synod that met in Ploërmel in October 1562, and thus the meeting in Blain could not have been a formal synod; he suggests that it was a "tumultuously assembled colloquy, or a synodical council, or an extraordinary consistory." Whatever the label, it is a good example of the kind of ad hoc meetings to deal with immediate concerns to the churches that the Discipline would eventually regularize as the colloquy. At the same time, the meeting also serves as a reminder of the limitations of the Discipline and the acts of the national synods as a source for the practice of the churches: the situation on the ground varied a great deal, and the provinces frequently had to act on their own in the face of local circumstances in ways not regulated by the Discipline or the national synods. Pastoral supervision, in any event, remained primarily in the

---

[13]Since no known copy of the 1562 Discipline survives, I have taken the provisions of this article from the acts of the national synod, Quick, 3–Orléans–1562, chap. 2, art. 5 (23), cf. ANS, 3–Orléans–1562, 5; it appears in a corrupted form as art. 20 in the Geneva BPU Archives Tronchin vol. 10 version of the 1563 Discipline and in purer forms in later editions of the Discipline as well.

[14]The 1559 Discipline had already assigned the provincial synod the responsibility to settle disputes over the loan and return of ministers (art. 11).

hands of the provincial synod, as demonstrated by the synod of Roche-Bernard (1563). This synod took a number of actions relating to pastoral supervision and discipline, including dealing with a conflict over where a minister was to serve, designating *proposants,* assigning ministers to churches, and deputing a minister and elder to a count to call on him to accept the Discipline and his church to abide by it or be declared schismatic.[15]

The fourth national synod met in Lyon, 1563, under the moderatorship of Pierre Viret. This synod made one important structural change to the Discipline: rather than leave it as a simple collection of articles, the synod ordered that the document be organized into chapters. The structure and content of this reorganization show that the colloquy had not yet been adopted systematically within the French Reformed churches: the chapter on collective government, *Des synodes,* continued to use *colloque* as a synonym of *concile* and *synode,* and it continued to rely on ad hoc meetings of local pastors and on the provincial synods for pastoral discipline. Even the few pieces of legislation dealing with pastoral supervision left this basic approach intact. The synod modified the article from the third national synod that regulated the "loaning" of ministers, adding that pastors were not to leave their church without the church's (i.e., the consistory's) consent given in consultation with neighboring ministers, and that these pastors could not take on another church without the "authority" of the provincial synod.[16] The national synod also gave the provincial synods the right to assign a minister either temporarily or permanently to another congregation with the consent of his home church.[17] These articles followed the earlier approach of assigning oversight of pastors to as local a level as possible, with the provincial synod becoming involved as needed.[18] The national synod also continued the practice of only calling the nearby churches or ministers to meet on an ad hoc basis to deal with specific issues; there was no provision as yet for regular meetings, and it would even have been possible in principle for different groups of "nearby ministers" to deal with different issues arising within a single church. In short, as late as the fourth

[15]Le Noir, *Histoire ecclésiastique de Bretagne,* 95–96, 104–5.

[16]Quick, 4–Lyon–1563, chap. 5, art. 15 (33), cf. ANS, 4–Lyon–1563, 9. Curiously, the change is not reflected in the manuscript copies of the Discipline.

[17]Quick, 4–Lyon–1563, chap. 5, art. 14; chap. 11, art. 8 (33, 35), cf. ANS, 4–Lyon–1563, 8. Once again, "church" probably means "consistory."

[18]The desire to resolve issues on as local a level as possible did not always apply to questions involving elders and deacons: the national synod decided that members of same family could serve on the consistory unless the provincial synod (not the nearby churches) determined that it was inappropriate in a particular situation; Quick, 4–Lyon–1563, chap. 3, art. 9; chap. 12, art. 14 (32, 36), cf. ANS, 4–Lyon–1563, 13.

national synod, there was no provision for regularly scheduled or even clearly defined assemblies of representatives from neighboring churches.

Two years later, however, the Discipline issued by the fifth national synod (Paris, 1565) marked the beginning of a trend that would lead to the acceptance of the colloquy as a formal structural element of the French Reformed churches. A variety of articles illustrate this. In one case, an article from earlier editions of the Discipline was modified specifically to legitimize the colloquies' right—where it existed—to nominate ministers;[19] in several other new articles, the colloquy was included as an accepted element in the church structure. Thus in places where there were no ministers, magistrates were to admonish believers "following the order of the Discipline by consistories, colloquies, and synods."[20] In a later chapter on provincial synods, the national synod added an article indicating that church government was to be so regulated that colloquies and provincial synods did not interfere with each other's work.[21] These articles suggest that the colloquy, though not yet universal, was becoming more widespread. At the same time, nearby ministers continued in their other responsibilities for pastoral oversight; the colloquy had not yet replaced these informal groups in any systematic way. The final responsibility for overseeing pastors continued to rest with the provincial synod; for example, in addition to their earlier duties, the national synod authorized them to handle complaints from pastors about unpaid wages.[22] Significantly, in some respects the local church's rights were preserved even in the face of decisions of a provincial synod: if a church loaned a minister to another for a set period of time, and that time expired, the church could recall the minister; if the receiving church refused to relinquish him, it was given six months to do so, after which the minister was to return to his home church "even if the authority of the provincial synod had intervened."[23] Thus even in 1565 the authority of the local church continued to be upheld by the national synod, a striking example of the continuing strength of congregational autonomy in the French Reformed churches.

[19]DE 1565, "Des ministres," 4; given the ad hoc way the Discipline developed, this article was probably modified in response to a specific situation in one of the provinces.

[20][S]elon l'ordre es Discipline par les consistoires, colloques et synodes. DE 1565, "Des ministres," 24. This change originated in the "faits pariculiers" of the previous national synod (Lyon, 1563). In the acts of the national synod, the text reads *par les classes et synodes,* reflecting perhaps the influence of Viret. After the acts of the national synod were circulated to the provinces, the text was inserted into the Discipline, *consistoire* was added, and *classe* was replaced by *colloque.*

[21]DE 1565, "Des synodes provinciaux," 6.

[22]DE 1565, "Des ministres," 34.

[23][S]ans que la dessus intervienne l'authorité d'un synode. DE 1565, "Des ministres," 18. Note that this quotation simply refers to *synodes* without specifying the level. It probably refers to the provincial synod, since the national synod tried to distance itself from these sorts of disputes; Quick

The sixth national synod (Vertueil, 1567) continued to elaborate on the role of colloquies and neighboring ministers in matters of pastoral selection and oversight. The colloquy or provincial synod was to examine and approve any potential pastors requested by a local congregation; if approved the colloquy or synod was to send him back to preach at the church accompanied by two or three other ministers, who together with the consistory, would ordain him as a pastor if the congregation agreed.[24] If a pastor had been promised time off to study, he had to get the permission of the colloquy or [provincial] synod before leaving, even if he had the church's prior approval. Neighboring ministers still performed their old roles plus a new one: no one was to be named a vagrant *(coureur)* until discipline administered by the neighboring churches had failed to restore him. Nonetheless, the provincial synod retained final authority over ministers: if a minister was charged with leaving his church without permission, he was to be brought before the provincial synod, not a colloquy or a group of neighboring ministers.[25]

Although the sixth national synod followed precedent by relying on colloquies and neighboring ministers primarily for pastoral supervision and selection, it also began to expand the role of the colloquy beyond these areas. It specified that in cases where the consistory of a local church could not resolve a problem, the problem was to be brought to the colloquy or *classe;* if this assembly could not resolve it, the problem was to be brought to the provincial synod.[26] This was, of course, simply an application of the general principle that issues be handled at as local a level as possible. It is nonetheless a significant indicator of the growing presence of the colloquy within the collective government of the French Reformed churches.

The colloquy took a long step forward at the seventh national synod, meeting in La Rochelle in 1571. The colloquy figures more prominently in the 1571 Discipline than in any previous edition. For example, in regions where they existed,

---

understood it this way. Alternately, if "synod" is taken as a nontechnical term, it could conceivably refer to either a colloquy or a provincial synod, though that seems less likely since there are no clear examples in the Discipline where the term is used that loosely.

[24]Quick, 6–Vertueil- 1567, chap. 8, art. 4 (75). The twelfth national synod (Vitré, 1583) imposed the additional qualification that any controversies which arose in the church over the selection of a minister must be reported to the colloquy or provincial synod; Quick, 12–Vitré–1583, chap. 3, art. 1, par. 4 (147).

[25]Quick, 6–Vertueil–1567, chap. 1, art. 1, 5 (where again "church" equals "consistory"), 13 (70). Art. 1 may have been related to a disciplinary case involving a minister from Normandy named Sylvester, who was permitted to continue in his office while being investigated for some unspecified crimes, Quick, 6–Vertueil–1567, chap. 7, art. 3 (74).

[26]Quick, 6–Vertueil–1567, chap. 1, art. 5, chap. 3, art. 19 (72), cf. ANS, 6–Vertueil–1567, 19.

colloquies were to take over most of the tasks that had been assigned to the ad hoc meetings of nearby ministers. Additional duties were assigned as well, most of which were related to pastoral supervision or the regulation of unusual circumstances that might face ministers of an unsanctioned, minority religion. The colloquies were to adjudicate cases where there was conflict over the "loan," return, and reassignment of ministers; they also were to oversee pastors who left their churches to avoid persecution or because their ministry had been rejected.[27] Similarly, colloquies or provincial synods were to investigate claims by pastors that they had not been paid their due wages, and if the minister's complaint was sustained, the colloquy or synod was to permit him to move to another church; in this circumstance, the colloquy or synod was also permitted to censure the church up to the point of excommunication.[28] At the same time, other aspects of pastoral discipline were kept specifically in the hands of the provincial synod, including, for example, the naming of *coureurs*[29] and the other areas where earlier editions of the Discipline had assigned the provincial synods a direct role in pastoral oversight.

Colloquies were also assigned an expanded range of duties in other areas, though these were almost inevitably related to discipline or to oversight of church officers. For example, professors of theology were named by and subject to colloquies and provincial synods; questions or conflicts over doctrine were to be resolved by the colloquy, subject to appeal to the provincial synod. The colloquy was also to act as a court of appeal, both for deposed elders or deacons and for members of the congregation who had been excommunicated or suspended from the Lord's Supper.[30]

With the 1571 redaction of the Discipline, we thus see a tremendous expansion in the amount of detail in the regulations as well as an expansion of the specific roles assigned to the colloquy. Earlier legislation was clarified, and the role of colloquies was developed in a far more systematic way. The decade between 1561 and 1571 was thus critical in the development of colloquies in France: in 1561, colloquies existed, but were not widespread; the Discipline of 1571 suggests that colloquies had become more and more common, and that most

[27]DE 1571, "Des ministres," 10, 12, 17, 18.

[28]DE 1571, "Des ministres," 27; Quick, 7–La Rochelle–1571, chap. 5, art. 22 (108). The eighth national synod (Nîmes, 1572) assigned the responsibility of investigating claims of nonpayment of wages specifically to colloquies, rather than to either colloquies or provincial synods; since this synod also placed a chapter on colloquies in the Discipline, it is likely that this change was at least in part a result of the new status of the colloquy in the ecclesiastical structure.

[29]DE 1571, "Des coureurs," 1.

[30]DE 1571, "Des professeurs en théologie," 1; "Du consistoire," 11; "Des anciens et diacres," 8; "Des censures," 1, 3.

churches were included in one. All that was left, then, was to incorporate a chapter on colloquies in the Discipline, signaling that it was now an integral part of the church structure. This change was introduced in 1572 at the eighth national synod meeting in Nîmes. Though most of the regulations relating to the colloquy continued to be scattered throughout other chapters of the Discipline, a new chapter entitled "Des colloques" made its appearance in 1572. The single article in this chapter dealt with procedural issues: churches were to be organized into colloquies, which were to meet four times each year to discuss matters of mutual interest and to deal with difficulties in the churches.[31] In addition, new responsibilities continued to be assigned to colloquies elsewhere in the 1572 Discipline. Specifically, the colloquy was to oversee the use of plays as a teaching tool in schools, and was responsible for church planting.[32] Thus as the colloquy became a mandated feature of the ecclesiastical structure of the French Reformed churches, its functions expanded far beyond the roles assigned to the ad hoc groups of nearby ministers that were its ancestors.[33]

From the eighth national synod on, the number of articles dealing with colloquies skyrocketed. Most of this new legislation expanded on precedents set by national synods; for example, since the colloquy was now established as an integral element of the church order, some of the tasks assigned to neighboring ministers or to either the colloquy or provincial synod were changed to refer specifically to the colloquy. As one might expect, many of the articles dealing with colloquies had to do with their role in overseeing pastors of local churches. Some of these were general regulations: for example, as early as 1581, provincial synods and colloquies were to determine the boundaries of areas of ministry, and in 1594 they were to ensure as much as possible that ministers remain in residence with their churches.[34] Other regulations concerned oversight of the work of the consistory,

---

[31]The tenth national synod (Figeac, 1579) decreased the number of meetings per year to two; Quick, 10–Figeac–1579, chap. 2, art. 6 (130); cf. 11–La Rochelle–1581, chap. 3, art. 27 (137).

[32]DE 1572, "Des particuliers," 19, "Des consistoires," 2.

[33]Later synods would expand on these responsibilities further. For example, in an article reminiscent of the *colloques* of the Pays de Vaud, the ninth national synod (St. Foy, 1578) called on colloquies to return to the practice of having scriptural exposition at their meetings so that the ministers might be better equipped to preach; Quick, 9–St. Foy–1578, chap. 3, art. 13 (118); this was later moved into the chapter "Des colloques" in the Discipline; Quick, 12–Vitré–1583, chap. 3, art. 1, par. 13 (147). As noted in the previous chapter, the thirteenth national synod (Montauban, 1594) requested the provincial synods to send to the next national synod their opinions about whether to permit theological disputations at colloquial meetings; the fourteenth national synod (Saumur, 1596) decided that this was inappropriate.

[34]Quick, 11–La Rochelle–1581, chap. 3, art. 38 (139); 13–Montauban–1594, chap. 4, art. 10 (162).

particularly in situations where its actions might involve other churches. For example, in 1578, the provincial synod or colloquy was called upon to censure ministers and elders who gave letters of attestation to travelers without specifying their names, destinations, and dates of travel.[35] Most of the articles, however, dealt with more specific issues relating to pastoral placement, transfer, conflicts with their congregations, and discipline. These were for the most part judicial decisions which either were based upon or extended earlier legislation following the general principle that issues be decided with as little outside interference as possible.

Pastoral and Congregational Oversight: Specific Issues

The synods had been involved in mediating disputes between pastors and their congregations from very early on. Not surprisingly, most of these disputes were centered on the issue of pay.[36] This was a subject to which the national synods had to return repeatedly, starting with the second national synod (Poitiers, 1561). Article 19 of the acts of this synod decreed that congregations were to be exhorted to supply their pastors with a living; should they fail to do so, after a warning the pastor was free to leave.[37] Unfortunately, whether by accident or design this addition is omitted from the two surviving manuscript copies of the 1561 Discipline. According to Quick, the fourth national synod (Lyon, 1563) passed a measure very similar to that of the second.[38] Probably at a request for clarification from a provincial synod, the fifth national synod (Paris, 1565) outlined a more formal procedure for settling these cases: the pastor was to lodge a complaint of insufficient support with his provincial synod, which was to investigate the claim; if the claim was sustained, the synod could then move the pastor to another church.[39] The seventh national synod (La Rochelle, 1571) elaborated on this procedure.[40] It assigned the task of investigation to either the provincial synod or the colloquy, which was to give the church three months (or, in some cases, less) to pay the pastor if his complaint was determined to be valid, that is, if he was not paid and it was a case of ingratitude rather than poverty. If the church failed to pay the

[35]Quick, 9–St. Foy–1578, chap. 2, art. 10 (117).

[36]In fact, placement of ministers and disputes about pay were the most common issues dealing with local churches brought before the provincial synods of Languedoc.

[37]Although the acts of the national synod say this was to be added to art. 18 of the Discipline, judging from the 1563 Discipline, it should have been art. 20. Quick, Aymon, and MS Wb all read this article back to the 1559 Discipline, a good example of incorporating a later synod's decision into a text dated earlier.

[38]Quick, 4–Lyon–1563, chap. 16, art. 57 (44); this does not appear in MS Rb, the most reliable manuscript of the acts of the national synod.

[39]DE 1565, "Des ministres," 34; Quick, 5–Paris–1565, chap. 9, art. 18 (64).

[40]DE 1571, "Des ministres," 27; Quick, 7–La Rochelle–1571, chap. 3, art. 12 (94).

pastor within the allotted time, he could move to another church with the consent of the colloquy or provincial synod, and the provincial synod or colloquy could excommunicate the "ungrateful" church.[41] The eighth national synod (Nîmes, 1572) softened this somewhat by calling on the colloquy to decide on the appropriate action to take with regard to the defaulting church.[42]

Along with setting up a process for mediating disputes between pastors and their congregations, the national synods took pains to establish procedures for dealing with discipline of church officers, which was considered a matter of common interest and thus outside of the competency of an individual church's consistory. From the first edition of the Discipline, the French Reformed churches were very concerned with maintaining high standards of conduct, doctrine, and training for their ministers. For example, DE 1559, article 16, deposes all ministers who taught wrong doctrine, lived a scandalous life worthy of punishment by the magistrate or by excommunication, or were disobedient to the consistory or inadequate in performing their functions (except because of old age, disease, or other infirmity). Further, article 17 specifies that any serious crimes—even if committed before the pastor was converted to the Reformed faith—were grounds for deposition as well. Articles 19 and 20 specify a basic procedure for deposing ministers: in cases of crimes, the consistory plus two or three nonsuspect ministers—presumably from neighboring churches—were to remove the minister from office, though if he claimed witnesses perjured themselves, he could appeal to the provincial synod; when a minister was deposed, the reasons were not to be revealed to the congregation unless the consistory judged it necessary.[43] Elders and deacons were to be deposed by the consistory for the same reasons as ministers and were suspended from office during any appeals.[44]

---

[41]This shows that the concern was less that the pastor be paid than that the church be worthy of the ministry; if it was "ungrateful," another, more grateful, church was to receive the benefits of the ministry. The distinction between ingratitude and poverty would be discussed again at the fifteenth national synod; Quick, 15–Montpellier–1598, chap. 3, art. 4 (193).

[42]Quick, 8–Nîmes–1572, chap. 5, art. 22 (108). This ruling does not seem to have been adequate, however; the ninth national synod (St. Foy, 1578) instructed colloquies and provincial synods to take action against churches which withheld their minister's salary; Quick, 9–St. Foy–1578, chap. 2, art. 3 (116), indicating that the colloquies were somewhat lax in this respect: this same national synod dealt with two cases in which churches had failed to pay their pastors what was owed them. The synod ruled against a church which failed to defray its pastor's moving expenses, instructing the colloquy or provincial synod to censure the church; and against another for failing to support its retired minister, ordering the congregation to pay him his due; Quick, 9–St. Foy–1578, chap. 8, art. 6, 10 (124). These cases probably moved the national synod to push the colloquies and provincial synods to deal with the problem.

[43]Roussel, "Discipline," art. 18. Cf. Quick, 12–Vitré–1583, chap. 3, art. 1, par., 55 (147).

[44]DE 1559, art. 24; this regulation was repeated by the eleventh national synod, Quick, 11–La

Although the first national synod (Paris, 1559) did not address the issue, the second (Poitiers, 1561) was obliged to discuss the problem of "vagrants" *(coureurs),* that is, persons who claimed to be ministers but who typically were never ordained in any church, were deposed from the ministry, or were otherwise deemed unqualified to be pastors. This synod allowed provincial synods to declare persons to be vagrants with the full authority of the national synod.[45]

These basic regulations were expanded considerably over the course of the century, mostly through additions to procedures or to the list of crimes for which a minister could be deposed rather than through fundamental changes to the legislation. The fourth national synod (Lyon, 1563) began this process. It ruled that officers of the church who committed "idolatry"—that is, participated in the Mass—as a result of persecution be deposed and suspended from the Lord's Supper until they had performed public penance; nonofficers were suspended until they performed a penance determined by the consistory.[46] Further, all churches were to be notified of those declared to be vagrants, heretics, or schismatics.[47] In two discipline cases, the synod added working as a lawyer rather than a pastor and extorting marriage promises by force to the grounds for deposition from the pastoral ministry.[48] The sixth national synod (Vertueil, 1567) ruled that no one be declared a vagrant until discipline from the "neighboring churches" had failed to restore him, an additional indication that the protocolloquy was involved in pastoral discipline even if its ability to depose offenders was restricted. The synod also ruled that the list of vagrants be kept

---

Rochelle–1581, chap. 2, art. 14 (137). An example of the procedure comes from the second national synod; Quick, 2–Poitiers–1561, chap. 6, art. 22 (19), cf. ANS, 2–Poitiers–1561, "faits particuliers," 28. Note that the first national synod ruled on an appeal that incompetence was not a sufficient ground for deposition of elders unless they were incapable of performing their office; Quick, 1–Paris–1559, chap. 3, art. 11 (8), cf. ANS, 1–Paris–1559, "faits particuliers," 13.

[45]DE 1561, 50; cf. 2–Poitiers–1561, "faits particuliers," 18; Quick, 2–Poitiers–1561, chap. 4, art. 15 (15).

[46]DE 1563, "Des excommunications," 50; cf. 4–Lyon–1563, "faits particuliers," 43; Quick, 4–Lyon–1563, chap. 4, art. 11 (32); chap. 16, art. 22 (39).

[47]DE 1563, "Des excommunications," 49; cf. Quick, 4–Lyon–1563, chap. 9, art. 25 (34); chap. 11, art. 5 (35); ANS, 4–Lyon–1563, 5. The seventh national synod (La Rochelle, 1571) added that all provinces were to be informed of deposed ministers; Quick, 7–La Rochelle–1571, chap. 4, art. 2 (94). The twelfth national synod (Vitré, 1583) instructed the provincial synods to bring the list of deposed ministers and vagrants to the national synod as well; Quick, 12–Vitré–1583, chap. 3, art. 1, par. 56, 59 (147, 148).

[48]Quick, 4–Lyon–1563, chap. 14, art. 1 (36); chap. 16, art. 35 (41); cf. ANS, 4–Lyon–1563, "faits particuliers," 1b, 9.

distinct from the acts of the national synods.[49] On the other hand, if the national synod placed someone on the list of vagrants, only a subsequent national synod could remove him.[50]

The seventh national synod (La Rochelle, 1571) introduced the first significant changes to the content of the disciplinary articles from 1559. This synod decreed that ministers and elders deposed for serious crimes could never be restored to their office; those deposed for lesser crimes could only be reinstated to serve in a church in a different province in order to avoid causing scandal.[51] The eighth national synod (Nîmes, 1572) declared that though the provincial synod could depose ministers, if the deposition was disputed the national synod would decide the case; the pastor was to continue in his ministry during the appeal.[52] This synod also limited the right to restore ministers deposed for heresy to the provincial synod, thus restricting the rights of the colloquy to "bind and loose" pastors.[53]

The development of the colloquy and the regulations for pastoral selection, discipline, and deposition evolved gradually, largely through ad hoc responses to specific situations that arose in the churches. Certain basic theological principles guided these responses, notably an insistence on the relative autonomy of churches tempered by awareness that the role of the pastor as the custodian of the marks of the church set him in a class apart. It was this unique role which made pastoral selection and supervision the responsibility of several churches, not one alone. These principles were implicitly challenged by a pair of documents brought before the third national synod, held at Orléans in 1562.

Viret, Morély, and the Third National Synod (Orléans, 1562)

The period between the second and third national synods, 1561 to 1562, was

---

[49]Quick, 6–Vertueil–1567, chap. 1, art. 1 (70); cf. ANS, 6–Vertueil–1567, "faits generaux," 1.

[50]Quick, 6–Vertueil–1567, chap. 4, art. 21 (72), cf. ANS, 6–Vertueil–1567, "faits generaux," 21. A precedent for this had been set by the third national synod (Orléans, 1562), which deposed a minister with the stipulation that he could only be restored by a subsequent national synod; Quick, 3–Orléans–1562, chap. 3, art. 2 (26–27); cf. ANS, 3–Orléans–1562, "faits particuliers," 2. The sixth national synod did in fact restore two vagrants to the ministry; Quick, 6–Vertueil–1567, chap. 5, art. 2 (72); chap. 6, art. 13 (73); cf. ANS, 6–Vertueil–1567, "faits particuliers," 24, 35.

[51]DE 1571, "Des ministres," 33; Quick, 7–La Rochelle–1571, chap. 12, art. 2, par. 3 (101). This article was reiterated by the thirteenth national synod, Quick, 13–Montauban–1594, chap. 4, art. 50 (166).

[52]Quick, 8–Nîmes–1572, chap. 5, art. 24 (108).

[53]Quick, 8–Nîmes–1572, chap. 3, art. 8 (105). This regulation was extended somewhat by the twelfth national synod (Vitré, 1583), which permitted ministers deposed for "slighter faults" (presumably minor crimes instead of heresy) to be reinstated by the provincial synod rather than the national synod; Quick, 12–Vitré–1583, chap. 3, art. 1, par. 57 (148).

quite an eventful time for French Protestant ecclesiology. Pierre Viret, newly arrived in Nîmes from Geneva, prepared a provincial church order for Languedoc in 1562 which was adopted there and in Dauphiné. The provincial synod of Nîmes (February 1561 [1562 n.s.]) indicated that the order contained some provisions which the national synod needed to address. Then Jean Morély published his *Traicté de la discipline et police Chrestienne,* timing its appearance so that it would arrive just before the meeting of the national synod.[54] This ignited the largest internal controversy faced up to that time by the French Reformed churches, one which would occupy nobles, churches, colloquies, and provincial and national synods in France as well as the church of Geneva for the next ten years. The third national synod (Orléans, 1562) had quite a bit of extra work that related to church order, along with its ongoing efforts to adjust and elaborate the Discipline.

Pierre Viret was one of the best known and most popular preachers of the francophone Reformation. A native of the Pays de Vaud, he had been recruited into the ministry by Guillaume Farel and later worked with the French reformer in Geneva. Viret may even have been present when Farel pressured Calvin to join him in Geneva. When Calvin and Farel were exiled, Viret went to Lausanne, where he became a professor at the academy and one of the principal leaders of the church. He continued to play an active role in Geneva as well: he helped smooth the way for Calvin's return to the city and aided his friend on several occasions through the 1540s and 1550s. Viret worked very closely with his younger colleague Beza to establish a more systematic approach to discipline in the Pays de Vaud, an effort which was resisted by the authorities in Berne. This controversy came to a head in 1559, and Viret was exiled from the Pays de Vaud. Beza had left earlier over the same issue, and Viret followed him to Geneva. While there he took an active interest in the Protestant churches in France, writing a series of letters to encourage them in their faith. In 1561 he left Geneva for health reasons to go to the Midi. He found himself in Nîmes and began to work in the newly established church there. In 1562, he left for Montpellier; later that year, he went to Lyon, where he assumed the pastorate. In 1563, the church of Lyon requested and obtained a formal transfer of his ministry from the church of Geneva. That same year, Viret was also appointed the moderator of the fourth national synod, which was held in Lyon, and undoubtedly was involved in that synod's redaction of the Discipline. In 1565, he was expelled from Lyon as a foreigner and eventually arrived in Pau, where he worked closely with Jeanne d'Albret in establishing a Reformed church in Navarre.

---

[54]Jean Morély, *Traicté de la discipline et police Chrestienne* (Lyon: Ian de Tournes, 1562; Geneva: Slatkine Reprints, 1968).

Viret's church order was prepared as part of his ministry at Nîmes.[55] Article 8 of the acts of the provincial synod held at Nîmes in February 1562, states:

> In addition, a very good church order has been organized by M. Viret, covering both collective and local government, which is very much in accord with doctrine. This order has been communicated to this synod and has been found to be very good for the most part, but because there are certain things to correct, it has been decided to communicate it to the future General Synod at Orléans in order to add to or take away from it in accordance with that synod's advice, and afterwards a copy will be given to each church in the province.[56]

The following articles in the acts of the synod outline Viret's church order.[57] Article 11 introduced a new element into the French Reformed Church structure, the *classe:*

> And because the province is large and it is inconvenient to meet together because of the distances involved, the province has been divided into five *classes* according to geographic proximity. All the ministers of the churches in a *classe,* together with one deacon or elder, are to meet every three months to resolve questions from the churches, and whatever the *classe* cannot resolve itself is to be sent to the provincial synod. And a minister is to be elected in each *classe* who is to visit all of the churches of the *classe* during the three months

---

[55]Viret's was not the only provincial church order; the first provincial synod of Brittany adopted a *police* for the province, dated 20 August 1561. Consisting of the decisions of the synod in fourteen articles, the document was sent to all the churches of the province and was to be examined for conformity to the Discipline; Le Noir, *Histoire ecclésiastique de Bretagne,* 70.

[56]En outre a esté dressé par Monsieur Viret un fort bon ordre concernant le fait des eglises tant en general qu'en particulier, auquel est convenable beaucoup de doctrine, lequel estant communiqué audit synode, a esté trouvé fort bon en la pluspart; mais parce qu'il y avoit certaines choses à corriger, a esté arresté qu'on le communiqueroit au synode general futur à Orleans, pour y adjouster ou diminuer selon que sera advisé, et en seroit apres donné copie par toutes les eglises de ladite province. Auzière, fol. 2v; cf. *Documents protestants inédits,* 42.

[57]Arnaud, *Documents protestants inédits,* 72–78, believed otherwise. He identified *La forme de dresser un consistoire* found in the Grenoble manuscripts with the *Articles polytiques* as Viret's church order, cf. ibid. 88–89. This is almost certainly mistaken: *La forme de dresser un consistoire* may have been written by Viret (cf. Bernard Roussel, "Pierre Viret en France," *BSHPF* 144 [1998]: 825), but it deals only with local church structure, whereas the article from the provincial synod cited above indicates that Viret's church order also included provisions for collective government. Further, art. 11 and 12 of the acts of the provincial synod include provisions almost identical to the church structure of the Pays de Vaud where Viret spent most of his ministry. It is more likely that Viret's church order was preserved in the acts of the provincial synod than in *La forme de dresser un consistoire.*

[between meetings] to hear the complaints of the ministers and the churches. And the provincial synod [is to elect] another whose charge is to visit all of the *classes* each year, and along with this to convoke the next synod.[58]

Article 12 deals with colloquies and their relationship to the *classe:*

And because the *classe* is large, it has been divided into several specific colloquies geographically. All of the ministers with a deacon or elder of each church are to meet together in one of the principal cities of the colloquy on a monthly or biweekly basis and there discuss the affairs of their churches. And one is to be elected to visit the colloquy every three months and to report to the *classe.* And all this is to rotate [among the churches].[59]

Both of these articles show the influence of the Pays de Vaud: the *classe* does not appear anywhere else in France, and the "visitor" in Viret's church order corresponds closely to the *doyen* and *jurés* in the Pays de Vaud; in fact, in Dauphiné, where Viret's church order was adopted,[60] this office was even called the *doyen* of the *classe.*[61] A parallel office to the *doyen* was also to be established on the provincial level by analogy to the *classe.* Although the rotation of officers and meeting sites

[58]Et pour ce que la province est grande, et estoit incommode s'assembler de bien loin, a esté divisée en cinq classes selon la proximité des lieux, et que en chaque classe s'assembleront de trois en trois mois tous les ministres avec un diacre ou surveillant de quelcune desdites eglises, pour resoudre des doutes des eglises; et ce qui ne se pourra resoudre a ladite classe, sera renvoyé audit synode provincial. Et sera esleu en ladite classe un ministre d'icelle, lequel aura charge dans lesdits trois mois de visiter toutes les eglises de ladite classe, ouyr les plaintes tant des ministres que desdites eglises, et aussi audit synode provincial un autre qui aura charge une fois l'année de visiter toutes les classes, avec celle de convoquer ledit synode futur. Auzière, fol. 3; cf. *Documents protestants inédits,* 43.

[59]Et pour ce que la classe seroit grande, auroit esté divisée en plusieurs colloques particuliers selon la distance des lieux, ausquels s'assembleront tous les ministres en l'une des villes principales dudit colloque avec un diacre de chacune eglise ou surveillant, et ce de mois en mois ou de quinzaine en quinzaine; et là communiqueront des affaires, et sera esleu un pour visiter le colloque dans trois mois et le rapporter à la classe, et le tout sera ambulatoire. Auzière, fol. 3r–3v; *Documents protestants inédits,* 44.

[60]This province introduced a *classe* system at the provincial synod of Montélimar (1562); *Documents protestants inédits,* 37; the Grenoble manuscripts published by Arnaud include the provincial synod of Languedoc which contained Viret's church order.

[61]Assembly of Valence, 1563, in *Documents protestants inédits, 52.* Robert Kingdon, in *Geneva and the Consolidation of French Protestantism 1564–1572: A Contribution to the History of Congregationalism, Presbyterianism, and Calvinist Resistance Theory* (Madison: University of Wisconsin Press, 1967), 61, notes that the only francophone churches to use the term "dean" were those of the Pays de Vaud and the Chablais, another indication of the Vaudois roots of this church order and thus of Viret's probable role in preparing it (*Geneva and the Consolidation,* 61).

provided for in article 12 as well as in article 10 dealing with provincial synods was intended to prevent an ecclesiastical hierarchy from developing, the requirement that the colloquy meet in one of its "principal cities" suggests that these were also its principal churches, in practice if not in theory. This provision may simply have been a matter of convenience, of course, though the parallel with the Pays de Vaud—whose *classes* met in and were named after their principal cities and whose overall structure followed a "central place" model—is striking.

The provincial synod noted that Viret's order needed to be corrected at some points and sent it to the third national synod, meeting at Orléans in 1562. The *classe* was relatively uncontroversial and was not discussed until 1571. The provisions for visitation were highly suspect among French Protestants, however, and the national synod immediately struck them down. Arguing that sending ministers to visit churches could have "dangerous consequences," the synod specifically banned this practice.[62] In view of the foundational principles of French Protestant ecclesiology, the synod probably reasoned that visitation violated the autonomy of the congregation, involved persons not directly concerned with local problems in their solution, and gave the visiting minister a greater de facto authority than the pastor himself in his own church; the records of the synod are not sufficiently detailed to prove this conclusively, however.

There is an irony here: the thirteenth national synod (Montauban, 1594) called on colloquies or, failing that, provincial synods to appoint two to three ministers to oversee problems in the churches to try to prevent abuses which were occurring; the synod did not change the Discipline, however.[63] Viret's approach was thus vindicated thirty-two years after it had been struck down, though it never became a regular feature of the church order.

The *classe* did not become an element of synodical government in many provinces either.[64] The fourth national synod (Lyon, 1563)[65] and the sixth national synod (Vertueil, 1567)[66] both mention it in connection with tasks usually associated with the colloquy, but aside from that, the *classe* was completely ignored by

---

[62]Quick, 3–Orléans–1562, chap. 2, art. 14 (24), cf. ANS, 3–Orléans–1562, 17. Dauphiné seems to have either ignored this prohibition or redefined the office of *doyen*.

[63]Quick, 13–Montauban–1594, chap. 4, art. 6 (161).

[64]Le Noir mentions a *classe* in Brittany c.1570 (*Histoire ecclésiastique de Bretagne*, 159). It seems to have been a district within the province, but there is no indication that its churches ever met as an assembly within the ecclesiastical government.

[65]Quick, 4–Lyon–1563, chap. 15 (36–37); note, however, that the 1565 Discipline changed "par les classes et synodes" to "par les consistoires, colloques et synodes" (DE 1565, "Des ministres," 24).

[66]Quick, 6–Vertueil–1567, chap. 3, art. 19 (72); Aymon, 6–Vertueil–1567, "articles générales," 30 (76) omits it.

the national synod's. In Languedoc, the *classe* was introduced to help deal with the large size of the province and seems to have functioned reasonably well until 1571. In that year—perhaps not coincidentally the year of Viret's death—the seventh national synod meeting at La Rochelle instructed Languedoc to conform to the practice of the other provinces of the kingdom and suppress the *classe,* leaving the consistory, colloquy, and provincial synod as the only remaining organs of ecclesiastical government.[67] The province moved toward compliance: the synod of Nîmes held in June 1571 noted the abolition of *classes,*[68] and subsequent lists of deputies to provincial synods were arranged by colloquy rather than *classe.* The only reference to the *classes* in the later provincial records comes from the *Assemblée extraordinaire* held in Nîmes in 1573.[69] This may imply that they were still functioning two years after the national synod called for their abolition, though it may simply have been a habitual reference on the part of the scribe. One way or another, the *classe* soon passed completely out of the ecclesiastical structure of the French churches.

Another challenge to basic elements of the French Reformed churches' ecclesiology was raised by Jean Morély, sire de Villiers.[70] To understand some of the dimensions of this controversy, it is necessary to know something of Morély's background and dealings with the city of Geneva. His father was a regent master of the faculty of medicine at the University of Paris, eventually becoming a personal physician of Francis I. Morély's father was thus ennobled and acquired a number of small seigneuries. His marriage to Catherine Bonnet, daughter of a *procureur* of the Parlement of Paris, cemented his position among the lower ranks of the *noblesse de la robe.* Jean, his oldest son, was given a solid humanist education. After his father's death in 1543, Jean left France to continue his studies in Zurich, Lausanne, and Geneva. Jean Rott and Philippe Denis believe he was converted to Protestantism during his time in Switzerland through the influence of Farel, Viret, and Calvin; this would explain Morély's strong emphasis on discipline in his subsequent writings.[71] He himself placed his conversion to about 1547, which was during his first trip to Switzerland. In 1548, Morély returned to

---

[67]This does not appear in the acts of the national synod but is contained in the report to the provincial synod of Nîmes (1571) given by the provinces' deputies to the national synod; Auzière, fol. 44v.

[68]Auzière, fol. 44v.

[69]Auzière, fol. 76r.

[70]The best biography of Morély and the most complete discussion of his ideas is Philippe Denis and Jean Rott, *Jean Morély (ca. 1524–ca.1594) et l'Utopie d'une démocratie dans l'église,* Travaux d'Humanisme et Renaissance 278 (Geneva: Droz, 1993). See also Kingdon, *Geneva and the Consolidation,* 37–148.

[71]Denis and Rott, *Jean Morély,* 23.

Paris, then went to Wittenberg to study with Philip Melanchthon in 1549. In 1550 Morély was back in Lausanne, where he took the side of Farel and Viret in their dispute with the Bernese authorities over church discipline. After returning to Paris and traveling to England on a mysterious errand for the Reformed cause, Morély once again returned to Geneva, becoming a legal resident and purchasing a house in a prosperous neighborhood within the old walls of the city in 1554.

Morély conducted more diplomatic missions for Geneva before running afoul of the pastors and the city council in 1560. He had returned from France some months after the Conjuration of Amboise (18 March 1560), and reported that Chandieu had been sent by the pastors of Geneva to Paris with a message that approved of taking action under the direction of the First Prince of the Blood in response to the renewed persecutions in the country, and that indicated that Beza especially had given his support and consent to the project. Unfortunately, word of Morély's remarks made its way to Beza and Calvin, who brought the matter before the Small Council of Geneva. This was a very alarming development: the French government already suspected Genevan involvement in the events at Amboise, and if Morély's words became public, it would cause severe diplomatic and possibly military difficulties for Geneva. The Genevan pastors, including Calvin and Beza, denied any involvement in the plot. Beza was particularly emphatic in his denials, claiming that Morély's report had some grains of truth but distorted the essence of his communications to the French. Chandieu also gave a statement which "tended to exonerate" the Genevan pastors.[72] Because of the sensitivity of the matter, Morély was put on trial secretly. He was censured for speaking so lightly about serious matters and for calumny and was ordered to pay a fine of 500 écus and to acknowledge his error. Morély paid his fine and apologized for his words, saying he never intended to defame the ministers of Geneva.

Two years later, Morély published his *Treatise on Church Discipline and Polity*. Although he had originally planned to dedicate the work to Henri II or one of his sons or to Henri of Navarre, the work was finally dedicated to Pierre Viret. In the dedication, Morély indicated that he had presented a copy to Viret, who held it "for some time" but was unable to read it in its entirety due to his sudden departure from Geneva; this enables us to date the work to sometime before September 1561.[73] Calvin was also given a copy, but declined to read it; as Robert M. Kingdon points out, much trouble might have been averted had either of these men read and commented on the book before it was published.[74] Morély's treatise is

[72]Kingdon, *Geneva and the Consolidation*, 45.
[73]Denis and Rott, *Jean Morély*, 53.
[74]Kingdon, *Geneva and the Consolidation*, 48.

analyzed in detail by Rott and Denis, and there is no need here to go into all of the details of his argument; an outline of some of his main points and particularly the ones at the center of the controversy is sufficient for present purposes.

Morély was a firm believer in church discipline, but he was unhappy with its state in any of the churches in Europe. Reforming discipline meant reforming church structures to place authority in the right hands, and to Morély, the only scriptural body that could be given that authority was the individual church as a whole. This authority could not and should not be delegated to any other, neither to the secular government nor to the leadership of the church, that is, the consistory; it must remain directly in the hands of the members of the church, that is, those who have signed the Confession of Faith. Thus Morély stripped the consistory of its most basic function in Calvinist polity; its role was reduced to administrative matters, such as preparing the agenda for and running church meetings, and to carrying out the church's decisions.[75] Further, the consistory only served at the pleasure of the people: the church as a whole was responsible for selecting and deposing its ministers, including both pastors and elders.[76] This was in sharp contrast with the Discipline, which required several surrounding ministers to be involved in selecting pastors and gave the provincial synod significant authority in judging issues of pastoral discipline. As for elders, the Discipline allowed them to be selected by the congregation when a church was first established, but once a church was established, new elders were to be selected by co-optation by the consistory; in other words, the consistory would nominate elders and the church would then be asked to ratify them. The ratification vote was taken very seriously; it was certainly not intended to be a routine endorsement of the consistory's candidates. This procedure nonetheless placed the task of screening candidates with the consistory rather than with the congregation, which was only brought in at the last step in the process.[77]

An important qualification needs to be made here. Morély viewed the individual church as the embodiment of the universal church, thus having "true liberty"

---

[75]As discussed in chap. 6, there was precedent within French Protestant churches for an administrative consistory; Morély was thus picking up here on one strand of French Protestant tradition.

[76]At the same time, Morély recommends that each province establish a university to provide theological training, implying that pastors should meet some educational standards. Further, the universities could recommend pastors to churches in outlying towns, subject to their approval. Kingdon, *Geneva and the Consolidation*, 53.

[77]Morély also gave the congregation the right to judge doctrinal questions. Although the Discipline had yet to make a statement on this, Calvin gave that task to the pastors and doctors (at least in theory). The national synod would follow him on this once they were asked to make a pronouncement on it; DE 1571, "Des professeurs en théologie," 1.

to conduct its own affairs. But the "individual church" existed at the level of the *bailliage*, or in larger cities at the level of a parish or quarter, not at the level of the church meeting in each village or town; in England, Morély saw this as the episcopal diocese. In France, each *bailliage* was to have a mother church which was responsible for overseeing pastoral and congregational discipline in the local churches. The mother church was to hold weekly ecclesiastical assemblies to discuss church affairs. This assembly, which was composed of either the pastors or "the churches" if the matters to be discussed were generally known, was to elect a moderator for a two-year term. Morély described this officer as an "overseer" *(surveillant),* though he noted that the office was commonly called the *doyen.* Although Morély does not make the connection explicitly, this officer was presumably the same as one which was to be elected within the mother church of each *bailliage* to preside over the church and to report lapses in doctrine or practice to "the consistory" (presumably the consistory of the mother church). To assist him in this work, pastors were to be deputed to check on the doctrine of the ministers and people of the *bailliage* and to report the results either to the consistories of the local churches or to the mother church. Morély did not consider the mother church as being in a hierarchical relationship above the others; rather, it was a question of different functions and degrees of responsibility within a single, structured church; in any event, proper organization of the church was a question of polity, not doctrine, and was not discussed in Scripture; there was thus no binding model that the churches had to follow.[78]

Morély's proposals for the mother church in the *bailliage* are sufficiently vague that they have caused some confusion among analysts of his church structure. One issue involves whether the structures Morély proposed for the *bailliage* should be considered as part of the collective government of the church. Kingdon argues that they should be, and that the *bailliage* was the equivalent of the French Reformed Church's colloquy. On the other hand, in 1562 the colloquy was not yet a standard element of the government of the French Reformed churches. Further, although the *bailliage* was made up of a number of individual congregations, Morély did not seem to view these as independent churches. Again, the individual church existed as a structured whole at the level of the *bailliage;* thus the assembly should not be seen on a theoretical level as being part of the collective government of the church, but rather as the assembly of a single church. An analogy can be drawn to the Genevan Consistory or the Company of Pastors, both of which included representatives from all of the churches both in the city and in the surrounding hinterland and yet were seen as part of a single church. If Geneva had a

[78]See Denis and Rott, *Jean Morély,* 166–67, 199–200, and Morély, *Traité,* 283–85.

single church for the multiple local congregations in its territory, then so could the *bailliage*. Yet unlike in Geneva, the individual churches in the *bailliage* had their own consistories, and thus the consistory of the mother church of necessity had different functions from the Genevan Consistory. Further, Morély's model for the mother church and the officers of the *bailliage* was clearly drawn from the Vaudois *classe:* the term *doyen* was used in only two Protestant areas, the Pays de Vaud and the Chablais in Savoy, both under the control of Berne.[79] Furthermore, the assistants to the *doyen* performed essentially the same role as the Vaudois *jurés*. Yet the *classe* was indisputably an element of collective government. Morély's discussion is sufficiently imprecise to resolve these issues definitively, though the weight of his discussion suggests that the *bailliage* ought to be considered part of the government of the individual church.

Morély did offer some proposals for collective government in the church, however. Above the *bailliage*, he recommended the creation of a provincial synod to meet annually if possible, and biennially if not. Such synods, which were to be held in the "metropolitan church," were essential for maintaining the unity of the churches. In addition to administrative duties, the provincial synod was to discuss difficult issues concerning doctrine, discipline, or liturgy, and to write remonstrances and exhortations to political rulers about their duties as Christians. Higher-level synods could be called at great need, with national synods summoned by the prince. These national and even ecumenical synods performed much the same functions as the provincial synods. In no case did any of these synods have the right to pass laws or decrees which were binding on the local church; they were purely deliberative and advisory, with no authority over the churches.[80] Although Morély's synods addressed the same sorts of issues as those of the French Reformed churches—even the ad hoc nature of the national synod corresponded to the 1559 Discipline—their lack of authority was an important difference that challenged not only the Discipline itself but the entire approach taken by the churches as they had begun the process of organizing French Protestantism just three years before.

Morély's program faced stiff opposition within the leadership of the French Reformed churches on several fronts, all of them revolving around the authority of the individual congregation: Morély allowed the church as a whole to select

---

[79]Kingdon, *Geneva and the Consolidation*, 55, 61.

[80]This may have been influenced by the churches' use of the *droit des corps* to integrate themselves into the public law of the kingdom: churches tried to identify themselves as legal corporations, giving them the right to regulate their "legitimate interests." Since in France all *corps* were local (except the Catholic clergy), there was no legal precedent for synods, and thus they had no right to regulate even the "legitimate interests" of the churches.

and depose church officers, to administer discipline, and to decide doctrine, he stripped the consistory of its basic function of administering discipline, and the consistory and the synods lost authority to make decisions. Given the treatise's dedication to Viret and a number of points where the Vaudois reformer seems to have had some sympathy for Morély's ideas,[81] he may have expected Viret's presence at Orléans to provide him with some measure of support. Unfortunately, the conditions under which the synod met worked against Morély: Catholic and Protestant armies were mobilizing for the first war of religion, and Orléans was the base of operations for Condé, the commander of the Protestant armies, as well as his means of controlling the Loire valley. The turmoil prevented many deputies from coming to the synod, including Viret. To make matters worse, Beza and Chandieu were both present, neither of whom had particularly fond memories of Morély's comments about their respective roles in the Conjuration of Amboise. With Beza's support, Chandieu was elected moderator of the synod, making the environment less than hospitable for Morély's ideas. It was not an open-and-shut case, however: Morély's book was debated extensively, and Beza and Chandieu both worked hard to change the minds of his supporters. They succeeded, and the book was condemned in a simple and terse statement recorded in the acts of the synod:

> As to the book entitled, *Treatise on Christian Discipline and Polity*, composed and published by Jean Morély, the Council judges that, with respect to the points concerning the Discipline of the Church by which he pretends to condemn and overturn the accustomed order of the churches, founded on the Word of God, that the aforementioned book contains evil doctrine tending to the confusion and dissipation of the Church, and thus the Council exhorts all the faithful to be on guard against its doctrine.[82]

This was not the end of the Morély conflict. For our purposes, the rest of the story can be told briefly. Geneva got involved as well: the consistory excommunicated Morély on one of his trips to the city for refusing to recant his views and

---

[81]See Philippe Denis, "Viret et Morély: Les Raisons d'un Silence," *Bibliothèque d'Humanisme et Renaissance* 54 (1992): 395–409.

[82]Quant au livre intitulé "Traitté de la Discipline et Police chrestienne", composé et publié par Jean Morely, le concile est d'avis, quant aux points concernant la discipline de l'eglise par lesquels il pretend condamner et renverser l'ordre accoutumé des eglises, et fondé sur la parole de Dieu, que ledit livre contient mauvaise doctrine et tendant a confusion et dissipation de l'eglise, et pourtant le concile exhorte tous fideles de se donner garde de la susdite doctrine. ANS, 3–Orléans–1562, "faits particuliers," 13.

ordered him to appear before the Council. At this Morély fled, whereupon he was convicted of contempt and disobedience to the Council, and his book was burned. No amount of later apologies or attempts at reconciliation by Morély would persuade the Genevan church to lift the excommunication. In France, the national synod's decision did not end the controversy either. On several occasions, provincial synods in the Ile de France attempted to rehabilitate Morély and even got him to admit that there were errors in his book, but these attempts always fell apart due to Genevan intransigence and the influence of Chandieu. Morély always managed to find supporters at key times: in 1565 it was Odet de Coligny, the Huguenot cardinal of Châtillon and brother of Admiral Coligny; in 1566, it was Jeanne d'Albret; and from 1567 to 1572, Pierre Ramus. The national synods continued their involvement in the controversy: the fourth (Lyon, 1563), presided over by Viret, did not address the Morély affair, but the fifth (Paris, 1565), presided over by Nicholas des Gallars, then minister of Orléans but formerly of Geneva, the seventh (La Rochelle, 1571), presided over by Beza, and eighth (Nîmes, 1572) all did.[83] Predictably, these synods condemned Morély's program at every opportunity. In particular, the 1565 national synod commissioned Chandieu to write a refutation of Morély, which appeared in 1566 as *La Confirmation de la Discipline ecclésiastique, observee es Eglises reformees du Royaume de France.* This work was essentially the official defense of the Discipline, though it omitted any discussion of collective government because Protestant synodical meetings were illegal at that point, a fact which Morély attempted to use to his advantage on occasion.[84] The controversy only came to an end later in 1572, when the St. Bartholomew's Day massacres claimed the lives of a number of those involved in the debate and gave the French Reformed churches bigger things to worry about.

The Morély controversy was obviously quite a complex, messy affair. Personal egos and animosities were part of it, particularly in Morély's relationships with Beza and Chandieu, as were conflicts between loyalty to the Huguenot political leadership and loyalty to Geneva. For our purposes, the case is particularly important for the light it sheds on the tension between congregational autonomy and collective government in the early years of the French Reformed Church. As we have seen, the autonomy of the local church was an important element of French Protestantism, a point made by many scholars with respect to Morély. Unfortunately, the efforts of the Discipline to preserve a relatively high degree of

---

[83]The sixth national synod (Vertueil, 1567) may have as well: art. 11 indicates that the deputies were each asked if their churches had any doubts about the Discipline; all responded that their churches agreed with it and that those who disrupt the order of the churches should be censured.

[84]Denis and Rott, *Jean Morély,* 201–2; Kingdon, *Geneva and the Consolidation,* 70.

congregational independence have not been as widely recognized, due in part to the lack of reliable editions of the early versions of the Discipline. The general trend has been to assume that the French Reformed churches had a highly organized, even hierarchical synodical structure; this was simply not the case, especially at the time the controversy broke out. This assumption has led to many misunderstandings of the nature of the Morély affair. It has been interpreted as a battle pitting congregational autonomy against a top-down church order where authority flowed from the national synod through the provincial synods to the colloquies and thence to the local church, or as indigenous French congregationalism resisting Genevan centralization. This is a serious misinterpretation of the Discipline, and especially the early redactions such as that of 1561 which was in force (in theory) when Morély's book was published. The Discipline emphasizes local autonomy except in matters of general concern, where one congregation's decisions could affect another's. In these cases, local autonomy meant that no individual church had the right to impose its will, and hence there was recourse to various synodical bodies to reach a collective decision. This was very similar to the approach taken by Morély, except that his synods had no right to enforce their recommendations: the differences between the systems can easily be exaggerated.[85]

To demonstrate that the issues at stake did not center on hierarchical versus nonhierarchical government, one need look no further than the acts of the third national synod (Orléans, 1562). This synod also quashed the portions of Viret's church order that proposed a system of visitation within the province: it violated the autonomy of the local church and established a de facto hierarchy by giving the officers of the *classe* authority to oversee the local church. Yet this was the very same national synod which first condemned Morély's "congregationalism"![86]

If the issue was not hierarchy, then what was it? As Kingdon suggests, the difference between the Discipline and Morély lay in the high degree of anticlericalism in Morély's program, or to put it differently, in his emphasis on the authority of the congregation as a whole rather than that of the consistory (or the synods).[87] Morély refused to allow officers or councils to have any real authority in the church; everything was finally and completely vested in the laity. In contrast, the Discipline held a high view of pastors, elders, and deacons and their collective

---

[85]Given that Protestant synods had been banned in France at the time, Chandieu's defense of the Discipline does not discuss this aspect of the problem in any detail; this also has contributed to the misunderstandings of the nature of the controversy.

[86]In one respect, Morély's program was more hierarchical than the Discipline: "mother churches" in the *bailliage* and metropolitan churches in the provinces, for example, set up a de facto hierarchy within the churches, Morély's protests to the contrary notwithstanding.

[87]Kingdon, *Geneva and the Consolidation,* 59.

authority within the church. This led to such elements of the church order as special rules for "clerical" discipline (that is, oversight of church officers), co-optation of officers by the consistory subject to the ratification of the congregation, and the involvement of neighboring churches in choosing pastors, the most critical of all of the offices. It also contributed to the authority of synods, though paradoxically so did the insistence on congregational autonomy.

The Discipline was thus something of an elitist document, and for good reason, as far as its supporters were concerned. The very same elements in early French Protestantism which were closest to Morély—its emphasis on complete congregational autonomy, combined with a "Gallican" tendency toward anticlericalism—had also led to the sectarianism that had so plagued and divided French Protestantism from its earliest days. The Confession and Discipline were written to end this division and to create a uniform Protestant Church within the kingdom.[88] Morély's challenge of the church leadership and of the synodical system was more than simply an issue of church government: it was a threat to the very foundations of the *Eglises Réformées*. The condemnation of Morély was thus the result of a basic distrust of the ability of the uneducated to make responsible decisions about church leadership and discipline, combined with a fear that a congregationalist polity would lead to the continuation of the sort of divisions within the Protestant camp that the Discipline and the Confession were adopted to end. In essence, the condemnation represented the French Reformed churches' characteristic attempt to find a via media between episcopacy and congregationalism, or as they would have seen it, between hierarchy and anarchy.

THE COLLECTIVE GOVERNMENT OF THE FRENCH REFORMED CHURCHES

The organs of collective government and the ecclesiastical structure of the French Reformed churches evolved considerably over the first thirteen years of its existence, though it remained consistent with the basic principles of polity articulated in both the Gallican Confession and in the first edition of the Discipline. The churches' insistence on the equality of all pastors and the autonomy of churches led them to reject any form of hierarchy and to try as much as possible to deal with problems on as local a level as possible; conversely, more general problems would properly be addressed by assemblies having broader competence than the local church. Initially, the churches had two basic levels of government, the consistory and the provincial synod, with national synods and meetings of neighbor-

---

[88]Morély himself may have recognized sectarianism as a potential problem: his synods were intended to promote unity within the church, though their lack of teeth would seem to limit their effectiveness.

ing pastors and elders to be held on an ad hoc basis. The national synod was quickly defined as a regular unit within the synodical structure, however, and thus a clear three-level church government was established. Still later, the ad hoc meetings of local pastors and elders emerged as the colloquy, which became an officially recognized element in the church structure with its own chapter in the Discipline in 1572, though its existence and role in the church had been acknowledged earlier.

To understand this development and its implications for the evolution of French Reformed ecclesiastical structures, it is helpful to trace chronologically the changing nature of these various bodies and the approach to representation in them. As can be seen in fig. 1, the 1559 Discipline had one regular element of collective church government, the provincial synod, and ad hoc meetings of the national synod and neighboring churches; the individual churches sent representatives to each of these directly. The next edition of the Discipline (1561) maintained the ad hoc meetings of neighboring churches, but made the national synod a regular element of the church government; further, rather than individual churches' sending representatives to the national synod, the provinces did (fig. 2). In Languedoc, the nearly contemporary provincial church order drafted by Pierre Viret set up two intermediate levels between the provincial synod and the local

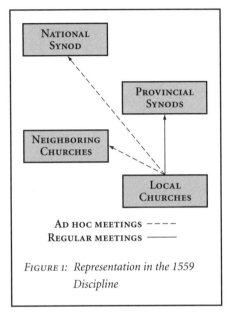

AD HOC MEETINGS ----
REGULAR MEETINGS ———

FIGURE 1: *Representation in the 1559 Discipline*

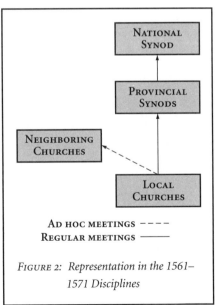

AD HOC MEETINGS ----
REGULAR MEETINGS ———

FIGURE 2: *Representation in the 1561– 1571 Disciplines*

church. Churches in close geographic proximity were grouped into colloquies, and neighboring colloquies were grouped into *classes* (fig. 3). This organization was largely administrative, however; local churches sent representatives to each of these bodies, though the *classe* was also to organize visitation of the colloquies. Since the church order was designed to operate within the province, it did not address the issue of the national synod. In 1571, the national synod abolished *classes*, but by that point, colloquies were generally well established within the French Reformed churches. Colloquies were incorporated into the Discipline at the next national synod (Nîmes, 1572), though without setting them into the same hierarchical structure as the provincial and national synods: rather than have the local church send deputies to the colloquy, and the colloquy send representatives to the provincial synod, local churches sent representatives to both the colloquy and the provincial synod directly (fig. 4). Although the colloquy was part of the chain in appeals of disciplinary decisions, it was not in terms of the system of representation. The mature system that emerged in 1572 continued

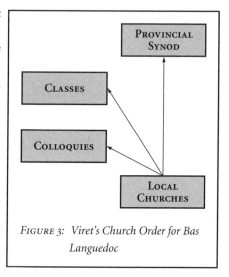

FIGURE 3: *Viret's Church Order for Bas Languedoc*

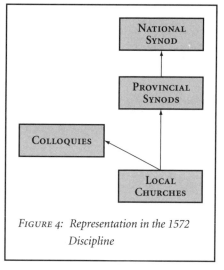

FIGURE 4: *Representation in the 1572 Discipline*

to emphasize the local church as the fundamental basis of the entire ecclesiastical structure, and the provincial synod as the key element in the collective government: provincial synods were composed of representatives of individual churches (unlike the national synod); they were always more active than colloquies; and they controlled access to the national synod. By the end of the century, the church began showing signs of increasing centralization as the national synod continued to accumulate more responsibility and authority, though the provincial synods continued to play a vitally important role within the system and never became completely overshadowed by the national synod.

One caveat needs to be added here. The insistence on the autonomy of the local church was never absolute, particularly in terms of pastoral selection, placement, and discipline. To be sure, Viret's system of visitation was vetoed because it compromised the equality of pastors and the right of the churches to operate without outside interference. But Morély's congregationalist approach was banned as well: the national synod continued to insist on co-optation of church officers by the consistory and on the necessity of neighboring churches (and later, the colloquy) to be involved in pastoral selection, though the reason for this probably had more to do with a distrust of the common laity than with a desire to see other churches involved in local matters. Just as the laity could not be trusted completely to select their own ministers, they also could not be trusted with issues of supervision and depositions. These were left primarily in the hands of the provincial synod, though in practical terms the synod could not provide the sort of immediate oversight needed in all the churches throughout the province. Thus ad hoc meetings of neighboring ministers were given authority to handle controversies in the churches; these eventually evolved into the colloquy. With its emergence as a regular element of the collective government of the churches, the colloquy acquired a number of other responsibilities beyond pastoral supervision as well.

A large percentage of this chapter is dedicated to the work of congregational and pastoral oversight. The next two chapters address the local church itself more directly, and specifically its officers and consistory. While in many ways local church structure followed a more or less standard Reformed model, a number of features of the diaconate in the French churches reveal a considerably more complex interaction between Reformed and non-Reformed elements than has generally been recognized.

Chapter 5

The French
Reformed Diaconate

Of all the offices in Christian churches, none has taken so many guises as the diaconate.[1] In many church traditions, deacons exist largely to fill gaps in the church's
hierarchy or ministry; in others, the office evolved into a step on the road to ordination as a priest. Many Reformed Protestants in the sixteenth century attempted
to restore what they understood to be the biblical role of the office by placing the
deacons in charge of the social welfare ministry of the church by, for example,
having them collect and distribute alms and take care of widows, orphans, and
the sick. Although the French Reformed churches accepted this as the principal
definition of the deacon's role, from the very beginning the French Reformed
diaconate took on many unique characteristics that set it apart from other versions of the office. Indeed, earlier forms of French Protestantism had an essentially non-Reformed view of the office, and it is from these roots that many of the
unusual aspects of the French Reformed diaconate developed. This chapter discusses some of these characteristics in light of the historical evolution of the
office. After a brief outline of the history of the diaconate in Western Europe, it
examines the background to the French Reformed diaconate as articulated in the
1557 *Articles polytiques* and then traces the legislative history of the liturgical and
catechetical roles of the French deacons from the 1559 Discipline through the
subsequent national synods. This study shows that these regulations reflect not

---

[1]Portions of this chapter have appeared in Glenn S. Sunshine, "Geneva Meets Rome: The Development of the French Reformed Diaconate," *Sixteenth Century Journal* 26 (1995): 329–46.

only Reformed but Roman Catholic influences on the structural development of the French Reformed Church.

DEVELOPMENT OF THE DIACONATE

The appointment of the Seven in Acts 6 was viewed as the origin of the diaconate by both Roman Catholic and Reformed thinkers in the sixteenth century, and it is the logical place to start in discussing the office.[2] The Seven were appointed to settle a controversy about distribution of food to widows between the Greek- and Hebrew-speaking communities in the Jerusalem church:

> Now in these days when the disciples were increasing in number, the Hellenists murmured against the Hebrews because their widows were neglected in the daily distribution. And the twelve summoned the body of the disciples and said, "It is not right that we should give up preaching the word of God to serve tables. Therefore, brethren, pick out from among you seven men of good repute, full of the Spirit and of wisdom, whom we may appoint to this duty. But we will devote ourselves to prayer and the ministry of the word." And what they said pleased the whole multitude, and they chose Stephen, a man full of faith and of the Holy Spirit, and Philip, and Prochorus, and Nicanor, and Timon and Parmenas, and Nicolaus, a proselyte of Antioch. These they set before the apostles, and they prayed and laid their hands upon them. (Acts 6:1–6, RSV)

The work of the Seven can be analyzed in terms of two interrelated functions: they were to relieve the Apostles of duties which strictly speaking were not an

---

[2]For a summary of the history of the diaconate, see Jeannine E. Olson, *One Ministry, Many Roles: Deacons and Deaconesses through the Centuries* (St. Louis: Concordia, 1992). Elsie Ann McKee, *John Calvin on the Diaconate and Liturgical Almsgiving,* Travaux d'Humanisme et Renaissance 197 (Geneva: Droz, 1984) provides a useful exegetical history of the key biblical passages dealing with the diaconate and outlines the various approaches to the office in more detail than is possible here; see 129–30 for a summary of the various types of diaconates. The identification of the Seven as the first deacons has been disputed recently for two principal reasons. First, it implies that the church of Jerusalem had a much more highly developed sense of structure and offices than is likely; it may be, however, that deacons evolved from the ministry of the Seven, even if they were not themselves deacons. Second, the Greek word *diakonos* does not appear in the text of Acts 6; on the other hand, the verbal form *diakoneo* does (vs. 2), weakening the force of the objection. Whatever the conclusion of this debate, the important point for present purposes is that sixteenth-century theologians of both the Catholic and Reformed camps considered the Seven the first deacons; see McKee, *Liturgical Almsgiving,* 138–58. Other passages were important for defining the diaconal office, notably 1 Tim. 3:8–13, but here the Acts passage serves to illustrate the different approaches to the diaconate.

essential element of their ministry, and specifically the Seven were to do this by administering the social welfare ministry of the church. These two aspects of the work of the Seven evolved into the two basic models of the diaconate used in Western Europe in the sixteenth century.

Although the early church tended to emphasize the social welfare role of the diaconate, the deacons performed a range of other duties as well. For example, they read or chanted the Gospel or epistles, assisted in the preparation and distribution of Communion, received offerings, and recorded donors. Their liturgical duties were cut back considerably under Gregory the Great, who in 595 assigned many of their chants to the cantors. But it was particularly the collection and distribution of alms that made the deacons important and powerful figures within the church hierarchy. The Council of Nicaea (A.D. 325) curbed their powers considerably, but they retained a great deal of influence in practice: both the Council of Toledo (A.D. 633) in the West and the Trullan Synod (A.D. 692) in the East had to stress that the office was hierarchically inferior to the priesthood.[3] In the Latin West, the diaconate continued to develop as a minor order until 1207, when Innocent III redefined it as the second of the four major orders, above subdeacon and below priest and bishop.[4] Although for various reasons some men remained deacons for life, in general the office had by this time become little more than a transitional step on the road to the priesthood.

By the end of the Middle Ages, deacons had accumulated a bewildering array of potential functions. They tended to fill whatever roles were necessary in local churches, particularly before their place in the hierarchy was established. As a result, precedents were set in different parts of Europe at different times which made it possible for deacons to take on a tremendous variety of tasks. By the late medieval period, the temporary nature of the office and a surplus of fully ordained priests meant that deacons rarely performed the tasks permitted them. Nonetheless, since canon law allowed all these functions, those Protestants who were trained in canon law could draw on these precedents in developing their own forms of the office. A brief survey of the principal roles permitted to the deacons—whether or not deacons actually performed them—provides important background for analyzing the development of Protestant forms of the office.

By the late Middle Ages, the deacons' functions were primarily liturgical.[5] First of all, they assisted the priest during the Mass: they laid out the altar, presented the

---

[3]"Deacon," *Oxford Dictionary of the Christian Church*, 2d ed.

[4]This change in focus is tied particularly to a specific interpretation of 1 Tim. 3:13; see McKee, *Calvin on the Diaconate*, 163–64.

[5]This discussion is a synthesis of: "Deacon," Herber Thurston, *The New Catholic Encyclopedia;* "Deacon," *The New Schaff-Herzog Encyclopedia of Religious Knowledge*, ed. Samuel Macauley Jackson;

unconsecrated bread and wine to the celebrant, exposed the consecrated elements, and placed them in the tabernacle after the benediction. Generally, they also held the paten when the priest distributed the bread, though when Communion was given in both kinds, the deacons distributed the wine. At need in the absence of a priest, they could distribute the consecrated bread; they were not permitted to perform the consecration themselves, however. In addition to their Eucharistic duties, the deacons had other liturgical roles. They chanted the Gospel and guided the congregation during the Mass by calling them to kneel or to pray and by proclaiming the Ite, missa est. On Holy Saturday, they sang the Exultet. And with special permission (generally in the absence of a priest), deacons could perform solemn baptism and hear deathbed confessions. Lastly, deacons could also teach catechism[6] and with special permission, they could preach.

By the sixteenth century in the Latin West the diaconate had been transformed from a permanent office responsible primarily for coordinating the church's charitable work to a temporary, transitional office to the priesthood with largely liturgical duties. Rather than emphasize the Seven's social welfare functions, the church focused on the deacons' role as assistants of the Apostles: the office's primary task was to assist the priests in the liturgy. For purposes of this study, forms of the diaconate which treat the office either as a pastoral assistant or in a preparatory stage before ordination as a pastor or priest will be considered as "Roman Catholic" models of the office. This terminology does not mean, of course, that this approach to the diaconate was unique to the Catholic Church; many Protestant churches followed this model as well. For example, in Zurich and Berne, deacons were essentially assistants to the pastors in cities or in large rural areas.[7] This practice was brought into the Suisse romande, including the Pays de Vaud, by the Bernese, and from there may have influenced French Protestantism, as will be seen below. But this holdover from Catholicism would not go unchallenged by the more institutionally minded Protestant Reformers, who wished to return to what they saw as a more biblical view of the office.

THE REFORMED DIACONATE
As with so many other aspects of ecclesiology later adopted by Reformed churches, one of the first advocates of the restoration of the diaconate as the

---

"Deacon," *Oxford Dictionary of the Christian Church*, 2d ed.; Lesage, *Catholicisme: Hier, aujourd'hui, demain;* "Diacre," J. Forget, *Dictionnaire de Théologie Catholique*.

    [6]Catechizing is listed as a task of deacons only in the *Dictionnaire de Théologie Catholique;* all other tasks listed in this and the preceding paragraph come from at least two of the encyclopedias listed in n. 5.

    [7]Henri Vuilleumier, *Histoire de l'Eglise Réformée du Pays de Vaud*, 1:269.

charitable arm of the church was Martin Bucer in Strasbourg. From the first articulation of his theory of the four ministries in the church through *De Regno Christi* in 1550, Bucer consistently argued that the church ought to be involved in poor relief, and that it was the deacons' responsibility to carry out this aspect of the church's ministry.[8] Unfortunately, he never succeeded in implementing this part of his reform program: the civil government of Strasbourg had earlier secularized the administration of charity, and thus the only role the churches had in poor relief was to provide a place to put the alms boxes.[9]

In addition to charitable functions, Bucer envisioned a larger role for the diaconate. Following the model of the early church, he argued that the deacons ought to have a wide range of additional roles following the patristic pattern of the office. For example, he argued that they should have liturgical functions, specifically as readers, in the distribution of the Eucharist, and even as preachers. He also argued that they should have pastoral and disciplinary responsibilities.[10] Bucer thus envisioned a role for deacons which centered their work on charity, but which also included aspects of the Roman Catholic model of the office, though without giving them the same place in the ecclesiastical hierarchy.

Although Bucer was stymied at several points in his attempt to reform the church at Strasbourg, other Reformers whom he influenced would have more success elsewhere. The most notable of these was John Calvin. Bucer had a profound influence on Calvin's ideas of church structure during the latter's stay in Strasbourg as an exile from Geneva (1538–41). In fact, Jacques Courvoisier goes so far as to argue that Calvin's entire approach to ecclesiology was the same as Bucer's, only explained more clearly.[11] While this evaluation is clearly exaggerated, there is no doubt that Calvin's ecclesiology was drawn largely from Bucer's; further, Calvin was able to design a church structure for Geneva with far less interference from the magistrate than Bucer had been able to do in Strasbourg. With respect to the diaconate, Calvin went one step beyond Bucer: in addition to rejecting the deacon's place in the hierarchy of offices, Calvin also eliminated many of the liturgical and pastoral duties drawn by Bucer from the practice of the early church. For Calvin, social welfare was the nearly exclusive focus of the diaconal ministry.

---

[8]Hammann, *Entre la secte et la cité*, 295.

[9]Miriam Usher Chrisman, *Strasbourg and the Reform: A Study in the Process of Change* (New Haven: Yale University Press, 1967), 275–83; cf. Ganoczy, *Calvin, théologien de l'église et du ministère*, 381.

[10]Hammann, *Entre la secte et la cité*, 296.

[11]Jacques Courvoisier, *La notion d'église chez Bucer dans son développement historique* (Paris: Librairie Félix Alcan, 1933), 137.

Even before Calvin's arrival, Geneva had a relatively efficient system of poor relief in place, centered on the General Hospital. Established on 19 November 1535, shortly after the end of episcopal power in the city, the General Hospital rationalized Geneva's previously disorganized system of poor relief, taking on responsibility for distribution of food, education of orphans, caring for elderly or infirm citizens, and similar duties. The Hospital had two types of officers: the procurators, who were essentially fund-raisers, and the hospitalers, who worked directly with the poor. As Elsie McKee notes, these two officers performed precisely the same tasks as the two types of deacons called for by Calvin's biblical exegesis.[12] Accordingly, Calvin's *Ecclesiastical Ordinances* of 1541[13] put in place a double diaconate which in effect "baptized" both the procurators and the hospitalers as ministers of the church of Geneva. Unlike Bucer, Calvin's reform of ecclesiastical institutions included co-optation of officers of the civil administration into the structure of the church.

Since only native Genevans were eligible for aid from the Hospital, each refugee community in the city established its own relief agency. These were known as *bourses,* the largest and best known of which was the *Bourse française.* Because the *bourses* were involved in poor relief, their officers were recognized as deacons together with the procurators and hospitalers; in fact, Jeannine Olson has shown that the *Ecclesiastical Ordinances* notwithstanding, the officers of the *bourse* were more commonly recognized as deacons than the hospitalers and procurators themselves.[14] Further support for her conclusions comes from a sermon on 1 Tim. 3:6–7 which Calvin preached in 1563. In it, Calvin calls the populace of Geneva— including the hospitalers and procurators themselves—to a renewed awareness that these officers are actually doing God's work rather than simply the state's.[15] It appears that Calvin's attempt to consecrate a secular office as a ministry of the church was not entirely successful, at least in the popular mind.

---

[12]McKee, *Calvin on the Diaconate,* 195–200. McKee argues that Calvin developed his interpretation of Rom. 12:8 independent of his experience in Geneva, whereas Robert M. Kingdon, "Calvin's Ideas about the Diaconate: Social or Theological in Origin?" in *Piety, Politics and Ethics: Reformation Studies in Honor of George Wolfgang Forell,* ed. Carter Lindberg (Kirksville, Mo.: Sixteenth Century Journal Publishers, 1984), 167–80, suggests that Calvin's exegesis was influenced by his encounter with the Genevan General Hospital, noting that he developed his interpretation of the diaconate during his first stay in Geneva, 1536–39.

[13]See the text, edited by Jean-François Bergier, in *RCP,* 1:1–13; cf. the English translation in idem, *John Calvin: Selections from His Writings,* 229–44.

[14]Jeannine Olson, *Calvin and Social Welfare: Deacons and the Bourse française* (Selinsgrove: Susquehanna University Press, 1989), 30–32.

[15]*CO* 53: 290–91, cf. Ganoczy, *Calvin, théologien de l'église et du ministère,* 383–84.

What was clearly successful, however, was a fundamental transformation of the conception of the diaconate as a stepping stone of the priesthood to a ministry aimed primarily at charity. For typological purposes, this shift in focus is the distinctive characteristic of the Reformed model of the diaconate, which defines the deacon's role in terms of poor relief. This does not necessarily mean that the deacons had no other duties. Calvin, for example, permitted them to collect alms as part of the liturgy and to hold the cup during the Lord's Supper;[16] Bucer added an even wider range of duties drawn from church tradition. Both, however, kept social welfare at the core of the office.

One final group of churches should be mentioned before moving to the diaconate in Protestant churches in the kingdom of France: the refugee churches of London and Glastonbury, the latter of which was moved to Frankfurt in 1554 as a result of the persecution of Protestants by Mary Tudor.[17] For the most part, these churches followed the Reformed model of the diaconate. The London churches included both French and German congregations and shared a common form of government developed by their de facto bishop, John à Lasco. The role of the deacons in these churches was limited to poor relief; their accounts were audited by the consistory monthly, and they participated in the mutual censure of the officers of the church, held quarterly.[18] The pastor of the church at Glastonbury was Valerand Poullain, a former priest who had been a pastor with Bucer in Strasbourg,[19] and like the London churches was under the supervision of Lasco. Poullain's

---

[16]The former task was a logical corollary of their social welfare role; the latter was a task that the deacons shared with the elders, who carried it out with far more regularity than did the deacons. Although *La forme des prières* of 1541 and 1545 places most of the stress on the deacon's role in the Lord's Supper while allowing the elders to hold the cup as well (see OS 2: 48–49; cf. *Ecclesiastical Ordinances,* RCP 1:9), in practice the registers of the Consistory show that the elders were called upon to perform this task far more often than the deacons, and that among the deacons, the *procureurs* were called upon more often than the *hospitaliers*. It is worth noting, however, that the scribe of the Consistory—who technically was a civil servant with no ecclesiastical office—occasionally held the cup along with the elders and the deacons. See for example, Archive d'Etat de Genève, *Registres du Consistoire* 19:33v (29 March 1562), which assigns several elders, plus Pierre Chappuis, *procureur de l'Hospital* and *conseiller,* plus P. Alliod, the scribe of the Consistory, to hold the cup during the Lord's Supper. (This volume was examined on microfilm in the Meeter Center for Calvin Studies, Calvin College, Grand Rapids, Mich.)

[17]F. de Schickler, *Les églises du refuge en Angleterre,* 3 vols. (Paris, Fischbacher, 1892), 1:71–72.

[18]John à Lasco, *Toute la forme et maniere du ministere ecclesiastique, en l'eglise des estrangers, dressée a Londres en Angleterre, par le prince tresfidele dudit pays, le Roy Edouard VI de ce nom: L'an apres l'incarnation de Christ 1550 avec le previlege de sa Majesté a lafin du livre,* trans. from Latin to French by Giles Ctematius [E. van der Erve] ([London?]: Giles Ctematius [E. van der Erve], 1556), fols. 11r–16v, 229v–39r.

[19]F. de Schickler, *Les églises du refuge en Angleterre,* 1:59.

church shared the same basic organization as the London churches, with one inno-vation: in addition to the "regular" deacons, who were elected annually, the pastor of the Glastonbury church was permitted to select a deacon himself. This deacon had special functions in the church: "And he is to serve in the administration of the sacraments and also to preach on Sundays after dinner and on other days when the superintendent [i.e., Lasco] or the pastor is absent."[20] According to F. de Schickler, this deacon was also to participate with the pastor(s), elders, and superintendent (if available) in the disciplinary meetings held Sunday evenings.[21] The appointed deacon seems to have been an assistant pastor, much like the deacons in Berne and the Pays de Vaud; he was involved in all of the duties of the pastorate—preaching, sacraments, and discipline—but without the full authority of the office. In other words, the Glastonbury church had a diaconate which followed the Reformed model as a result of its connection with the refugee churches of London, but also had what amounts to a second diaconate following the Roman Catholic model. This compound diaconate illustrates the diversity within the Reformed commu-nity over the interpretation of the diaconal office and anticipates in some ways one approach to the diaconate that would emerge in the French Reformed churches.

The French Reformed Diaconate

Although churches in such Reformed regions as the Pays de Vaud, Berne, and Geneva influenced the development of French Protestant ecclesiastical structures, the Huguenots' status as an unsanctioned religious minority within the kingdom made the sort of church-state cooperation found in majority Protestant areas impossible. This meant that for decades French Protestantism had no central authority dictating either doctrine or discipline, and thus had developed quite diverse practices in the churches. Even when the national synods started to meet, they often had to try to channel practices already in place in the churches into a single direction to lend the movement an air of unity in the eyes of the monarchy. Given the complexity of the diaconate historically, it is not surprising that the diaconate within French Protestantism prior to 1559 was quite diverse and that the French Reformed churches worked to develop an approach to the office that adapted this wide range of existing practices into the framework of Reformed the-ology. Accordingly, this section begins with a brief summary of the diaconate

---

[20]Et cestuy sert en l'administration des Sacremens, et aussi de prescher les dimanches apres le disner, et les autres jours en l'absence de Superintendant ou Pasteur. Lasco and Poullain, *L'ordre des prieres et ministere ecclesiastique, avec la forme de penitence pub. et certaines prieres de l'Eglise de Londres et la confession de foy de l'Eglise de Glastonbury en Somerset* (London: [S. Mierdman?], 1552), fol. 42v.

[21]*Les églises du refuge en Angleterre*, 1:65; Schickler does not identify his source for this, however; it does not come from *L'ordre des prieres*.

described in the *Articles polytiques* of 1557, the clearest evidence we have of a French Protestant diaconate prior to the Discipline. The section then analyzes the Discipline of 1559 and its development by subsequent national synods in light of both the Articles and the two models of the diaconate discussed above. Given the broad range of functions the diaconate fulfilled in French Protestant churches and its close connection with other aspects of ecclesiology, the discussion is divided between this chapter and the next, which deals with the consistory.

FRENCH PROTESTANTISM PRIOR TO 1559:
THE *ARTICLES POLYTIQUES* (1557) AND THE CHURCH AT LE MANS (1561)
It is difficult to treat the diaconate described in the *Articles polytiques* in isolation from the elders, since the roles of these two offices overlap a great deal. The standard division of labor in Calvinist ecclesiology assigns social welfare to the deacons and discipline to the elders; in the *Articles polytiques,* however, both offices had disciplinary, financial, and charitable functions. In terms of disciplinary duties, deacons were "to catechize those who are named for introduction to the assembly and to enquire diligently into their life and conversation"; further, they were to "watch diligently and closely over the morals of the flock, making every effort to confront and rebuke vice and scandal."[22] Elders were to perform largely the same tasks: "The charge of elders is to watch diligently and closely with the deacons over vice and scandal, to remonstrate and rebuke [it], to call before the consistory all those of the assembly who live an evil and scandalous life...."[23] In fact, the chapter "Charge commune" in the *Articles polytiques* deals with responsibilities which elders and deacons had in common, most of which involved overseeing the life, morals, and faith of the people residing in their neighborhoods.[24]

At the same time, the *Articles polytiques* assigned social welfare and financial tasks to both offices. Deacons were "to visit the sick and those in prison for the Word of God and to look after the needs of the poor."[25] The elders were also

---

[22]"[D]e catechiser ceux qui seront nommez pour estre introduits en l'assemblée et de s'enquerir diligemment de leur vie et conversation"; "[de] regard[er] diligemment et de près sur les moeurs du troupeau, feront tout devoir de taxer et reprendre les vices et scandales." *Articles polytiques,* "Des diacres," 1, 2 (7).

[23]La charge des anciens est de veiller avec les diacres diligemment et de près sur les vices et scandales de remonstrer et reprendre, de faire appeler au consistoire tous ceux de l'assemblée qui meneront vie mauvaise et scandaleuse.... *Articles polytiques,* "Des anciens," 1 (8).

[24]This chapter also includes administrative roles shared by elders and deacons, notably identifying places to hold *predications.* The role of deacons in discipline is discussed further in chap. 6.

[25]La charge des diacres sera de visiter les malades et ceux qui seront prisonniers pour la parolle de Dieu, de regarder sur l'indigence des povres.... *Articles polytiques,* "Des diacres," 1 (7).

involved in at least p irt of this work, since they were to "plead diligently the cause of those who are prisoners for the Word of God."[26] More to the point, alms for the poor, though collected by a deacon, were to be distributed by the deacons and elders together:

> The collection for the poor is to be taken at the end of every sermon. And [the amount of] this collection is to be written by the hand of the minister in the deacon's book and [the money] kept by this deacon to be placed into the hands of the bursar on the day the consistory meets. And this money is to be distributed by the deacons *or elders* who visit the poor and find out about their needs, having first taken the counsel and advice of the consistory.[27]

The *Articles polytiques* does not take a "Reformed" view of the offices of elder and deacon; each was to be involved in the ministry which standard Reformed ecclesiology assigns to the other, but the deacons described in the Articles had other roles as well. In addition to disciplinary and financial duties, deacons were given responsibilities in three general areas. First, they had liturgical roles: "Deacons are to pray in the assembly in the absence of ministers and always and whenever they are committed and sent to do this by the minister.... And while waiting for the people to meet and the minister to begin preaching, one of the deacons is to read from the books of the Bible."[28]

Second, they were to be catechists. Not only were they to visit people in their homes to teach them, but the deacons had responsibilities that went well beyond private instruction: "[Deacons] are to catechize one day per week, or more often if necessary, not simply the young but also older people who are little instructed in the principal points of religion, and they are to work at this particularly before the celebration of the Lord's Supper in order to prepare well those of the district over

---

[26][S]olliciteront diligemment la cause de povres fideles qui seront prisonniers pour la parolle de Dieu.... *Articles polytiques,* "Des anciens," 2 (8).

[27]La collecte des povres se fera par chacune predication a la fin d'icelle et sera la dite collecte escrite par la main du ministre au papier du diacre et gardé par le d.t diacre pour estre mis es mains du boursier au jour du consistoire, et fera la distribution des dits deniers par les dits diacres *ou anciens* qui visiteront les povres, et s'inform=ront de leur indigence, sur ce premierement prins le conseil et advis du consistoire (emphasis added). *Articles polytiques,* "Articles politiques," 3 (12).

[28]Les diacres feront les prieres en l'assemblée en l'absence des ministres, et toutes fois et quantes qu'ils seront commis et envoyez pour ce faire par les dits ministres....

Et en attendant que le peuple soit congregé et que le ministre comence la predication l'un des diacres fera lecture des livres de la Bible. *Articles polytiques,* "Des diacres," 2, 3 (7). To some extent, this article follows Bucer's recommendations on the liturgical duties of deacons.

which each deacon has charge."[29] These catechetical duties seem to have been related to the deacons' role in examining and approving persons wishing to join the church:

> No one is permitted to bring or to introduce anyone to the assembly unless they have been named to the deacons, who are to examine their life and conversation, and unless they are catechized and instructed in doctrine, discipline and ecclesiastical order by the brothers of the church.

> Strangers asking to be received in the assembly…shall talk to the deacons to be questioned and heard before being admitted to the services.[30]

Lastly, the deacons had administrative tasks, notably in terms of keeping records of baptisms, marriages, and burials as well as keeping the consistory registers and other acts of the church.[31] In a logical extension of their task as examiners of prospective members, the deacons were to maintain a register of all church members.[32]

The church structure described in the *Articles politiques* was almost certainly based on the church at Poitiers, where the document was drafted, though lack of surviving records makes it impossible to confirm this. On the other hand, records from the church at Le Mans, one of whose pastors (Salvert) had been ordained at Poitiers, do survive and indicate that the church structure described in the *Articles politiques* paralleled to some extent the structure of some Protestant churches in the region.

The church at Le Mans was founded on 1 January 1561; the consistory records also begin on this date. Unfortunately, no systematic description of the

---

[29]Catechiseront un jour de la septmaine plus souvent s'il est besoin non seulement la jeunesse mais aussi les grands qui seront peu instruitz es principaux poincts de la religion et singulierement y travailleront devant l'administration de la S. cene [*sic*] pour y bien preparer ceux du quartier duquel chacun diacre aura charge. *Articles politiques*, "Des diacres," 4 (7).

[30]Ne sera loisible a aucun de l'assemblée amener ne introduire personne en icelle sinon qu'ils ayent este nommez aux diacres, lesquels s'informeront de sa vie et conversation, et par les freres de l'eglise seront catechisez et instruits en la doctrine pollice et ordre ecclesiastique.

Les estrangers demandants a estre receus en l'assemblée…parleront aux diacres pour estre interrogez et ouys premierement que d'estre receus aux predications. *Articles politiques*, "Articles politiques," 8, 9 (13). It is somewhat curious that the article specifies that "the brothers of the church" rather than the deacons were to catechize prospective members; it may be that this was a technical term for the consistory or some subset of the church leadership.

[31]*Articles politiques*, "Des diacres," 5 (8).

[32]*Articles politiques*, "Articles politiques," 25 (17).

ecclesiastical offices is given at the beginning of the document, and it is necessary to reconstruct their roles from the minutes of the meetings.[33] The picture that emerges is significantly at odds with what one would expect, given that the *Discipline ecclésiastique* had been adopted nearly two years earlier; in fact, the church at Le Mans seems to have been completely unaware of the new church order. Deacons were involved in church discipline as members of the *consistoire de la censure;* they also had responsibilities for administrative matters as members of the *consistoire de la police.* They shared with the *surveillants*—the office corresponding to *anciens* in the *Articles polytiques* and the Discipline—responsibilities to read martyrologies before sermons, to visit prisoners and to ensure that everyone paid their "taxes" to the church. They also were to catechize those who wished to join the congregation.[34] On the other hand, they do not seem to have had any direct responsibility for poor relief.

This structure bears little resemblance to the diaconate of the Discipline; despite the chronology, the original organization of the Le Mans church was essentially a holdover from pre-1559 practices. The church did not keep this structure for long, however: by the middle of March 1561 persecution forced the church to suspend services. Pastor Salvert was reassigned to Angers over the objections of the deacons of Le Mans,[35] and Poinsson, their other minister, fled to Alençon.[36] Five months later, the church reopened under the leadership of Pierre Merlin, a newly arrived minister from Geneva[37] who completely revamped the structure of the church, making it far more conformable to the Discipline and to Calvinist ecclesiology.

[33]This is a particularly tricky problem, since the church included offices—or at least names for offices—which have no counterparts in other Reformed churches of the period.

[34]Le Mans, 3, 4, 7–8, 10.

[35]This is the most likely interpretation of the minutes of the consistory, though no record of the event is found in the acts of the national synod of Poitiers. The relevant section of the consistory register reads: "mon dict sieur Salvert, ministre, s'en alla au synode général assigné en la ville de Poictiers, où il fut ordonné, sans avoir égard à la remonstrance des diacres de nostre Eglise, les quelz avoient esté envoyez à ceste fin, qu'ils retourneroit à Angers pour y continuer le ministère de la parolle de Dieu et y entretenir l'ordre et police de l'église, selon les articles de la discipline arrestez au synode du dict Poictiers...." Le Mans, 7.

[36]Le Mans, 7.

[37]Kingdon, *Geneva and the Coming,* 79, notes that the Genevan archives indicate that a Pierre Merlin was sent to France in 1561, but that the same name appears in later lists of missionaries as well; Kingdon suggested that the 1561 reference was a mistake, and that the correct name should have been Jehan Remond Merlin, a pastor who was definitely sent to France in 1561. The register of Le Mans, however, shows that Pierre Merlin did in fact come to France in 1561; presumably, the later references indicate that he returned to Geneva and was subsequently dispatched back to France.

Despite its ephemeral character, the original organization of the church at Le Mans provides important evidence for early French Protestant interpretations of ecclesiastical structures. In particular, the diaconate described at Le Mans and prescribed in the *Articles polytiques* was fundamentally non-Reformed in character: it was not centered on charitable duties, and those which it did have were largely shared with the elders (at least in the case of the Articles); similarly, the elders shared their disciplinary role with the deacons. This diaconate was in fact much closer to the Catholic model of the office—perhaps as mediated by the Pays de Vaud or some other Protestant area—than to the Reformed, even in its Bucerian form. The similarities are clearest when the liturgical and catechetical roles assigned to the deacons in the *Articles polytiques* are compared with the non-Eucharistic tasks permitted to Catholic deacons: deacons acted as substitutes (within limits) when pastors were absent, they read Scripture, they were involved in public and private catechizing. Although it is not stated directly, the deacons at Poitiers may have been a form of assistant pastor, given the wide range of duties assigned to them. This impression is reinforced by the structure of the *Articles polytiques:* the section on deacons is placed between the sections on pastors and on elders, suggesting that deacons were in some sense a "higher office" than elders. This may indicate a Vaudois influence, which was itself essentially a holdover from Catholicism, or it may have been adapted directly from Catholicism, which had, after all, been in place in France for centuries.

The Diaconate in the Discipline

While the *Articles polytiques* presents an essentially non-Reformed view of church offices, a new force was growing in the kingdom in the second half of the 1550s that changed the ecclesiastical structure of the French Protestant churches permanently. This force was, of course, the Genevan-trained pastors, such as Pierre Merlin, who brought with them a militantly Reformed theology, including the concern for ecclesiology that characterized Calvin's reforms in Geneva.[38] These pastors—particularly Anthoine de la Roche Chandieu and François Morel—were instrumental in organizing the first national synod (Paris, 1559) which produced the *Discipline ecclésiastique*. It is thus not surprising that the Discipline has a far more Reformed understanding of church offices than does the *Articles polytiques*.

With respect to the diaconate, this shift toward Reformed ecclesiology was signaled in the Gallican Confession, article 29, which states that churches should

---

[38]Kingdon, *Geneva and the Coming*, traces the "flood" of missionary pastors from Geneva into France; 61 percent of the missionaries sent between 1555 and 1562 arrived in the period 1557–59 (145).

have deacons "so that…the poor and all who are in affliction may be helped in their necessities."[39] The 1559 Discipline spells out what this was to mean. Article 23 reads: "As for deacons, their charge is to visit the poor, the prisoners and the sick, and to go to homes to catechize."[40] The second national synod, meeting at Poitiers in 1561, clarified these responsibilities as follows: "As for deacons, their charge is to receive and distribute alms under the direction of the consistory to the poor, the prisoners, and the sick, and to visit them, and to go from house to house to catechize.…"[41] Although the responsibilities of deacons, especially in the article's original version, are similar to those outlined in the *Articles polytiques,* there are critical differences: elders are not mentioned in connection with distribution of alms or other social welfare tasks;[42] similarly, no disciplinary tasks are assigned to deacons. In other words, instead of following a Catholic model of the diaconate as in the *Articles polytiques,* the defining roles of both elders and deacons are drawn from Reformed theology.

On the other hand, the emerging French Reformed churches had to find ways of integrating existing churches and religious leaders into their organization. Provisions for bringing pastors into the French Reformed churches are examined in chapter 4; here, we consider the problem of what to do with elected or charismatic lay leaders and preachers in local churches. The solution, as it has been in a variety of other situations in church history, was to expand the functions of the diaconate. Unlike "elder," the term "deacon" was readily recognizable in France from the Catholic Church; some French Protestant churches already had deacons in place, and many of these lay leaders were performing roles similar to those of Catholic deacons. The 1559 Discipline based its primary approach to the diaconate on the Reformed model of the office, focusing on their social welfare responsibilities, but grafted onto that a number of important additions to the office that distinguished French Reformed deacons from their Genevan counterparts. A relatively minor example is the visitation of prisoners, which Geneva's

---

[39][A]fin que…les pauvres et tous autres affligés soient secourus en leurs nécessités.… *Creeds of Christendom,* 376–77. This interpretation could be questioned on the grounds that the diaconal office is not directly linked to the above clause, but the obvious parallelism in the sentence makes such a linkage the only tenable interpretation of the article.

[40]Quant aux diacres, leur charge sera de visiter les pauvres, les prisonniers et les malades, et d'aller par les maisons pour catechiser. Roussel, "Discipline," art. 21.

[41]Quant aux diacres, leur charge sera de recueillir et distribuer par l'avis du consistoire les deniers des pauvres, des prisonniers et des malades, et les visiter et aller par les maisons pour catechiser.… ANS, 2–Poitiers–1561, 9; DE 1561, art. 28.

[42]This was the theory, at least; in practice, elders sometimes distributed alms. See the discussion of the loss of the diaconal office in the next chapter.

Ecclesiastical Ordinances of 1541 assigns to pastors, not deacons.[43] This provision was probably a response to persecution in France, which made it difficult (and dangerous) for pastors to enter prisons controlled by the Catholic authorities. But there were bigger differences as well. For example, the deacons were to be involved in the consistory and were eligible to be deputies to national and provincial synods; they continued in their liturgical activities with some new restrictions; they could teach catechism, again with some new restrictions.[44] The remainder of this chapter is devoted to an examination of their liturgical and catechetical roles, while their role in church government is discussed in chapter 6.

The 1559 Discipline permits deacons to perform certain liturgical duties. Some of these are described in rather vague terms. Article 24 states: "The office of the deacons is not to preach the Word of God nor to administer the Sacraments, even though they may assist in them...."[45] Preaching and administering the Sacraments were the responsibility solely of pastors. But the last clause in this quotation permits participation by deacons in public worship as an assistant to the pastor, though the lack of precision distinguishing what deacons could and could not do makes it difficult to determine what the article allowed them to do. This clause probably reflects the influence of existing church practice supported by the example of the early church, perhaps as mediated by Bucer, which gave the deacons responsibilities for reading Scripture, assisting in the Eucharist, and other liturgical duties. Whatever its intent, the clause was dropped from the Discipline by the second national synod (Poitiers, 1561) as part of a clarification of the duties of elders and deacons.[46] The motivation for the change is a matter of speculation, though its effect was to distance the deacons from some of their traditional liturgical duties, at least in theory.

The issue of deacons functioning as liturgical assistants during the Lord's Supper did not go away after 1561, however. The fourth national synod (Lyon, 1563) was asked to decide whether anyone other than the pastor ought to administer the cup to the congregation during the Lord's Supper. Since the pastor was the only one permitted to consecrate the elements and always distributed the bread, the question here was virtually whether anyone could "assist" the pastor in the celebration of the Lord's Supper. Given that there was a severe shortage of pastors in the kingdom, the French churches decided to ask Geneva's advice on this matter.

---

[43]*RCP,* 1:10.

[44]DE 1559, art. 3, 5, 21; Roussel, "Discipline," art. 19; DE 1559, art. 23, Roussel, "Discipline," art. 21; DE 1559, art. 24, Roussel, "Discipline," art. 21; DE 1559, art. 25, Roussel, "Discipline," art. 23.

[45]L'office des diacres n'est pas de prescher la parolle, ni d'administrer les sacrements, combien qu'ils y puissent aider.... DE 1559, art. 24.

[46]ANS, 2–Poitiers–1561, 9; DE 1561, art. 28.

Geneva responded that, although it would be better if a pastor distributed the bread and wine, if this was not practical elders and deacons could do so after the pastor consecrated the elements.[47] The advice from Geneva was adopted by the synod as policy for the churches: "The churches shall be warned that only the ministers are to present the cup at the Lord's Supper if at all possible in order to prevent any evil consequences."[48] Significantly, the synod did not restrict the handling of the cup to deacons, or even to church officers more generally. During the course of the century, the practice seems to have become increasingly lax; by 1601, the national synod had to adopt an article restricting the handling of the elements to the elders.[49]

Other liturgical duties for the deacons were specified more precisely in the 1559 Discipline, primarily in an attempt to get control over existing practice within the churches. Article 25 states, "In the absence of the minister, whether because of sickness or some other reason, the deacon can say the prayers and read some passage of Holy Scripture without any form of preaching."[50] Judging from the provincial synods of Dauphiné in the early 1560s, deacons were quite active as readers in services and often went beyond the bare scriptural texts. The provincial synod of Die, held 31 July 1561, essentially repeats the article from the Discipline, specifying that deacons were to read Scripture (and only Scripture) in churches where there were no ministers.[51] This regulation was repeated at the provincial synod of Lyon, 25 November 1561, with the addition that no sermons—not even M. Calvin's—were to be read in churches.[52] Later synods indicate that deacons also did much of the reading of Scripture even when the minister was present, but again, even in that context, the deacons tried to work in their own material. The provincial synod of Montélimar (6 March 1562) states: "Deacons and other readers of Holy Scripture reading in the assembly before the sermon are not to explain

---

[47]Quick, 4–Lyon–1563, chap. 21, art. 4 (53). As discussed earlier in this chapter, this advice reflects Genevan practice, where elders and occasionally deacons held the cup during the Supper.

[48]Les eglises seront averties que c'est aux ministres seuls d'administrer la coupe en la sainte Cene autant que faire se pourra, et ce pour obvier aux mauvaises consequences. ANS, 4–Lyon–1563, art. 4, cf. Quick, 4–Lyon–1563, chap. 10, art. 26, chap. 11, art. 4 (35).

[49]Quick, 16–Gergeau–1601, chap. 5, art. 7 (217).

[50]En l'absence du ministre, ou lors qu'il sera malade ou aura quelque autre nécessité, le diacre pourra faire les prieres et lire quelque passage de l'Escriture, sans forme de predication. DE 1559, art. 25; Roussel, "Discipline," art. 23. The text actually says "do the prayers"; since even pastors were not permitted to pray extemporaneously except at the Lord's Supper, the deacons were undoubtedly reading liturgical prayers at these services.

[51]*Documents protestants inédits,* 21–22.

[52]*Documents protestants inédits,* 31. Although the article does not mention the absence of the pastor, it seems clear that this was the situation envisioned.

nor to add to or take away from the text, but only to read it with due honor and reverence." The same provincial synod assigned deacons the task of conducting services each morning, though it did not permit preaching at these services.[53] These examples show that deacons were attempting to continue the French Protestant tradition of lay preaching; the Discipline, on the other hand, was attempting to curb it while still permitting these lay-preachers-turned-deacons some liturgical responsibilities.

All of this highlights the practical need for liturgists in the churches, whether the pastors were present or absent. Though Catholic precedent made the deacons logical choices to fill this role, there was no reason elders could not have performed the role as well; in fact, in many churches elders rather than deacons did read the Scriptures and lead the prayers.[54] In Le Mans, for example, after Merlin's arrival, the consistory decided that someone should read Scripture before the sermon, and assigned the task to an elder.[55] In this case, the register suggests that the church was not particularly concerned whether the task was done by an elder or a deacon. In Brittany, at the instigation of Du Gravier (a visiting pastor), the Protestants of Casson elected an *ancien* to read the Bible and lead the prayers when they assembled without a minister. On the other hand, at Chateaubriand, Du Fossé had set up a deacon to read in the services and "to talk about things he had read in order to teach the people" (i.e., to catechize).[56] So in one case the liturgist was an elder, in the other, a deacon. To further confuse the issue, in some cases it appears that elders and deacons were not clearly distinguished. Thus in Isabeau d'Albret's house church, when the minister was not preaching, prayers were read by an elder or a "domestic reader"; Le Noir comments that the household church sometimes had a regular minister, and sometimes simply the diaconate, apparently referring

[53]Que les diacres et autres lecteurs de l'Escriture sainte lisant en l'assemblée avant les presches, n'exposeront et n'ajousteront ou diminueront du dit texte, mais tant seulement feront leur lecture avec deub honneur et reverence. *Documents protestants inédits*, 37, 39.

[54]See Raymond A. Mentzer, "Laity and Liturgy in the French Reformed Tradition," in *The Past Has Many Voices*, ed. Lee Palmer Wandel (Kirksville, Mo: Truman State University Press, 2003), for extensive documentation of elders as liturgists and readers. Mentzer's evidence suggests that elders may have performed these roles more often than deacons, though if this is the case it is difficult to understand the absence of elders as liturgists in the acts of the national synods. In fact, the Discipline does not mention elders in connection with liturgical roles until the eleventh national synod (La Rochelle, 1581) permitted them to read the prayers; reading Scripture was added to this only in the seventeenth century, Quick, 11–La Rochelle–1581, chap. 2, art. 12 (137).

[55]Le Mans, 43.

[56]Le Noir, *Histoire ecclésiastique de Bretagne*, 54, 55. Interestingly enough, the deacon of Chateaubriand was a paraplegic, and so the church—as Le Noir describes it, even though it only had a "feeble foundation of the diaconate"—met in the deacon's home.

to the elder.[57] This sort of confusion may have contributed to the de facto loss of the office of deacon described in the next chapter. Perhaps as a result of this diversity of practice, the article from the 1559 Discipline that deals with liturgical reading by deacons was dropped at the second national synod (Poitiers, 1561) as part of the clarification of the role of elders and deacons.

While the national synods were placing increasing restrictions on what deacons could read or say during services, they were expanding the deacons' responsibilities as catechists. Article 23 of the 1559 Discipline stated that the deacons were "to go to homes to catechize."[58] This is one of the tasks assigned to deacons in the *Articles polytiques*,[59] though the differences in wording again suggest that the earlier document was not the model for this article; this in turn implies that teaching catechism in private houses had been a common duty among French deacons prior to 1559. This practice carried over into Viret's church order for Languedoc as well, which added catechizing to administering alms in the list of diaconal duties.[60] The 1571 Discipline permitted both elders and deacons to catechize "by families," a change that remained in force through the 1659 edition of the Discipline.[61]

On the whole, private catechizing does not seem to have been a particularly controversial task for deacons and, later, elders.[62] Public catechizing such as that permitted in the *Articles polytiques* raised more problems, however, and the 1559 Discipline thus tried to eliminate the practice. The reason is unclear: the framers of the Discipline may have feared that public catechesis could turn into preaching;

[57]Le Noir, *Histoire ecclésiastique de Bretagne,* 62.

[58]Quant aux diacres, leur charge sera...d'aller par les maisons pour catéchiser. DE 1559, art. 23; Roussel, "Discipline," art. 21.

[59][V]isiteront les maisons de ceux de l'assemblée pour l'instruction de leur famille.... *Articles polytiques,* "Des diacres," 2.

[60]Synod of Nîmes (February 1561 [1562 n.s.]), Auzière, fol. 3v, cf. *Documents protestants inédits,* 44. Roussel, "Viret en France," 831, suggests on the basis of *La forme de dresser un consistoire* that this may be related to the deacons' role in almsgiving, since the amount the deacons distributed was to depend on the recipients' relationship to the church.

[61][P]ar les familles, DE 1571, "Des anciens et diacres," 3. There is no indication of when this change was made in any of the acts of the national synods, and the lack of surviving copy of DE 1567 makes dating the change difficult. The original wording version of the article giving the deacons the responsibility to catechize in homes was still in force in 1565; most likely, the article was modified in 1571 as part of the revision of the Discipline adopted at that time. See also "Des anciens et des diacres," 5, in Méjan, *Discipline de l'Eglise Réformée de France,* 224.

[62]A useful list of which officers conducted catechism is in Raymond A. Mentzer, "The Printed Catechism and Religious Instruction in the French Reformed Churches," in *Books Have Their Own Destiny: Essays in Honor of Robert V. Schnucker,* ed. Robin B. Barnes, Robert A. Kolb, and Paula L. Presley, Sixteenth Century Essays & Studies 50 (Kirksville, Mo: Thomas Jefferson University Press, 1998), 97.

they could have been concerned about the theological training or orthodoxy of the deacons; or the omission of public catechesis could simply have been an oversight. Whatever the reason, the next national synod (Poitiers, 1561) relaxed the ban somewhat. Like Poullain in the refugee church of Glastonbury, the national synod added a second category of deacons: "And in the case where one of them [i.e., the deacons] is found ready and able to do it, having promised to dedicate and consecrate himself perpetually to the service of God and to the ministry, he can then be chosen by the ministers and the consistory to catechize in public according to the formulary received by the Church to test him more fully, though without authority to administer the sacraments."[63] The rest of the deacons did not hold their offices permanently and could not catechize publicly.[64]

The reintroduction of the public catechizing by a subcategory of deacons in 1561 suggests that the practice was sufficiently widespread that it could not be easily eliminated; the national synod thus moved to regulate and restrict it. Significantly, one of the most important of these restrictions was that these deacons had to be preparing to enter the pastoral ministry, thereby reintroducing a critical element of the "Catholic" model of the diaconate into the French Reformed churches. This appears to be another example of integrating lay preachers into the church structure by placing them in the diaconate: if lay preachers were to continue to preach, they needed to become ministers of the Word; setting them on the road to the ministry by making them "catechizing deacons" adapted the familiar Catholic model of the diaconate to the peculiar needs of the churches as they emerged from the "magnificent religious anarchy" of early French Protestantism.[65]

Once again, the provincial synods of Dauphiné provide an interesting commentary on this stage in the development of the French Reformed churches' stand on diaconal catechizing. These synods show that late in 1561, the province changed its approach to the diaconate by creating a separate class of catechizing deacons. The provincial synod of Lyon, 25 November 1561, reached the following decision: "*Item:* it has been decided that before deacons are received into their charge by the consistory, their faith and doctrine are to be duly examined in order to know if they are able to catechize. And if one is found who has been received

---

[63] Et au cas qu'il s'en trouva quelqu'un propre et capable, lequel promette de se desdier et consacrer perpetuellement au service de Dieu et au ministere, alors pourra estre esleu par les ministres et consistoire pour catechiser en public selon le formulaire receu en l'eglise pour estre plus amplement esprouvé et sans administrer les sacrements. DE 1561, art. 28. Cf. Quick, 2–Poitiers–1561, chap. 3, art. 7 (19).

[64] DE 1561, art. 29. Cf. Quick, 2–Poitiers–1561, chap. 3, art. 7 (19).

[65] It is worth noting that the purpose of allowing such prospective pastors to catechize was to test them; whether the test was of their abilities as teachers or of their orthodoxy is left unstated.

into office without being examined, he is to be examined."[66] Four months later, the provincial synod of Montélimar, 6 March 1562, provided additional regulations for the new class of deacons: "Catechizing deacons are not permitted to administer the holy Sacraments nor to bless marriages; these are to be left to the ministers. Ministers and consistories cannot receive nor admit catechizing deacons before they are received and admitted by the colloquy."[67] These articles point to the creation of a new class of deacons engaged in public catechizing in Dauphiné between the second and third national synods.[68] Given the timing, it seems likely that the impetus for this change came from the regulations adopted by the national synod in 1561.

One difficulty with this interpretation is that the restrictions on diaconal catechesis in Dauphiné do not directly correspond to those in the Discipline: although the deacons are to be examined in faith and doctrine and approved by the colloquy, nothing is said about their being committed to entering the pastoral ministry. On the other hand, since the synod of Montélimar thought it necessary to prohibit deacon-catechists from celebrating the sacraments and blessing marriages—tasks performed by ministers of the Word—at least some churches must have seen an association between the two offices; given the historical context, it is quite likely that such deacons were viewed as pastoral trainees. Further, if deacon-catechists were viewed as *proposants* (i.e., pastoral candidates), examination by the colloquy would be a logical step in the selection process, especially considering the colloquy's emerging role in approving ministerial candidates.[69] At the same time, catechesis was not considered a standard diaconal responsibility in Dauphiné; for example, *La forme de dresser un consistoire,* a document included in the same manuscript set as the provincial synods, does not assign any catechetical roles to the deacons. On the whole, the evidence strongly suggests that the provincial

---

[66]Item a esté arresté que les diacres avant qu'ils soyent receus en leur charge par le consistoire seront deuëment examinez de leur foy et doctrine, afin de savoir s'ils sont capables pour catechiser, et s'il en trouve qui ayent esté receus sans estre examinez, on les examinera. *Documents protestants inédits,* 33.

[67]Que ne sera loisible aux diacres catechisants d'administrer les saints sacrements ny la benediction du mariage, ains les laisseront faire aux ministres. Que les ministres et consistoires ne pourront recevoir ne admettre les diacres catechisants, ains qu'ils seront receus et admis par les colloques. *Documents protestants inédits,* 38.

[68]Although the text does not specifically mention *public* catechizing, private catechizing was uncontroversial for deacons. Further, the 1562 provincial synod was detailing public functions that "catechizing" deacons were or were not permitted to perform; it is logical to assume that the catechetical instruction was public as well.

[69]See, for example, DE 1565, 4, which specifies that where there is a colloquy, it is to work with the consistory in choosing a new pastor, unless the provincial synod can do so.

synods of Dauphiné were doing their best to conform with the direction set by the national synod and the Discipline.

Even as Dauphiné began to incorporate deacon-catechists into their church structure, other churches were moving in the opposite direction. This can be seen in the de facto local Discipline Merlin introduced into the consistory register at Le Mans on 16 August 1561. Among other things, these minutes explain the roles and functions of the offices of the church. The section "Deacons" reads as follows:

> As for deacons, their work is to receive the money given for the poor, to give an account of it to the consistory each week, and to distribute it under the direction of the consistory to the poor or for other necessities of the church. And for this, they must enquire about those who are in need to give them solace, and even visit the sick; and if these need consolation and doctrine, [the deacons] are to call the minister. And if they wish to dedicate themselves entirely to the service of the church they can catechize privately.[70]

The last clause is particularly interesting, since Merlin took a more restrictive stand on this issue than did the national synod: while the national synod and the Discipline limited *public* catechizing to deacons who planned to enter the ministry, Merlin placed the same limitation on *private* catechizing and by implication completely banned *public* catechizing by deacons. Both from Merlin's experience in Geneva and from a Reformed model of the office, this made sense: the diaconate was responsible for social welfare, not catechesis. Nonetheless, Merlin and other Reformed pastors were forced to compromise on this definition of the diaconate because of the established practice of the local churches; thus even in Le Mans deacons who planned to enter the ministry could catechize privately. This compromise also points to the continuing influence of the Catholic model of the diaconate, since it allows at least some deacons to be viewed as pastors-in-training.

The decision of the national synod of Poitiers to permit "preministerial" deacons to catechize publicly was challenged at the very next national synod, held at Orléans in 1562. This synod moved to restrict public catechizing by deacons even further until a final decision on the matter could be reached:

---

[70]Quant aux diacres, leur debvoir est de recepvoir l'argent qui sera donné pour les pauvres, et en rendre compte toutes les sepmaines au consistoire, et le distribuer aux dicts pauvres par l'ordre du consistoire, ou bien l'employer aux aultres nécessitez de l'église. Et pour ce, il fault qu'ils s'enquièrent de ceulx qui sont nécessiteux pour les soulaiger, et mesmes qu'ils visitent les malades, et s'ils ont besoing de consolation et de doctrine qu'ils y appellent le ministre, et s'ils veullent se dédier du tout au service de l'église ils pourront cathéchiser en particulier. Le Mans, 18.

As for those deacons in some provinces who are accustomed to cate-chizing publicly, having heard and weighed the problems which have come from this and which could come later, the Council has placed the entire decision of this matter in the hands of the next General Council. Nonetheless, it exhorts the churches where this custom has not been introduced to abstain from it. As for the others where this custom is practiced, they are similarly exhorted to see to it that those deacons capable of it be called into the ministry of the Gospel as soon as possible.[71]

Significantly, despite the "problems" that the practice had caused, the synod did not prohibit it while it was under study. This again suggests that it was sufficiently widespread and well entrenched that, despite the difficulties it had created, it could not be eliminated entirely.

The restrictions set by Orléans did not sit well with some churches; in fact, the next national synod, held at Lyon in 1563, was called upon to resolve a case from Normandy in which a church used the earlier form of the article as an excuse for practices that went well beyond the letter of the law:

The church at Caen has been sending *proposants* here and there to preach, such that scandal has resulted because they have sent men of evil life contrary to the decision [against that practice] taken by [the provincial synod of] Rouen. Their justification is that according to the Council of Poitiers, deacons are permitted to catechize; also, they could not lay hands on [i.e., ordain] these men first because they were still neophytes. Further, they send them into places that could not support a minister. They ask if they have done something worthy of rebuke in this.

Because the synod of Poitiers never mentioned *proposants* but only deacons who had resolved in all things to serve God in the ministry when they were called to it, those who sent these *proposants* are indeed worthy of rebuke, inasmuch as the synod of Rouen had prohibited it.[72]

---

[71]Quant aux diacres, qui ont acoutumé de catechiser publiquement en quelque province, ouis et pesez les inconvenients qui en sont avenus et pourroient avenir ci apres, le concile a remis l'entiere deci-sion de ce fait au concile general prochain venant. Et cependant exhorte les eglises ou cette coutume n'est introduitte, de s'en abstenir. Et quant aux autres ou ladite coutume a lieu, elles seront pareillement exhortees de faire que lesdits diacres a ce capables se rangent au ministere de l'Evangile le plutost qu'il sera possible. ANS, 3–Orléans–1562, art. 27; cf. Quick, 3–Orléans–1562, chap. 2, art. 24 (25).

[72]Ceux de Caen envoyent des proposans ça et la prescher, tellement que scandale en seroit

The record of this case is interesting for several reasons. Caen defended its actions on the basis of the decision by the national synod of Poitiers giving deacons the authority to catechize publicly; Caen extended that to preaching, and pointed out that the *proposants* who were sent out could not be ordained as ministers right away because they were "neophytes." The church was thus identifying *proposants* with deacons. Caen was not alone in this: the provincial synod of Rennes, meeting in 1561, set aside Jean de la Favède, an elder at le Roche-Bernard and a physician by training, for the ministry and named him a *diacre perpétuel;* in his chronicle of this period, seventeenth-century pastor Le Noir notes that this position had since been renamed the *proposant.*[73] The national synod had other ideas. The decision against Caen was based on a distinction between *proposant* and *diacre,* which Caen evidently did not make, along with the observation that Poitiers did not speak of all deacons, but only those who had dedicated their lives to the ministry. The national synod did not distinguish between preaching and catechizing. This case highlights a conflict on the conception of the diaconate: while the national synod permitted *some* deacons to catechize as part of their training for the ministry, the church at Caen simply identified *proposants* with deacons. This demonstrates a degree of continuity with the *Articles polytiques,* which seems to have considered deacons to be pastors-in-training. This identification of deacons with *proposants* continued even later in the century. For example, in 1595–96 the deacon of the church at Clairac was explicitly a pastoral trainee.[74] Clairac and Caen thus reveal the continuing influence of a Catholic model of the diaconate in an increasingly Reformed ecclesiastical structure.

Despite the practices of some of the churches, the restrictions on diaconal catechizing established at Orléans were incorporated into the Discipline by the next national synod, which met in Paris in 1565;[75] these restrictions then

---

ensuivy pour y envoyé gens de mauvaise vie contre ce qui avoit esté arreté a Rouen. Leurs raisons sont que par le concile de Poitiers, il estoit permis aux diacres de catechiser; aussi qu'ils ne pouvoient du premier coup leur imposer les mains pour ce qu'ils estoient encore neophites, et aussi qu'il les envoyent aux lieux qui n'eussent peu entretenir un ministre. On demande si en cela ont fait chose reprehensible.

Pour ce qu'au synode de Poitiers n'est fait mention des proposans, mais seulement des diacres du tout resolus de servir a Dieu par le ministere quand ils y seront appellez, ceux qui ont envoyé lesdits proposans sont reprehensibles, d'autant memement que l'admonition en avoit esté faite par le synode de Rouen. ANS, 4–Lyon–1563, "faits particuliers," 13, cf. Quick, 4–Lyon–1563, chap. 16, art. 34 (41).

[73]Le Noir, *Histoire ecclésiastique de Bretagne,* 72–73. M. de la Favède was ordained a minister in 1562 (90).

[74]Janine Garrisson, *Les Protestants au XVIe siècle* (Paris: Fayard, 1988), 370 n. 25.

[75]DE 1565, "Des anciens et diacres," 4.

remained in force with only minor modifications in wording all the way up to the revocation of the Edict of Nantes in 1685.[76]

THE NON-REFORMED ROOTS OF THE FRENCH DIACONATE

It is obvious that the French Reformed diaconate did not simply apply principles of Reformed theology to the situation in the kingdom. The diaconate described in the first years of the *Eglises Réformées* was heavily influenced by the same practices that shaped the *Articles politiques,* practices which had non-Reformed roots. These were integrated into a Calvinist view of the office to produce a new form of diaconate, which blended elements of both the Reformed and the Catholic models while integrating existing lay leaders and preachers into the emerging structure of the French Reformed churches.

This blending of the two models of the diaconate can be seen in the deacons' role as liturgical assistants. In Calvin's ecclesiology, the pastorate was the only office in the church whose work was defined in terms of liturgical tasks (preaching and administering the sacraments); Reformed churches thus tended to assign all liturgical tasks to pastors, including reading of Scripture and public prayer. Deacons were to be responsible for social welfare, and elders for discipline. Although the *Articles polytiques* ignored this division of labor, the Discipline followed it reasonably closely, assigning to the deacons the ministry to the poor, the prisoners, and the sick, and specifically excluding them from administering the sacraments or preaching. But the 1559 Discipline left open the possibility that deacons might assist the pastor in these tasks, much as the Roman Catholic deacon assisted the priest at Mass. Although this article was quickly rewritten, the 1559 Discipline suggests that the national synod was open to some elements of Roman Catholic practice that had been adopted by earlier French Protestant churches even though they diverged from a strictly Calvinist interpretation of the diaconate.

Similarly, though the pastor would logically be expected to read Scripture and pray at public services, this was not a theological necessity; it was possible in principle to permit others in the church to perform these tasks. Accordingly, the Discipline again followed existing practice in the churches reflected in the *Articles polytiques* by extending to the deacons the right to read Scripture and the prayers publicly, at least when the pastor was absent. Presumably, when he was present, the close connection between Scripture reading, liturgical prayer, preaching, and the sacraments made it undesirable to allow the deacons to lead the liturgy lest they appear to be encroaching on the pastor's office.

---

[76]See the text in François Méjan, *Discipline de l'Eglise Réformée de France,* "Les anciens et diacres," 4 (224–25).

Although precedent in both Catholicism and French Protestantism may have suggested deacons as the logical candidates for liturgical assistants in the initial draft of the Discipline, in practice it seems that elders did these tasks at least as often as deacons across the French Protestant communities. The second national synod (Poitiers, 1561) dropped the specific reference to deacons' reading Scripture and leading in the prayers, leaving unregulated the question of who was to assist the pastor in these areas. Nonetheless, the initial assignment of liturgical roles to the deacons is significant, and is most easily explained as a holdover from Roman Catholic practice. Put simply, there was ample precedent for the national synod to view deacons as liturgical assistants and no theological reason not to, at least as a secondary role. Although the Catholic deacon's sacramental duties were largely rejected by French Protestants on the basis of Reformed doctrine, their other tasks could be adapted to Protestant worship fairly easily, especially in the absence of the pastor. Both Martin Bucer's understanding of the office of deacon and the example of the early church would tend to reinforce this Catholic influence on the French Reformed churches. The lack of any obvious model for liturgical roles for elders—the office does not exist in Catholicism and is not defined in liturgical terms in Reformed theology—initially led the national synod away from discussing them as liturgical assistants. The practice in the churches, however, quickly forced the national synod to modify the Discipline to leave open the question of which office might read Scripture and lead the prayers in the services.

The development of the legislation concerning liturgical duties seems largely to be a movement away from a Catholic-influenced system, with a decreasing emphasis over the first years of the French Reformed churches on deacons as liturgical assistants. Legislation concerning public catechism moves in the opposite direction. The 1559 Discipline says nothing about the issue, nor is there any hint of identifying deacons as prospective pastors. But as the *Articles polytiques* shows, deacons had already been teaching catechism publicly in some Protestant churches in France, probably following the lead of their Catholic counterparts (or at least of canon law). To regulate and restrict this rather troublesome holdover from the pre-1559 churches, the second national synod of Poitiers (1561) grafted another element of the Catholic model which had been in use among French Protestants—deacons as a ministers-in-training—into a Reformed diaconate. There can be no serious doubt that the synod was aware of the parallel they were creating between their own and the Catholic diaconates; it would have been obvious to anyone in sixteenth-century Europe with even a modest knowledge of ecclesiology. Perhaps that was one reason why the decision proved to be controversial, though it seems just as likely that the synod was concerned about the orthodoxy or theological knowledge of the deacons. At any rate, the Protestant churches took a self-conscious step back toward the Roman Catholic model of the diaconate to try to gain some control over diaconal catechizing. The legislation enacted at Orléans was intended to restrict the practice further, with the probable goal of eventually eliminating it entirely. In the meantime, this legislation helped solve another problem in the churches by tapping into a promising pool of candidates to fill the shortage of pastors.

The French Reformed diaconate thus seems to have been shaped by two distinct influences. The first was Reformed theology, which gave them their primary task as ecclesiastical social workers. In addition, the Roman Catholic model of the diaconate contributed to the specific form that the diaconate took within the kingdom. This is particularly evident in the liturgical and catechetical duties assigned to deacons, the former in the earliest versions of the Discipline, the latter crystallizing a few years later. Both of these areas preserved roles that had been present in pre-1559 French Protestantism as shown by the *Articles polytiques* of 1557.

Although important, liturgical and catechetical duties were not the central issue that separated the French deacons from their Genevan counterparts. Of far greater significance was the participation of deacons in the government of the churches, their relationship to the elders, and their participation on the consistory, which is examined in the next chapter.

Chapter 6

The Consistory

The role of elders and deacons in the French Reformed churches can be clarified further by looking in more detail at the government of the local churches in the kingdom. The governing body in these churches was the consistory, an organization modeled largely on its Genevan counterpart. Like the Genevan Consistory, the French consistories were responsible primarily for church discipline in the sense of enforcement of morals; in fact, the Discipline devotes almost its entire discussion of the consistory to setting out procedures for handling disciplinary questions. The French consistories differed in several ways from their Genevan prototype: they were responsible for all aspects of ecclesiastical government, not only discipline; they generally included deacons; their relationship to the state was necessarily different because the Huguenots could not count on the luxury of having a Protestant magistrate. This chapter examines in detail the development of the French Reformed consistories, first with a brief survey of disciplinary institutions in three regions which influenced French Protestantism: Strasbourg, Berne, and the Pays de Vaud, as well as Geneva.[1] It then discusses the consistory in the 1557 *Articles polytiques* and traces the development of local church councils in

[1]These were not the only cities and regions that had elders and disciplinary institutions that might have influenced French Protestantism. John Oecolampadius in Basel, for example, argued in his *Oratio de reducenda excommunicatione* (1530) for discipline by lay elders and pastors together. This practice was adopted by the Basel council that same year. Two members of the council and an additional layman from each parish were to oversee the morals of their district; if someone refused to repent, the pastors were brought in as well. If the party still refused correction, that individual was excommunicated. If s/he did not seek restoration within a month, civil penalties followed. This was modified within six months, giving the council final say over excommunications. From 1532 to 1539,

the Discipline and the acts of the national synods. In the process, it analyzes the relationship between elders and deacons and the dynamics involved in the gradual merger of these offices.

PRECEDENTS FOR THE CONSISTORY OF THE FRENCH REFORMED CHURCHES

Bucer, Strasbourg, and England

Martin Bucer believed that church discipline was both an essential mark of the church and one of the primary tasks involved in the ministry of *Seelsorge*, the care of souls.[2] But he was never able to implement many of his ideas on discipline in Strasbourg, partly because of fears it would reintroduce a new "papal tyranny" within the city, partly because the government refused to share its power with the pastors in disciplinary matters. Church-state dynamics paralleled Bucer's difficulties in instituting a Reformed diaconate in the city, although in the case of discipline the city did at least act on the pastors' concerns by establishing a group of lay *Kirchenpfleger*. Each of the city's seven parishes contributed three *Kirchenpfleger*, one of whom was to be a senator, one a member of the *Schöffen*, a large governmental council elected by the guilds, and the third a lay resident. As originally instituted in 1531, the *Kirchenpfleger* were responsible solely for overseeing the doctrine and practice of the clergy. The Strasbourg Synod of 1533 and the church ordinance that grew out of it, however, assigned the officers the task of overseeing the laity as well, together with organizing the *Kirchenpfleger* more formally.[3] In principle, they took on much of the ministry of Bucer's "ruling elders."

From the perspective of the pastors, the system as implemented had several serious flaws, particularly with respect to the balance of authority between the different ministries of the church. The ordinance gave the *Kirchenpfleger* a great deal of authority over the clergy. They were to be present at the regular meetings of pastors and could take away the pastors' right to deal with difficult or controversial

---

a council of both pastors and lay elders was appointed to oversee church discipline, but that too was dissolved and the council took over this task as well. See Walther Köhler, *Zürcher Ehegericht und Genfer Konsistorium,* Quellen und Abhandlung zur Schweizerischen Reformationsgeschichte 7, 10 (Leipzig: Heinsius, 1932–1942), vol. 1, *Das Zürcher Ehegericht und seine Auswirkung in der deutschen Schweiz zur Zeit Zwinglis,* chap. 8. Strasbourg, Berne, and Geneva were far more direct influences on the Huguenots, however.

[2]See Glenn S. Sunshine, "Discipline as the Third Mark of the Church: Three Views," 469–80, for a discussion of the views of Bucer and others on discipline as a mark of the church.

[3]Amy Nelson Burnett, *The Yoke of Christ: Martin Bucer and Christian Discipline,* Sixteenth Century Essays & Studies 26 (Kirksville, Mo.: Sixteenth Century Journal Publishers, 1994), 66, 69. The ordinance was not approved until 1534.

issues. The pastors were also forbidden from making any important decisions without the knowledge of the senate.[4] Further, though the Synod recommended that the pastors be included in the oversight of their parishioners, the ordinance actually placed that task completely in the hands of the *Kirchenpfleger*, who could ask the pastors' advice if they wished but were not required to do so. To make matters worse, the vast majority of the *Kirchenpfleger* did not carry out their disciplinary responsibilities with the rigor that Bucer believed was needed.

Bucer responded to the pastors' lack of disciplinary authority and the laxness of the *Kirchenpfleger* by setting up "Christian fellowships" within the parishes of the city. These were composed of individuals who voluntarily agreed to submit themselves to pastoral discipline. Initially, a group of lay elders would be chosen from the most godly men in the community; after they were trained, they were to join the pastors and *Kirchenpfleger* as overseers of the "fellowship." These leaders would then examine the parishioners on doctrine and explain the nature of Christian fellowship. The parishioners would then be encouraged to make a confession of faith (to be repeated annually) and to promise obedience to the pastors and elders, who would then visit them annually to remind them of their promise. Participation in the fellowship involved a commitment to send children to catechism classes, to accept fraternal admonition, to receive private instruction in the faith (as needed), and to visit the pastor before receiving the Lord's Supper. All of these were essential elements of discipline for Bucer, who understood the term to include all of the actions taken by the church to encourage growth in godliness. Except for an initial meeting of the entire parish where the concept of "Christian fellowships" was to be explained, at no time were all of the people who committed themselves to the fellowship actually to meet together.[5]

The first "fellowships" were instituted in 1546, apparently with the senate's approval; they caused a fair amount of controversy, however, including most seriously a charge that they were promoting schism (October 1547).[6] The magistrate suspended their activities, and they were not reinstated for the duration of Bucer's ministry in the city.

---

[4]Burnett, *Yoke of Christ,* 69, cf. idem, *Penance and Church Discipline in the Thought of Martin Bucer* (Ph.D. diss., University of Wisconsin–Madison, 1989), 149–50.

[5]Burnett, *Yoke of Christ,* 180 n. 2, notes that the term "Christian fellowship" was typically used by Bucer in the abstract, e.g., "to devote oneself to Christian fellowship"; he did not use it as a designation for the groups he formed in the parishes, though secondary literature typically does. In this chapter, I follow Burnett's convention of setting the term off in quotation marks to indicate this. See also ibid., 185; idem, *Penance and Church Discipline,* 356.

[6]Burnett, *Penance and Church Discipline,* 352, 360.

When Bucer immigrated to England, his ecclesiology had a profound effect on the organization of the Refugee Church in London under John à Lasco; in fact, this church was essentially a direct application of most of the principles of Bucer's theology. It was led by a "superintendent"—essentially a bishop—and had two basic "orders" of ministers, the elders and deacons. Elders (Bucer's *Seelsorgen*) consisted of the superintendent, the doctors (Bucer's *Leren*), the pastors, and the elders (Bucer's two classes of *Hirten*). At the same time, the church was careful to insist that there were a multiplicity of ministries within the church. The church maintained the Bucerian distinction between public and private discipline, and defined a careful gradation of steps to be followed before public censure; catechism was also considered part of discipline. Just as confession and mutual admonition were expected from the congregation, so too did the leaders take part in mutual censure and admonition.[7]

Many of these elements would become commonplaces in Reformed churches throughout Europe and had in fact been implemented in Geneva for several years before the founding of the church in London. Nonetheless, Lasco's church order is both a striking illustration of how many of the details Bucer's concepts of church structure were intended to function, and a possible influence on the development of the French churches. The breakup of the London church after Mary Tudor ascended the throne makes an immediate connection between this church and the early national synods unlikely, although the Glastonbury congregation, which immigrated en masse to Frankfurt, and the printed church orders could have influenced elements of the Discipline. Such connections are a matter of speculation at this point.

Strasbourg followed an essentially Zwinglian or Erastian model of reform, in which the civil government controlled the church; this ultimately prevented any effective disciplinary structures from being established within the city, since the *Kirchenpfleger* did not carry out their duties and the city refused to extend to the pastors any rights to oversee the laity. But this model of church-state relations did not inevitably produce the same results all over. In Berne, where the civil government also had complete authority over the church, an effective disciplinary structure was instituted, one which was predominantly lay controlled but which included limited involvement by preachers.

Berne and the Pays de Vaud
The morals court of Berne was the *Chorgericht*, founded in 1528 on the heels of

---

[7]Lasco, *Toute la forme et maniere du ministere ecclesiastique*, fols. 1v–2r, 11r, 160r, 161, 162; cf. Hammann, *Entre la secte et la cité*, 165, 281–87.

the reform of the city. Two of its members were drawn from the Small Council, four from the Council of Two Hundred, and two from among the preachers of the city, with the city's chief magistrate as its presiding officer; it also employed a scribe. The members of the council were elected annually, though they often served for several years in succession. The *Chorgericht*'s primary responsibility was marital law, particularly divorce, but it also handled discipline of ministers and violations of divine law which did not require a civil or criminal trial: gluttony, conspicuous consumption, drunkenness, sexual immorality, usury, gambling, disrespect for parents, impiety, incredulity, superstition, oaths and blasphemy, and other moral offenses. Unlike the *Kirchenpfleger* of Strasbourg, the Bernese *Chorgericht* seems to have been very active in its work of policing morals. Also unlike the *Kirchenpfleger*, the *Chorgericht* had the authority to mete out a wide range of punishments for violations of Christian behavior, including admonitions, censures, and even such penalties usually associated with the civil and criminal courts as public or private *amendes honorables*, fines, imprisonment, and banishment. Interestingly enough, however, Berne shared with Strasbourg the fear of a return to "papal tyranny," though for the Bernese, the crucial question was not discipline, confession, and so on, but excommunication. Thus this was the one penalty forbidden to the *Chorgericht*.[8]

In the German-speaking sections of the canton, courts similar to the capital's were established in the 1530s, with largely the same competence except that especially serious offenses, including recidivism, were sent to the court of the *bailliage*, to the Small Council, or to the *Chorgericht*. Further, divorces could only be pronounced by the *Chorgericht* in Berne. The state thus worked with the church in enforcing morality. Although the Reformation Edict of 1536 provided for the establishment of similar courts (called "consistories") in the French-speaking areas of the canton, only the *bailliage* of Thonon set up such a court until 1558, when consistories were established in each parish. Their competence had by this time been extended to rooting out vestiges of Roman Catholicism and superstition, and conversely, on checking parishioners' doctrinal knowledge, regular attendance at services, and participation in the Lord's Supper. These courts proved to be quite controversial: not only did they raise significantly more opposition in the Pays de Vaud than they had in the German-speaking sections of the canton, but Viret and many other Vaudois pastors, with the support of Calvin, objected to the courts' inability to excommunicate offenders. Nonetheless, by the end of the sixteenth century, consistories had become established as an effective

---

[8]Vuilleumier, *Histoire de l'Eglise Réformée du Pays de Vaud*, 1:255–56, 299.

means of social control in the Pays de Vaud as they had been for decades in other parts of the canton.[9]

In Strasbourg and Berne, the control of morals was left to the civil authorities, who by law controlled the church as well. In Strasbourg, the result seems to have been relatively unsuccessful, at least from the pastors' point of view; in Berne, it was considerably more successful, though again certain aspects of the system were not completely satisfactory from the perspective of the pastors of the Pays de Vaud. In Geneva, Calvin developed a disciplinary system which integrated both civil and ecclesiastical government into an even more effective method of social control than was available to the Bernese church. The church continued to be a branch of the state, albeit a relatively independent one, but both pastors and lay elders were responsible for maintaining discipline within the church via the institution most closely associated with Calvin, the Genevan Consistory.

The Genevan Consistory

The consistory included personnel from both the church and the civil government. Its members included the pastors—who were technically civil servants—plus a group of lay elders elected annually by the Small Council in consultation with the pastors. Each of the twelve quarters of the city was to be represented by an elder, whose job it was "to keep an eye on everybody." Six of the elders were to be chosen from the Council of Two Hundred, four from the Council of Sixty, and two from the Small Council; one of these last was the first syndic of the city, who presided over the consistory's meetings. In addition, the city employed a scribe to keep the registers and an "officer" whose responsibility was "to summon those whom they wished to admonish."[10]

The work of the consistory has been seriously misunderstood by historians. Although a nearly complete set of its registers survives, they are notoriously difficult to decipher. For Calvin's lifetime alone, there are twenty-one surviving folio volumes of notes written at high speed during the meetings, mostly by M. Pierre Alliod (or Aillod), whose hand is difficult to read at best. As a result, most researchers have relied on the extracts published in 1853 by Frédéric Auguste Cramer, the last person until very recently to read most of the documents.[11] In the late 1980s and early 1990s, however, a team under the direction of Robert M. Kingdon transcribed the complete records of the consistory during Calvin's lifetime

---

[9]Vuilleumier, *Histoire de l'Eglise Réformée du Pays de Vaud,* 1:299–301, 304–5.

[10]*RCP,* 1:6–7, 11; cf. *John Calvin, Selections from His Writings,* 235, 241.

[11]Frédéric Auguste Cramer, *Notes extraites des registres du Consistoire de l'Eglise de Genève, 1541–1814* (Geneva, 1853).

and has begun to publish them.[12] This project makes it clear that Cramer's extracts focus on the most colorful cases and do not accurately represent the more typical work of the consistory. As a result, much of what has been written about this agency needs to be reevaluated. The following is a preliminary assessment based on this new work of the types of cases brought before the consistory and the sanctions it imposed.

Although the consistory is most often described as a morals court, the most common type of problem it addressed in its first years was some form of religious misbelief.[13] Most often, this involved either a holdover from Catholic beliefs and practices or some type of superstition, though occasionally such heresies as anabaptist beliefs or antitrinitarianism arose. Especially in its first years, the consistory seems to have called people in for no other reason than to check to see if they knew the Creed, the Ten Commandments, and the Lord's Prayer in a language they understood; they almost systematically checked for this in people brought in for other reasons as well. The usual "sanction" imposed for this or other forms of misbelief was an order to attend more sermons and to see a pastor to be better instructed in the faith.

The second most common type of problem encountered among residents of the city proper—and the third most common among people in the outlying rural areas—was serious quarreling. This category included excessive beating of children or wives (or occasionally husbands), nagging of husbands by wives (or occasionally of wives by husbands), disobedience or beating of parents, neighborhood quarrels—in short, virtually anything which was public enough to "cause scandal." The usual sanction here was a severe scolding, followed by an admonition to live peaceably in the future and not to be called back to the consistory at the risk of being sent to the civil magistrate for further punishment.

The third most common offense in the city and second most common in the country was sexual misconduct. This included not only such activities as premarital sex and adultery, but also breach of promise of marriage. Once again, the

---

[12]Two volumes have been published: *Registres du Consistoire de Genève au temps de Calvin,* vol. 1 (1542–1544), ed. Thomas A. Lambert and Isabella M. Watt under the direction of Robert M. Kingdon with the assistance of Jeffrey R. Watt (Geneva: Droz, 1996); vol. 2 (1545–1546), ed. Thomas A. Lambert, Isabella M. Watt, and Wallace McDonald, under the direction of Robert M. Kingdon (Geneva: Droz, 2001). Vol. 1 has been translated into English as: *Registers of the Consistory of Geneva in the Time of Calvin,* vol. 1: 1542–1544, Robert M. Kingdon, general editor; ed. Thomas A. Lambert and Isabella M. Watt with the assistance of Jeffrey R. Watt; trans. M. Wallace McDonald (Grand Rapids: Meeter Center for Calvin Studies; Grand Rapids: Eerdmans, 2000).

[13]Robert M. Kingdon, "The Geneva Consistory as Established by John Calvin," *On the Way: Occasional Papers of the Wisconsin Conference of the United Church of Christ* 7 (Autumn, 1990): 34.

most common punishment administered by the consistory was a tongue-lashing, though the offenders were often sent to the civil courts for additional penalties.

The most serious punishment available to the consistory itself was excommunication, a right unsuccessfully sought by the pastors of both Strasbourg and the Pays de Vaud. This generally took the form of a ban on participation in the sacraments until the offender demonstrated his or her repentance to the consistory. Excommunication was thus a very effective sanction, partly because of the sociological function of the Lord's Supper in the Reformed churches—it was the identifying mark of membership within the community—but also because excommunication carried social penalties as well, including particularly the inability to act as a godparent at baptisms. As a result, most excommunicated people sought to be readmitted to the sacrament either before the next celebration of the Supper or after missing it once.

Although the idea of church discipline certainly did not originate with Calvin, no one is more closely associated with the development of disciplinary institutions within the church, and for good reason: the Genevan Consistory proved to be a very effective method of social control in the city, resulting in a standard of morality that astonished visitors. With Calvin's growing stature as a theologian, the favorable impression left on refugees in Geneva by the conduct of its citizens, and the large number of missionary pastors trained there, it is small wonder that the consistory became a model for similar institutions in emerging Reformed churches in Scotland, the Netherlands, and especially France.

THE CONSISTORY IN FRANCE

French Protestantism prior to the Discipline ecclésiastique
In France, consistories had been established in at least some French Protestant churches prior to the 1559 Discipline, though these bodies took a different form from their counterpart in Geneva. In terms of composition, French churches tended to include deacons in the consistories, as shown not only by the subsequent history of the institution but also by the *Articles polytiques* of Poitiers: "The consistory is to meet each week for remonstrance, correction and purgation of the vice and scandal of the flock, and the aforementioned deacons and elders are to attend this consistory....."[14] This should come as no surprise in view of the role the Articles give to deacons in the church. What is something of a surprise, however, is that

---

[14]Il se tiendra toutes les septmaines un consistoire pour la remonstrance, correction et purgation des vices et scandales du troupeau, et seront tenus se trouver au consistoire les dits diacres et anciens....., *Articles polytiques*, "Articles politiques," 4 (12).

the pastors apparently were not included in the consistory; not only are they not listed in the quotation above, but they are nowhere mentioned in connection with the work of the consistory. This approach was obviously not based on Geneva; although similar in some respects to Strasbourg, the tensions there between the pastors and the civil magistrate make it an unlikely model for disciplinary institutions elsewhere. The Pays de Vaud provides a more promising model,[15] though anticlericalism may have been a factor as well. Although many Protestant regions mistrusted pastors, regarding their efforts at discipline as a return to "papal tyranny," anticlericalism was particularly prominent in France even within the Catholic Church. Technically, pastors were not clerics in the same sense as Catholic priests; nonetheless, they would be the logical target of continuing distrust of clergy within the Protestant community.[16]

In addition to detailing the composition of the consistory, the quotation above also outlines its basic function in the French churches: it was primarily charged with the enforcement of morals. But along with this role, the Poitiers church assigned additional duties to the consistory: "The consistory is to meet on another day during the week if needed to consult, deliberate and decide upon the affairs of the church, at which time all the deacons, elders and deputies are to attend to set in order all the affairs as the occasion may require, and if one of them fails to attend, he is to be severely reproved unless he has a legitimate excuse."[17]

One question raised by this quotation is to whom the term "deputies" refers. Earlier in the Articles, a form of the word is used to describe those sent from a local church to a synod;[18] presumably the word has the same meaning here, since otherwise it is left completely undefined. The implication is that the consistory

[15]As it did to some extent for Beza's provisions in the *Confession*, where ministers were not assigned disciplinary duties. See the discussion in chap. 2.

[16]See Roussel, "Discipline," 184–86, on the nonclerical nature of Huguenot church leaders. Another factor in keeping pastors out of disciplinary roles in the Articles may have been xenophobia. With the beginnings of Genevan mission efforts in France in 1555 and the increasing "flood" of pastors in 1557 (Kingdon, *Geneva and the Coming*, 145), it was becoming increasingly common for pastors to be outsiders in the communities in which they ministered. In the next decades, this would generate a fair amount of tension in French Protestant churches. For example, Janine Garrisson, *Protestants du Midi*, 123–41, documents some of the social, cultural, and linguistic differences between pastors and their parishioners in the southern provinces together with the difficulties faced by pastors in this region generally. The Articles give no indication that they were addressing this problem, however, which only later seems to have become a significant issue within French Protestantism.

[17]Il se tiendra consistoire a certain autre jour de la septmaine s'il est requis pour adviser deliberer et conclure des affaires de l'eglise la ou tous les diacres anciens et deputez seront tenuz se trouver pour pouvoir donner ordre a tous les affaires selon l'exigence d'iceux, et si aucun d'iceux y defaillent seront aigrement reprins sinon qu'il y eust excuse legitime. *Articles polytiques*, "Articles politiques," 7 (13).

[18]…ceux qui seront deputez d'une chacune eglise. *Articles polytiques*, "Articles politiques," 1 (11).

could "depute" individuals who were not elders or deacons to the synods. If it did so, these individuals would quite naturally be included in the meetings dealing with church affairs, since, after all, they represented the church at synods which themselves dealt with administrative matters.

Thus together with their duties with regard to church discipline, the consistory was to take on the administration of the church as well, although at meetings held on a different day from the regular disciplinary sessions and, at least potentially, with expanded personnel. These administrative functions break with the pattern established by the disciplinary bodies of virtually all other Reformed churches in the period, whether in Strasbourg, Geneva, Berne, the Pays de Vaud, or elsewhere. The reason for assigning administrative matters to the consistory in the kingdom of France is obvious: all of the other Reformed churches were established with the assistance of the civil government, and were in fact state churches; the civil government thus handled administration and limited the consistory's competence to strictly disciplinary matters. The French churches, on the other hand, generally had to contend with a Catholic magistrate and thus needed to regulate church affairs themselves. The consistory was the logical body to perform this task, since it included all of the leadership of the church (except the pastors in the case of the *Articles polytiques*). This would be the continuing practice in the Huguenot consistory throughout the sixteenth and seventeenth centuries.

Once again, it is instructive to compare the system outlined in the *Articles polytiques* with the early structure of the church in Le Mans prior to the arrival of Pierre Merlin. As in the case of the diaconate, the consistory's structure follows its own logic rather than the Discipline, and again provides a clue into the ecclesiastical structure of some pre-1559 Protestant churches in the kingdom. In terms of officers, the church included pastors, deacons as described in the previous chapter, overseers *(surveillants),* and *senieurs* (eminent members of the congregation). The roles of these last two offices can be better clarified by examining the consistorial structure within the church. Following the pattern established at Poitiers, there were two consistories at Le Mans. The first was responsible for "censures" and met on Saturday afternoons; it consisted of the ministers (unlike Poitiers), the deacons, and the overseers, plus a scribe. The second, which met on Sundays between 7:00 and 8:00 A.M., was charged with administrative affairs *(police).* It included ministers, deacons, overseers, and *senieurs,* together with the scribe.[19]

---

[19]The relevant articles summarized above read as follows: [1] "Qu'il y aura deux consistoires, l'un pour la police et l'aultre pour la censure." [2] "Que le consistoire de la censure tiendra aux jours de sabmedy à une heure après midi, et le consistoire de la police aux jours de dymenche entre sept et huict heures du matin." [3] "Que au dict consistoire de la censure y assisteront seullement messieurs les

Thus the "overseers" performed roughly the same function as elders in other Reformed churches, while the *senieurs* were perhaps closer to modern trustees, though the registers are not entirely clear on that point.

The *Articles polytiques* and the early structure of the church at Le Mans thus shared several important points. Both included two consistories, one charged with discipline, the other with administration. The details of composition varied somewhat, as did the terms used for the offices. The disciplinary consistory included deacons—though they did not have the same responsibilities as other Reformed deacons—and another officer whose primary task was oversight of the congregation; in Le Mans it included the pastors as well. The administrative consistory added to these another office (deputy or *senieur*). The differences in terminology and in the composition of the consistories provide an important caution against overgeneralizing on the basis of such limited evidence. Nonetheless, it is clear that at least some of the churches in the kingdom established a structure involving a consistory charged with enforcing discipline, and a second "expanded consistory" responsible for administration.[20] This tradition of bi-level consistories would be an ongoing issue in the early years of the French Reformed churches.

The Consistory in the Discipline
In the early years of the French Reformed churches, there is a surprising lack of specificity in the provisions for local church structures. The 1559 Discipline contains two terms describing local church councils, *senat* and *consistoire*. The two terms have been taken to be virtually synonymous,[21] especially since the eighth national synod (Nîmes, 1572) eliminated the term *senat* altogether in favor of *consistoire*. Further, as Roussel points out, there is considerable precedent for the use of "senate" as a synonym of consistory.[22] On the other hand, the local Discipline of the church at Saint-Lô (1563) distinguishes between the consistory and the *Sénat ecclésiastique*.[23] In view of this, as well as the dual consistories in the *Articles polytiques* and the registers of the consistory of Le Mans, the assumption

---

ministres, diacres, surveillans et scribe, et au consistoire de la police tous les susdicts et oultre les senieurs." Le Mans, 3.

[20]Contra my earlier discussions of these churches as including two consistories, Roussel (Roussel, "Discipline," p. 179) prefers to view this as a single consistory with variable size: the smaller consistory handled censures, while the "enlarged" consistory dealt with other matters (Roussel, "Discipline," p. 179). Given the overlap in personnel, this is a clearer description of the structure of these churches.

[21]The only exception I have found to this is Janine Garrisson, *Les Protestants au XVIe siècle*, 200, who notes that the *senat* is the *consistoire* plus the deacons.

[22]Roussel, "Discipline," pp. 178–79.

[23]"Police et Discipline de l'Eglise de Saint-Lô (1563)," "Des Anciens ou Surveillans," art. 3.

that *senat* and *consistoire* refer to the same body in the 1559 Discipline needs to be examined carefully.

The term *senat* appears in only one article in Roussel's edition of the Discipline: "The elders and deacons are the senate of the church, over which should preside the ministers of the Word,"[24] which suggests that the pastors were technically not part of the senate. This separate status is reinforced by another article that appears in a number of manuscripts on the selection of elders and deacons: "In places where the church order is not yet established, deacons as well as elders will be elected by the common voice of the people with their pastor. But where the Discipline is in place, the senate of the church with the pastors will elect them."[25]

At this point, technical arguments about the manuscript evidence become important. The base manuscript of Roussel's published text of the 1559 Discipline omits a number of articles (including this one) which are attested by a variety of other manuscripts. Although these manuscripts are demonstrably corrupt at a number of points, the key question is whether there is evidence of corruption in this particular article. Roussel rejects the article for three basic reasons: it is missing from his base manuscript; he argues that local custom dictated how church officers were to be selected; the article's appearance in other manuscripts, including MSS Wb, Ra, Rb, and Pithou, is a result of its introduction by the second national synod (Poitiers, 1561).[26] The third point seems critical here: Roussel points out that the article was included in the 1561 Discipline (art. 30), but on the other hand there is no indication in the acts of the national synod that it had been added in 1561 despite the fact that the acts record other changes and additions to the Discipline. There is no manuscript evidence that the article was added in 1561, and some evidence, albeit not always the most reliable, that dates it to 1559. It thus seems reasonable to date the article to 1559, even though it was not included in all textual traditions of that edition of the Discipline.

This article provides an interesting parallel to the procedure for electing pastors: "Ministers will be elected to the consistory by the elders and deacons and will be presented to the people for whom they are ordained."[27] In other words, ministers are to be elected by essentially the same officers who elect elders

---

[24]Les anciens et diacres sont le senat de l'eglise auquel doyvent presider les ministres de la parolle. DE 1559, art. 21, Roussel, "Discipline," art. 19); cf. Quick, art. 23; *Histoire ecclésiastique*, art. 20.

[25]Es lieux ou l'ordre de l'eglise n'est point encore dresse, tant les diacres que les anciens seront esleus par les voix communes du peuple avec leur pasteur. Mays ou la Discipline sera dressee, ce sera au senat de l'eglise avec les pasteurs de les elire. DE 1559, MSS Wb, Rb art. 27; cf. Quick, art. 26; Aymon, art. 27. The article is omitted in the *Histoire ecclésiastique*.

[26]Roussel, "Discipline," 189 n. 87.

[27]Les ministres seront esleus au consistoire par les anciens et diacres, et seront presentez au peuple,

and deacons;[28] once again, pastors are treated as a separate class from other church officers and are not even listed among the electors. The article then continues to give the consistory the right to decide the case should opposition arise (subject to appeal to the provincial synod). The article does not identify the original electors as the consistory, however; ministers are elected *to* the consistory, not *by* it.

Nowhere does the 1559 Discipline contain an article defining the consistory's membership, suggesting that it was indeed synonymous with *senat*. Two articles do place specific officers in this council, however. The first article, which states that ministers are to be elected to the consistory, is quoted above. The second explains that one of the tasks assigned to elders is to report scandals to the consistory.[29] Deacons were not explicitly mentioned as working with the consistory, however.

As implied in article 20 defining the role of elders, the consistory's primary responsibility was overseeing the moral and spiritual life of the congregation and its leaders. The framers of the Discipline were particularly concerned that the consistory be given authority over the ministers, and to a lesser extent, elders and deacons. For example, the consistory (plus a few neighboring ministers) could depose ministers for specified offenses and decide whether to make the reasons for the deposition public (art. 19, 20).[30] In addition to such direct powers, the consistory had authority over other aspects of the pastor's ministry as well. For example, ministers could not leave their church without consistory approval;[31] if they were sent elsewhere because they could not minister in their own church but refused to go, the consistory was responsible to judge the case (art. 11). A minister from another church could not preach without the pastor's consent or, in his absence, the consistory's (art. 9). Similarly, the consistory had the right to depose elders and deacons for the same reasons as pastors (art. 26).[32] It also was the first court of appeal for objections to elections of ministers (art. 6), and elders or deacons.[33]

---

pour lequel ils sont ordonnez. DE 1559, art. 6. MSS Rb and Pithou add "ministres" before "anciens et diacres."

  [28]As we saw in chap. 4, this article was modified by the second national synod of Poitiers in 1561 to state that ministers are to be elected by two or three ministers plus the consistory; this is essentially the version of the article included in the editions of Aymon and Quick.

  [29]"L'office des anciens sera de…rapporter les scandales au consistoire.…" DE 1559, art. 22, Roussel, "Discipline," art. 20.

  [30]Roussel, "Discipline," art. 19.

  [31]This article appears in DE 1559 in MSS Wb, Rb, and Pithou, and DE 1561; it does not appear to have been added by the second national synod, and thus probably dates from 1559.

  [32]Roussel, "Discipline," art. 24.

  [33]MSS Wb, Rb art. 27; cf. Quick, art. 26; Aymon, art. 27.

In addition to its responsibility to monitor the leadership of the church, the consistory was also to maintain discipline within the community. The elders reported scandals to this body (art. 22), and it then had the authority to take disciplinary action, including excommunication. This was a fairly controversial right, however, and the Discipline spent a fair amount of time regulating it. The Discipline specified the grounds for which someone could be excommunicated (one of which was rebellion against the consistory), and indicated that the consistory was to decide whether to prohibit a person from attending sermons as well as being banned from the sacraments (art. 28). People convicted of serious crimes such as heresy, contempt of God, schism, treason against the church, and the like were to be excommunicated and the reasons made known to the people; the consistory was also to decide whether to publicize the reason for excommunication of those guilty of lesser faults (art. 30, 31). In all cases, excommunicates could only be reconciled with the church by the consistory (art. 32).[34]

Lastly, the consistory played a role in the developing marital law within the Protestant community. First, after the marriage contract was made a couple had to "propose" the marriage to the consistory before proclaiming the banns; this procedure was to be followed unless prevented by some serious reason of which the consistory was aware (art. 35). If two young people wished to be married but the parents opposed the marriage unreasonably despite its being "holy and profitable," the consistory was to "advise" on the matter (art. 39). Finally, the consistory was to judge the validity of promises of marriage when questions arose (art. 40).[35]

At this point, a few observations are in order. Neither the 1559 Discipline nor the Gallican Confession assigns deacons disciplinary roles, yet all of the tasks assigned to the consistory involve discipline. Deacons were to be members of the *senat*, which was not associated with discipline in either article in which it appears, but are not listed as members of the consistory. In addition to their charitable work, deacons were permitted to be delegates to synods (art. 3, 5) and were involved in electing church officers, tasks that fall under the broad category of *police*. It is thus possible to interpret the 1559 Discipline as permitting the distinction between a *consistoire des censures* and a *consistoire de police* that we saw in the first church order in Le Mans and implicitly in the *Articles polytiques*. In this interpretation, the minister and elders are to handle discipline in the consistory,[36] particularly of church officers but also of those who violated the community's norms

---

[34]See Roussel, "Discipline," art. 20, 26, 27, 28 respectively.

[35]See Roussel, "Discipline," art. 31, 35, 36 respectively.

[36]This seems to have been the case at Saint-Lô in 1563, where the local discipline insisted that *only* the pastors and elders were responsible for congregational discipline, excluding teachers and deacons from this role ("Police et Discipline de l'Eglise de Saint-Lô," "Des censures," 3).

of conduct; when dissensions threatened to divide the community—whether from disputed elections, from conflict over promises to marry, or from parental opposition to a marriage desired by the couple—the consistory was to work to resolve the problem. The senate was an "enlarged consistory" which added the deacons to the other officers (but omitted pastors) and which was responsible for matters of polity such as selecting church officers and sending delegates to synods. At the same time, it is not clear that this division of labor was intended to be applied systematically. Although the Discipline can be read in such a way as to set up a two-level consistory, with the deacons contributing to *police* but not to *censures*, this is never explicit. The ambiguity may have been intentional: it permitted churches such as Poitiers to continue making the distinction between councils within the church without insisting that churches with a single consistory change their structure.

This compromise did not last for long, at least in terms of the legislation emanating from the national synod. The process of eliminating the potential distinction between the *senat* and the *consistoire* began with the second national synod (Poitiers, 1561). The acts of this synod specifically reject multiple consistories: "*Item:* it is resolved and recommended that there is to be but one consistory in each church, composed of ministers, elders and deacons exercising their charges, which when necessary can call whomever they think good for counsel and advice."[37] The status of this article poses a few problems. The manuscripts place this in the "faits particuliers" section of the acts, suggesting it was not intended to be incorporated into the Discipline; this is corroborated by the manuscripts of the 1561 Discipline. Aymon, however, classifies it as "faits généraux," 7; Quick has it in the "General Matters" section but separates it from the corrections and additions to the Discipline.[38] The balance of the evidence thus suggests that Poitiers did not add the article to the Discipline. But in the 1563 Discipline, the next surviving text after 1561, the article is included as "Des Consistoires" (art. 36); there is no indication that it had been added by either the third national synod (Orléans, 1562) or the fourth (Lyon, 1563).[39] When, precisely, the article was added to the Discipline is thus a mystery. On the other hand, whether it was supposed to be included in the Discipline in 1561, the article was intended

---

[37]Item a esté resolu et avisé qu'il n'y aura en chacune eglise qu'un consistoire, composé de ministres, anciens et diacres exerçant leurs charges, lequel pourra appeler pour conseil tels que bon luy semblera, quand l'affaire le requerra. ANS, 2–Poitiers–1561, "faits particuliers," 4.

[38]Aymon, 16–17; Quick, chap. 5, art. 1 (16).

[39]A similar though not identical issue was addressed by the fourth national synod, but only in answer to a specific query from a single church.

to be binding on the French Reformed churches from the time it was adopted[40] and was reinforced by changes this same national synod did introduce into the Discipline. The synod rewrote article 6 of the 1559 Discipline, which had specified that ministers be elected by the elders and deacons with the ministers, to include a direct reference to the consistory as the electing body: "A minister ought not to be elected for the present by one sole minister with his consistory, but by two or three ministers with the consistory, or by the provincial synod if possible...."[41] Similarly, the synod also modified article 3 of the 1561 Discipline, giving the consistory the right to select elders or deacons to accompany the minister to national synods: "Ministers will each bring to the aforementioned [national] synod one elder or deacon at the most, elected by those of the consistory...."[42] Two of the key tasks of the *consistoire de police* were thus assigned specifically to the consistory rather than implicitly to a larger body. Of course, since the consistory now specifically included all of the members of the *senat*, there was no longer any need to make the distinction between the regular and "enlarged" body. Although both articles on the senate continued to be included in the Discipline as articles 26 and 30, with the inclusion of the deacons in the consistory, the term *senat* had become metaphorical, as Roussel suggests. In fact, the 1565 Discipline includes a chapter entitled "Du senat ecclesiastique ou consistoire," making the identification of the two terms explicit. Curiously, this chapter retains both the article on the composition of the *senat* (art. 1) and the article specifying a single consistory composed of ministers, deacons, and elders (art. 6).

The second national synod did not end the confusion over the number and composition of councils within the church. The problem of the number of councils in the church came up before the fourth national synod (Lyon, 1563):

> On the matter raised by the church of Issoudun, concerning whether
> it would be good to have a council other than the consistory to handle
> the affairs of the church: after careful consideration, the synod is of

[40]For example, Pierre Merlin placed deacons on the consistory of the church at Le Mans in his reorganization of that church on his arrival in the city in August 1561, and this despite his not giving them any disciplinary responsibilities, Le Mans, 18. This church only included one council after Merlin's arrival: the distinction between the *"consistoire de la censure"* and the *"consistoire de la police"* had dropped out entirely.

[41]Un ministre ne doit estre esleu pour le present par un seul ministre avec son consistoire, mais par deux ou trois ministres avec le consistoire, ou par le synode provincial si fere se peult.... DE 1561, art. 9, cf. ANS, 2–Poitiers–1561, 4; Quick, chap. 3, art. 3 (13–14). Note that the minister is still treated as separate from the consistory.

[42]Audit synode les ministres ameneront cascun un ancien ou diacre pour le plus, esleu par ceux du consistoire.... DE 1561, art. 6; cf. ANS, 2–Poitiers–1561, 2; Quick, chap. 3, art. 1 (13).

> the opinion that consistories ought to decide all of the affairs of the church, without having for these matters a regular council composed of persons other than those who have a charge in the church.[43]

In this case, the situation seems to have been different from the "expanded" consistory of Poitiers or Le Mans: the second council evidently included members of the church who were neither elders nor deacons, presumably the *hommes de biens, notables,* or even *nobles* of the community, much like the *senieurs* of Le Mans but with independent status from the consistory.[44] The decision of the synod made it clear that there was to be no ongoing council within the church except those made up of the church's officers.[45] At the same time, though no permanent council that included people other than the ministers, elders, or deacons was permitted, the consistory remained free to call on others for advice on specific issues. Even after this decision, the issue still refused to go away: the sixth national synod (Vertueil, 1567) was alerted that "in some cities, there are councils other than the consistory which manage ecclesiastical affairs";[46] the synod noted that previous national synods had repeatedly decided that there was to be one and only one council in the church, and those churches that did not follow this regulation strictly were to be censured. The vitality of the dual-council tradition even in the face of repeated decisions banning this church structure is striking.

[43]Sur le fait propose par l'eglise d'Issoudun, assavoir s'il seroit bon d'avoir outre le consistoire un conseil pour vuider les affaires de l'eglise: apres diligent consideration, le synode est d'avis que les consistoires doivent decider de toutes les affaires de l'eglise, sans avoir pour cet egard conseil ordinaire compose d'autres personnes que de ceux qui ont charge en l'eglise. ANS, 4–Lyon–1563, "faits particuliers," 26, cf. Quick, chap. 16, art. 6 (38). Some manuscripts add: Jacoit qu'il soit bon aux affaires plus grandes et de grande importance d'appeler avec les anciens aucuns de plus discrets et de meilleur jugement d'entre ceux qui sont en l'eglise, encore qu'ils ne soient pas du cors du consistoire, ce neantmoins il n'y doit avoir autre compagnie ou forme de conseil pour les affaires ecclesiastiques, sinon du corps du consistoire ordinaire qui a est ordonné par l'eglise a ces fins, composées de personnes ayans charge publique en icelle, ce que les autres n'ont pas.

[44]Given that this synod met just one year after the beginnings of the Wars of Religion when the political and military leaders of the Huguenots largely assumed control of the movement, this issue may reflect a struggle for leadership of the community between the secular leaders of the party and the ministers of the church. Without more information on the circumstances, it is impossible to determine this with any degree of certainty.

[45]In principle, this would have permitted subcommittees within the consistory such as a board of deacons, but there is no evidence that any church created such a council. Further, in view of the Discipline's insistence that there be but one consistory to decide all ecclesiastical matters, it is unclear that such subcommittees would have been approved by the national synod, though if a subcommittee were supervised by the consistory it would probably have been accepted.

[46][E]n aucunes villes il y a des conseils autres que le consistoire, lesquels entreprennent le maniement des affaires eccles[iastique].... ANS, 6–Vertueil–1567, 30.

By this point, the composition and duties of the consistory should have been clear; in fact, no church again raised the issue of multiple consistories or councils within the church. However, the thorough revision of the Discipline presented at the seventh national synod held at La Rochelle, 1571, once again muddied the waters. "Des consistoires," article 4 of the 1571 Discipline, reads: "Ministers of the Word of God and elders make up the consistory of the church, over which the ministers ought to preside. And nonetheless deacons can be a part of the consistory with their approval."[47] In other words, deacons were not members of the consistory unless the elders and pastor(s) permitted them to be. Since the descriptions of the role of deacons in both the Confession and the Discipline never assigned them disciplinary duties, the primary task of the consistory, this change was consistent with basic theological principles; further, pastors and elders were solely responsible for discipline in the church order of Saint-Lô (1563)[48] and in Geneva, the home base for Theodore Beza, moderator of the seventh national synod. On the other hand, the effects of a full decade of acts and articles placing deacons on the consistory could not be eliminated so easily, and thus after consideration by the provincial synods this article was changed by the eighth national synod (Nîmes, 1572) to read that deacons can "and should" *(et devront)* be on the consistory. The synod explained this decision by adding at the end of the article: "seeing that out of the exigencies of the times our churches have employed the aforementioned deacons successfully in the government of the church as exercising also the charge of elder. And deacons elected hereafter or continuing their office are in charge of the government of the church with the pastors and elders."[49] This article effectively completed the development of the French Reformed consistory: contrary to some of its precedents, it had emerged as the only standing council in the church, and was responsible for handling all local ecclesiastical affairs. Unlike Geneva's Consistory, its membership included all the officers of the church, deacons as well as pastors and elders. But placing deacons on the consistory created something of a dilemma: since they performed all of the work of the elders, did they not become de facto elders as well as deacons? We turn to this issue next.

[47]Les ministres de la parole de Dieu et les anciens font le consistoire de l'eglise, auquel les ministres doivent presider. Et neantmoins les diacres pourront assister au consistoire par l'advis d'iceux. DE 1571, "Des consistoires," 4.

[48]"Police et Discipline de l'Eglise de Saint-Lô," "Des censures," 3.

[49][V]eu mesme que nos eglises pour les necessites des temps ont jusques icy employé heureusement lesdits diacres au gouvernement de l'eglise comme exerceans aussy la charge d'ancien. Et les diacres qui seront par cy apres ainsy esleux ou continues auront avec les pasteurs et anciens le gouvernement de l'eglise. DE 1572, "Des consistoires," 4.

Chapter 6

The Loss of the Diaconate
The evolution of the consistory was one of two interrelated developments that determined the peculiar shape of the local government of French Reformed churches; the other was a new form of diaconate. Although the Discipline and Confession continued to distinguish between elders and deacons, in practice on a local level the two tended to merge into a single office. In fact, the available evidence suggests that conformity to the Discipline in distinguishing the two offices was exceedingly rare. Janine Garrisson notes that except for the churches of Nîmes and Clairac, Huguenot churches tended to appoint an elder to be a deacon as well, in effect making the diaconal office a subcategory of elder.[50] Other exceptions to the rule included the church at Le Mans after the arrival of Pierre Merlin and the churches of Bayeux and Saint-Lô, if their local Disciplines are any indication of their actual practice. And the church at Clairac cited by Garrisson did not have a "proper" diaconate even though it maintained the distinction between elders and deacons: in 1595–96, the deacon was a *proposant* working as an assistant pastor as part of his training, thus returning to an essentially Roman Catholic view of the office.[51]

The church at Nîmes in the last decades of the sixteenth century provides an interesting—though apparently atypical—example of a church which attempted to maintain a diaconate along the lines of those described by the Discipline. Even here, however, the elders were heavily involved in the charitable work of the church. Thus, for example, one of the deacons (called the *basynier* or the *diacre du bassin des pauvres*) collected money for the poor, but an elder (called the *receveur des pauvres*) acted as the treasurer for the *bourse des pauvres* and arranged for pious bequests; elders and deacons together screened applicants for aid not previously approved by the consistory; initially, elders prepared the roll of the poor each January, which was then reviewed by the deacons and finalized by the consistory; later, this process was streamlined into a meeting of an elder, a deacon, and a pastor collectively preparing the roll of the poor; elders (not deacons) issued *billets* to permit those on the roll to collect their alms; elders and deacons together admonished the poor to engage in productive labor and not to beg on threat of losing their right to receive bread from the church.[52] The point is clear: even in this case, "diaconal ministry" was increasingly in the hands of not just the deacons, but

---

[50]Garrisson, *Les Protestants au XVIe siècle,* 200; cf. ibid., 370 n. 25, which cites the surviving consistorial records of the church at Nîmes and gives specific dates where the deacons' activities are discussed.

[51]Garrisson, *Les Protestants au XVIe siècle,* 370 n. 25.

[52]Raymond A. Mentzer, "Organizational Endeavour and Charitable Impulse in Sixteenth-Century France: The Case of Protestant Nîmes," *French History* 5 (1991): 8, 10, 19, 26.

the elders as well, even in this rare example of a church that maintained a separate diaconate.

In most other churches the elders virtually absorbed the deacons. In many churches, elders administered the funds for the poor. For example, the national synod of Poitiers (1561) decided that an elder who had misused the deniers he had collected should be examined before the consistory before being deposed; four years later, the fifth national synod (Paris, 1565) discussed elders who distributed alms.[53] Solange Bertheau found no trace of a distinction between the two offices in the consistory records of Moyen Poitou;[54] Jacques Pannier comments that the deacons in the Reformed church at Charenton had essentially merged with the elders by 1620;[55] and according to Elisabeth Labrousse, the consistory records in the church at Carla during the seventeenth century do not even mention the office of deacon; instead, charitable functions were assigned to elders.[56] Churches in the Midi also tended to designate certain elders as deacons; these men took on the administration of alms along with their normal duties on the consistory.[57] *La forme de dresser un consistoire* illustrates an early provision for this "doubling up" of offices. This document divided church offices up following standard Reformed ecclesiastical principles: ministers and elders make up the consistory, which was to be responsible for discipline; deacons were in charge of social welfare. But the offices of elder and deacon could be held by the same man, presumably in cases where there was an inadequate pool of candidates to fill both offices. The first article in the section on deacons reads: "Deacons are to be chosen from the large number [of godly men] mentioned above or from the elders if one of them finds himself able to attend to both charges, which are not in any way incompatible...."[58] While not expressly mandating that the deacons be chosen from elders, this is an early example of a practice which would soon become the norm in the churches.

---

[53] ANS, 2–Poitiers–1561, "faits particuliers," 8; 5–Paris–1565, "faits généraux," 21.

[54] Solange Bertheau, "Le Consistoire dans les Eglises Réformées du Moyen-Poitou au XVIIe siècle," *BSHPF* 116 (1970): 513.

[55] Jacques Pannier, *L'Eglise Réformée de Paris sous Louis XIII* (Paris: Librairie Honoré Champion, 1931), 306; cf. Paul de Félice, *Les Protestants d'autrefois: Vie intérieure des églises, moeurs et usages*, vol. 2, *Les Conseils ecclésiastiques: Consistoires, Colloques, Synodes* (Paris: Librairie Fischbacher, 1899), 9.

[56] Elisabeth Labrousse, "L'Eglise Réformée du Carla en 1672–1673 d'après le registre des délibérations de son Consistoire," *BSHPF* 106 (1960): 22–53, 191–231, esp. 28–33; *BSHPF* 107 (1961): 223–72.

[57] Garrisson, *Protestants du Midi*, 99–100.

[58] Les diacres soyent tirez du grand nombre cy dessu mentionné ou des anciens s'il s'en trouve qui puisse vacqer aux deux charges, lesquelles ne sont point incompatibles.... *Documents protestants inédits*, 75. It should be noted that even in Geneva, one could be an elder and a deacon simultaneously; see the list of deacons in the appendix to Robert M. Kingdon, "The Deacons of the Reformed Church

The acts of the provincial synods of Languedoc show a further deterioration of the diaconate over the course of the century. Initially, deacons and elders—the acts call them *"surveillants"*—were defined in terms corresponding fairly closely with the Gallican Confession and the Discipline: "deacons are in charge of catechizing, watching over the poor and administering their alms; elders [are] to report to the consistory the faults and insolences committed by those of the church and to indicate the truly polluted; the deacons are also to watch diligently over the other affairs of the church."[59] Yet the acts of later synods show a breakdown in the distinction between the two offices. Although the provincial synod of Nîmes (1575) assigned the distribution of alms in a particular case to deacons, no later synod did. Subsequent references to the charitable work of the churches do not include names or offices of those who were to distribute alms with three exceptions: the provincial synods of Montpellier (1578), Nîmes (1580), and Nîmes (1590) specifically designated elders for this task. All of this suggests that in the last quarter of the sixteenth century, the deacons of Bas Languedoc had lost much of the distinctive role assigned to them in the Discipline.[60]

This decline in the diaconate was not reflected in most of the legislation emanating out of the national synod, however; the last version of the Discipline prior to the revocation of the Edict of Nantes in 1685 contains a separate chapter on the diaconate, whereas earlier versions reflected practice more accurately (though unintentionally) by combining elders and deacons in one chapter. At the same time, the development of the consistory discussed above provides an obvious parallel for the development of the diaconate, and some of the articles dealing with the consistory give important supporting evidence of the merging of elders and deacons. For example, the seventh national synod (La Rochelle, 1571) reiterates in the "general matters" section of the acts that the deacons alone were to administer alms in the church.[61] The synod probably believed this

---

in Calvin's Geneva," in *Mélanges d'histoire du XVIe siècle offerts à Henri Meylan,* Travaux d'Humanisme et Renaissance 10 (Geneva: Droz, 1970), 81–90, esp. 88–89; names marked with an asterisk (•) held both offices in the specified year.

[59][L]es diacres auront charge de catechiser, veiller sur les povres et leur administrer leurs ausmosnes; les surveillans de rapporter au consistoire les fautes et insolences qui se commettront par ceux de leur eglise, indiquer les vrayment pollus; ausdits diacres, de veiller diligemment sur les autres affaires desdites eglises.... Provincial synod of Nîmes, February, 1561, *Documents protestants inédits,* 44. This is part of Viret's church order for the province discussed in chap. 4.

[60]Auzière, fols. 86, 128, 153v, 224v. The office of deacon had not completely dropped out, however, for as late as 1595—the last synod in the manuscript—some deputies were still designated as deacons (Auzière, fol. 292).

[61]Quick, 7–La Rochelle–1571, chap. 7, art. 1 (95).

article to be necessary because the deacon's distinctive role in the churches was being lost; in view of the evidence cited above, some churches may not have had deacons at all. More direct evidence for the blending of the roles of elders and deacons comes from the next national synod, held at Nîmes in 1572: again one of the reasons for recommending that deacons be included in the consistory was that they had been working successfully in many church governments in the capacity of elders. This is the only acknowledgment of the real relationship on a local level between elders and deacons in the acts of any of the national synods in the sixteenth century.

In addition to their role in local government, the Discipline gave the deacons virtually all of the extraconsistorial rights and responsibilities of elders. From the very first version of the Discipline, deacons were eligible to be deputies to provincial and national synods, though oddly enough when the chapter on colloquies was added to the Discipline in 1572, only pastors and elders were listed as deputies;[62] this may reflect the early stages of the breakdown of the distinction between elders and deacons, however. In Viret's church order for Languedoc, the deacons actually seem to have had precedence over elders as deputies to provincial synods: "once each year a provincial synod is to be held to which all of the ministers of the province must come with one deacon of each church which has two, or if there is only one an elder in place of the deacon."[63] The seventh national synod permitted deacons, like elders, to attend "propositions" by candidates for the ministry, to participate in censures, and to vote on all ecclesiastical matters except doctrine, which was reserved for ministers and "doctors" (i.e., teachers of theology).[64]

All of this suggests that distinguishing between deacons and elders, *senat* and *consistoire*, was not well suited to the realities of sixteenth-century French Protestantism. In other words, the merging of offices and councils in the local church seem to be a part of the same dynamic, caused to a large extent by the conditions under which the French Reformed churches had developed. The lack of state support, the small size of the churches, the shortage of qualified personnel to fill ecclesiastical offices, all contributed to the development of a system with less specialization among the church officers and, as a result, fewer councils than had been originally permitted by the Discipline. Under these conditions, deacons would have had to be included in the consistory to preserve plurality of

---

[62]Quick, 8–Nîmes–1572, chap. 3, art. 11 (106); cf. DE 1572, "Des colloques," 1.

[63][T]outes les années se tiendroit une fois le synode en ladite province, la ou seroient tous les ministres de ladite province tenus à venir avec un des diacres de chacune eglise ou il y en a deux; et ou il n'y en a qu'un, un surveillant au lieu d'un diacre.... Provincial synod of Nîmes, February 1561, *Documents protestants inédits*, 43.

[64]Quick, 7–La Rochelle–1571, chap. 7, art. 2 (95).

leadership.[65] It is likely that they also had to take on disciplinary and pastoral duties as well, but even if this was not immediately necessary their participation in the consistory would almost inevitably have led to this, since these duties remained this council's primary role. Once the deacons were on the consistory and performing all of the roles of elders, it was inevitable that the two offices be combined, with the diaconal responsibilities being assigned to a subset of the elders.

Church discipline was a highly controversial subject in all areas which attempted to set up consistories that were relatively autonomous from the civil government. In France, these "turf wars" were complicated by the fact that Protestantism did not have the backing of the state. To round out our view of Huguenot ecclesiastical structures, we must next examine how these institutions interacted with the various political powers within France as well as with various foreign churches.

[65]Garrisson, *Les Protestants au XVIe siècle*, 200.

Chapter 7

Church Institutions and the Wider World

Development of the French Reformed churches did not and could not exist apart from a complex web of political and theological relationships within France and beyond its borders. The churches, colloquies, and synods had no choice but to establish links with the power structures within France and with foreign churches and governments. These contacts were essential in order to obtain and maintain political, diplomatic, and even military pressure on the French government during the Wars of Religion. Within France itself, the churches needed to find a way to legitimize their doctrine and discipline to the monarchy; along with their intellectual defense in the Confession and the Discipline, they also had to lobby governmental bodies directly, including particularly the royal court. Less obviously, they also needed to establish ties with the Protestant political assemblies in the provinces and even with the Protestant nobility, whose churches were the most secure in France but did not participate in the colloquies and synods of the French Reformed churches. On a local level, a modus vivendi needed to be developed between the disciplinary work of the consistories and the work of the civil magistrate, whether Catholic or Protestant.

This chapter surveys some of the ways that the national and provincial synods attempted to integrate the French Reformed churches into the broader world. First, the problem of integrating the house churches of the nobility into the emerging organizational structure of the *Eglises Réformées* is examined. Next, relations with various secular authorities, including both the civil magistrate and the Protestant political assemblies and provincial estates, is surveyed, as well as the attempts of the provincial synods of Languedoc to get support from Henri de Montmorency, the governor of the province and former Huguenot supporter turned royalist. Finally, we turn to still broader issues of relations with the royal court and with foreign churches.

The *Eglises Réformées* and the Nobility

One of the main issues facing the emerging *Eglises Réformées* was integrating the kingdom's diverse Protestant churches into a single ecclesiastical organization. Although the center of gravity of French Protestantism had been in the towns, toward the end of the 1550s the nobility became an increasingly prominent part of the movement, a position confirmed by the Edict of January (1562). In this last-ditch attempt to avert civil war, Catherine de Médicis permitted the Huguenots limited rights to worship. The edict forbade the Huguenots to worship in towns, to assemble at night, or to meet under arms; they were free to assemble peacefully in the countryside. Although this left most of the Protestant population without any right to worship—Protestantism was still primarily an urban religion—it did leave the nobility free to organize and protect churches on their rural estates. Since Catherine's main concern was with the nobility who could raise armies and threaten civil war, the terms of the edict seemed an adequate solution to the problem. Unfortunately, it did not alleviate the most severe religious tensions in the kingdom, found primarily among the urban classes who formed the backbone of both militant Protestantism and militant Catholicism.[1] Thus both sides mobilized later that year for the first of what would become an interminable string of Wars of Religion.

The third national synod met in Orléans in 1562 during this mobilization, and for the first time a national synod addressed the issue of the noble churches directly. The synod added a rather lengthy article to the Discipline which asked the princes and other *seigneurs* at court who wished to establish churches in their houses to choose legitimately called Calvinist pastors who would sign the Discipline and the Confession. The article further asked these nobles to create a consistory made up of the minister and the "best approved" *(plus approuves) gens de biens* of the household to deal with scandals and vices. The ministers were invited to attend provincial synods and were eligible to be delegates to the national synod as well, though as always there was to be no primacy among the ministers. When the nobles were resident in areas where there was already an organized church, the

---

[1] Nonetheless, the provincial synod of Languedoc meeting at Nîmes in February 1561 (1562 n.s.), sent a letter to court urging the "ministers" there to abide by the edict (Auzière, fol. 2).

nobles' churches were asked to meet together with the local church "to eliminate all division" *(afin d'obvier a toute division).*[2]

Unfortunately, the growing militarization and politicization of Protestantism in France only increased tensions and "division" in the church. The Wars of Religion made the nobility the effective leaders within Protestantism instead of the pastors, though some pastors became involved in military activities as well, much to the chagrin of Calvin.[3] The various edicts ending the different Wars of Religion inevitably continued the trend begun by the Edict of January by reinforcing the privileges of the churches in noble houses and on their rural estates and weakening those of the churches in the towns.[4] Although the article requesting the integration of noble churches into the *Eglises Réformées* seems to have been honored for the most part, tensions still existed between the nobles, who were quite used to having their way, and the established order of the churches. The first evidence of this sort of tension to appear in the acts of the national synod is in the acts of the very next national synod (Lyon, 1563). In this period, communion was served first to all the men in the church, then to the women. A gentleman, however, insisted that his wife receive communion immediately after him, followed by the rest of the men and then the women; this was presumably intended to preserve his family's social preeminence even within the context of the Lord's Supper. The national synod replied that the gentleman must behave with more humility and follow the established practice in the churches; in fact, the synod adopted an article that made the existing practice the official approach to communion throughout the French Reformed churches.[5]

The next national synod (Paris, 1565) had to deal with other, more serious problems in the noble churches. Although the nobility was happy to accept the support of the French Reformed Church and to encourage churches they founded in towns and villages to join the *Eglises réformées,* their house churches never integrated themselves into the broader church unless they were tied to a local congregation. Doctrine was not an issue: Calvinism had largely won the day in France,

---

[2]ANS, 3–Orléans–1562, "faits généraux," 3; cf. DE 1565, "Des ministres," 14. N.B. There is no surviving exemplar of DE 1562.

[3]Léonard, *Histoire générale,* 2:112, 112 n. 4.

[4]For example, the fifth national synod (Paris, 1565) passed an article requiring ministers "in those places ordained by the king and in all others" not to receive anyone from a different church for communion without adequate references from the pastor or elder of her/his home church (ANS, 5–Paris–1565, "avertissemens generaux aux Eglises," 26). Presumably, the restrictions on places of worship encouraged people to travel to legal churches to receive communion when they could not do so in their own (illegal) churches.

[5]ANS, 4–Lyon–1563, "faits particuliers," 34, 35.

including among the nobility. The Discipline was more controversial, however. The nobles ignored the call to establish consistories in their churches, and at least some of the nobility viewed the pastors of their house churches as part of their personal staff: when the nobles traveled, they would take their pastor with them, leaving the church without a minister. The fifth national synod, meeting in Paris in 1565, addressed this issue by insisting that pastors were assigned to churches and not persons, even if their household was so large that it made up a church by itself; when nobles traveled, they did not have the right to take their minister with them if by so doing they would leave a local church without a pastor.[6] There are examples of this type of situation in Brittany, where some "seigneurial churches" were counted either as annexes to or parts of local churches; in these cases, the noble was not to take the pastor away from the congregation when the family left the area. In other cases, Le Noir identifies ministers as "domestic pastors" who presumably would be free to accompany the noble household as it traveled.[7] The fifth national synod also addressed a second problem in noble households. It decreed that *seigneurs* and *gentilhommes* were to be censured following the Discipline if, after being warned repeatedly, they continued to allow scandalous and incorrigible persons into their households, especially "priests chanting Mass or dogmatizing in order to debauch their servants," or if they received such persons into their service.[8] Both of these problems threatened the integrity of the French Reformed Church. If pastors were considered to be the personal servants of the nobility, this would call into question the right of churches on their estates to exist apart from the household; it would also imply that the noble churches were independent of the other Huguenot churches and that the local churches had no rights vis-à-vis the house churches of the nobility. And if nobles were to accept scandalous persons into their households, it would undermine the very discipline which was at the heart of much of Calvinist polity and piety; if nobles accepted Catholic priests into their entourage, it would not only endanger the virtue of their servants(!), but would call into question the authority of the pastor and elders and destroy the doctrinal purity of the church. Though the issues addressed by these decisions were serious, they also seem to have been relatively rare.[9]

[6]ANS, 5–Paris–1565, "Avertissemens generaux aux Eglises," 30.

[7]Le Noir, *Histoire ecclésiastique de Bretagne,* e.g., 108, 112, 114, 130, 131; cf. the reference to the formation of an *église domestique,* 156.

[8]Les Seigneurs et gentilhommes seront censurez selon la Discipline ecclesiastique si apres avoir esté plusieurs fois admonestez ils continuent d'entretenir en leurs maisons des personnes scandaleuses et incorrigibles, et sur tout s'ils y souffrent des prestres chantans messes ou dogmantisant pour debaucher leur domestiques, ou si de nouveau ils en prennent ou reçoivent a leur service. ANS, 5–Paris–1565, "Avertissemens generaux aux Eglises," 31.

[9]There were also problems with such issues as sumptuary laws and precedence at the Lord's Supper,

A more widespread problem was the lack of participation of the ministers from house churches at synods. While attendance at synods was spotty for many congregations, the absence of the noble churches seems to have been nearly universal. For example, in the surviving records of the provincial synods, colloquies, and *classes* of Bas Languedoc, covering over three hundred folios in a nineteenth-century copy, there are no clear references to noble house churches.[10] This does not mean that the nobility never participated in synods: the seventh national synod held at La Rochelle in 1571, the so-called "Synod of Princes," was attended by the most prominent Protestant nobility of France and Navarre, by any measure an exceptional event. In general, the nobility simply ignored the synods, viewing them as largely irrelevant to the Protestant cause. The synodical system was established by local, nonnoble churches to defend themselves against charges of sectarianism by a hostile monarchy; the system itself was established in large measure because of the lack of magisterial or political support for Protestantism. From the perspective of the Protestant nobility, which was led by several Princes of the Blood, these considerations were less than compelling. As far as they were concerned, the indigenous tradition of congregationalism provided an effective church structure under the watchful eye of the nobility: Protestant magistrates could work with churches to enforce discipline, and the nobility under the Protestant Princes of the Blood—whose military and political power enabled them to form a Party that even the monarchy had to respect—could provide leadership and a unifying force for French Protestantism. Synods thus were not necessary for the success of the Protestant cause, and so the banning of synods by the Edicts of Pacification was not a major issue from the perspective of the Huguenots' political leaders.

This general disregard for synodical government among the Protestant nobility was reflected in the proposals of Jean Morély—a French nobleman himself—concerning synods. Although he advocated holding synods as needed to discuss problems which arose in the churches, he argued that these synods had no right to issue "canons" or decrees: their decisions were strictly advisory. This approach to synods struck at the very heart of the French Reformed Church's provisions for collective government, though it has not received as much attention as his proposals

---

issues related more to the nobles' tendency to view themselves as a class apart rather than to the institutional problems raised by integrating their house churches into the broader French Reformed Church.

[10]This observation needs to be verified by identifying all of the churches represented at these sessions to see whether a noble house church might have been listed among the local churches, an item for further research which would help clarify the extent of the problem under consideration here.

concerning local church government. This lack of discussion dates back to the six-teenth century. Chandieu and the other defenders of the Discipline focused their attack on Morély almost entirely on his approach to local church governance, and since this was the primary battleground in the affair, quite naturally scholars have spent most of their time on this issue. This does not mean, of course, that Chandieu thought synods were unimportant. Rather, he decided to leave Morély's challenge to the synodical system unanswered because of the political situation faced by the French Reformed Church. Synods were illegal in 1562; the Huguenots held them anyway, but they could hardly afford to be too blatant about it for fear of provoking a royal reaction. In any event, recent scholars studying Morély's proposals have commented on the connection linking his ideas on synods and the local church with French Protestant traditions of congregationalism; what has not been noticed, however, is that Morély's approach to synods matches the indifference of the nobil-ity toward the collective government of the French Reformed Church. In essence, the nobility continued to be congregationalists; their attitude was that synods were nice but irrelevant. Overall policy was set by the Princes of the Blood, the Party, and the nobility themselves. The lack of representation by the house churches at synods suggests that the nobility were not much interested in synodical decisions even in ecclesiastical matters, perhaps because they did not want other people, especially commoners, telling them how to run churches which they sponsored in their own homes. The disinterest with which the nobility usually treated the synods was not far removed from reducing them to bodies that could advise but not legislate, as advocated by Morély.

All of this suggests that though the Protestant nobility shared a common theo-logical outlook with the French Reformed Church, though both looked to The-odore Beza and Geneva for leadership, though the French Reformed Church was recognized as the "official" Protestant church in the kingdom, yet the house churches of the nobility never fully integrated themselves into its institutional structures, particularly its provisions for collective government via synods. Indeed, the nobility seems to have considered themselves as a privileged class within the church as they were in society, and their goals and the goals of their Party did not always coincide with those of the Reformed Church. Other lines of evidence point in this direction as well, including the relationship of the civil magistrates with the consistories, and of the various political assemblies and provincial estates with the provincial synods. We turn to these issues in the next section.

The Church and the Civil Magistrate

The relationship between disciplinary institutions within the church and the civil magistrate had been a constant source of tension in many Protestant territories even though the church was never a completely separate institution from the state. In France, these issues were even more difficult to resolve because the kingdom was divided religiously. Not only did consistories in Protestant-controlled areas have to deal with the same sort of conflicts as foreign Reformed churches, but in most of the kingdom they had to deal with a Catholic magistracy that was even less sympathetic to Reformed disciplinary practices. As a persecuted minority wishing to be accepted as loyal subjects of the king, the Huguenots had to be very careful to avoid practices that might be seen as a challenge or threat to the existing order of society.[11]

The only known example of a church order from France which outlines precisely the role of the magistrate in the church is the Discipline of Saint-Lô. This Discipline described the office of magistrate as having a "public charge" in the church with the ministers, schoolmasters, elders and deacons, and, in terms reminiscent of Beza's *Confession,* referred to the magistrate as one of the church's "principal members." In conformity with Beza's Confession, the Discipline stated that the magistrate's charge was to "defend the authority of the Church of God against all those who hold it in contempt and who obstinately perturb [it]," and to "provide for civil justice and the reformation of external morals." The magistrate was thus to establish laws in conformity with the Law of God, the law of charity, and the edicts and ordinances of the king. The consistory, on the other hand, was responsible for overseeing the moral life of the congregation and maintaining good order in the church. This division of labor between the consistory and the magistrate not only followed that advocated by Beza, but it also paralleled the cooperation between church and magistrate found in Calvin's Geneva: the consistory regulated moral and religious practices and beliefs and issued ecclesiastical sanctions; the magistrate handled external morals and threats to the church and had recourse to civil and corporal penalties. Unfortunately, no sources survive which indicate whether this system was actually put into effect in Saint-Lô.[12]

[11]With the creation of *chambres mi-partie* (chambers in the parlements made up of equal numbers of Protestant and Catholic judges to ensure justice to Protestant litigants and defendants) by the Peace of Monsieur (1576), the situation had the potential to be even more complex. In these cases, Protestant judges would have joined their Catholic counterparts in making it clear that the consistories were not to overstep their bounds and trespass on secular jurisdiction. At the same time, there may have been disagreements between the judges on the appropriateness of some decisions of the consistories, though I know of no studies which have addressed that issue. Protestant magistrates did in some cases work to enforce the disciplinary decisions of the churches; it is difficult to imagine a situation where Catholic magistrates would do the same.

[12]"Police et Discipline de l'Eglise de Saint-Lô," "Quelle doit estre toute l'Eglise en général," 7 (43); "Du magistrat," 1, 2 (48–49), cf. Beza, *Confession,* vol. 42 (175).

However much the other Reformed churches of France might have liked to follow this same pattern, the largely Catholic magistracy made such cooperation between civil and Reformed ecclesiastical authorities unlikely at best. For one thing, the churches could hardly count on the magistrate "to defend the authority of the Church of God." Saint-Lô was an aberration to the usual pattern of church-state relations among Protestants in the kingdom. At the same time, the basic approach taken by Saint-Lô fit in with a broader pattern that the Protestant churches in the kingdom adopted to try to define the relationship between consistories and the magistrate. The central element of this approach involved integrating the churches into the public law of the kingdom by defining individual churches as legal bodies within the context of corporate law *(droit des corps)*.[13] This definition was largely based on wishful thinking, given that the churches were often illegal within the kingdom; during the various truces in the Wars of Religion, they were barely tolerated and severely restricted by the monarchy. Nonetheless, the *droit des corps* was a useful tool for the Protestants. It provided both a guiding principle for relations with the magistrate that was part of the recognized public law of the kingdom, and a quasi-legal justification for the churches' existence.

The *droit des corps* gave corporations the right to regulate their own affairs within the bounds of the legitimate interests of the *corps*. In other words, by assuming the *droit des corps* applied to them, the churches could freely regulate internal matters of faith and discipline. On the other hand, the *droit des corps* also gave royal officers the right to oversee the corporation (in this case, the church and specifically the consistory) to make sure it did not regulate matters which were beyond its rightful interests.[14] The presence of a civil magistrate at consistory meetings could make it difficult to administer discipline in the church effectively, especially in cases where criminal or civil offenses might be involved. Yet this was a trade-off that the churches were willing to accept. The fourth national synod (Lyon, 1563) dealt with this question, noting that magistrates "commonly" attended consistory meetings. The synod decided that although "it is a pernicious thing that the officers of the king, being strangers to the faith, are introduced into consistories by absolute authority," the problem was unavoidable and thus must be endured even though the magistrate might thus obtain evidence concerning

---

[13]Michel Reulos, "L'histoire de la Discipline des Eglises Réformées françaises, élément de l'histoire de la Réforme en France et de l'histoire du droit ecclésiastique réformée," in *La Storia del Diritto nel Quadro Delle Scienze Storiche* (Florence: Olschki, 1966), 542–43. French juridical history is a complex subject, particularly that of the late sixteenth century; this discussion is based largely on Reulos's work.

[14]Reulos, "L'histoire de la Discipline," 542–43.

criminal cases. Since the magistrates' presence might make it more difficult for "poor sinners to recognize and confess their faults," alternatives were to be sought to ensure that church discipline was maintained. Some possibilities included having a few elders meet with the offender to admonish him privately, or if the magistrate was Reformed, getting him to agree that if the consistory punished offenders appropriately, confessions made to it would not be used against the offenders in a court of law.[15]

The *droit des corps* also helped frame other aspects of the response of the French churches to the issue of their relationship to royal authority, and the national synod was careful not to overstep the bounds of its "legitimate interests" by legislating on issues which were properly civil matters. This can be seen most clearly in the response of the fourth national synod (Lyon, 1563) to a set of complaints sent to the synod by the "faithful" (i.e., Protestant) Estates of Languedoc concerning the ministers and consistories of the province. The issues raised and the synod's responses illustrate the tensions that could arise between the consistory and a Reformed magistracy, as well as the national synod's careful attempt to distinguish between civil and ecclesiastical jurisdiction. The complaints of the Estates involved ministers who did not study enough or who did not obey the magistrate by refusing to go where he wished to send them,[16] and overzealous consistories that summoned people for trivial reasons or that settled lawsuits. The Estates also added several requests, notably that magistrates be admitted to consistories, "*classes*," and synods, and that they be given the right to assign pastors to churches. The synod responded that it could do nothing about the ministers that neglected study since it did not know who they were, but it would warn the provincial synod to be aware of this problem, a solution in keeping with the provincial synods' responsibility to oversee ministers. Concerning the refusal of the ministers to obey the magistrate, the synod did not address the question directly

---

[15]"C'a esté une chose pernicieuse que les officiers du Roy estans estrangers de la foy fussent introduits par puissance absolue aux consistoires." ANS, 4–Lyon–1563, "faits particuliers," 53. The responses to the complaints, though not the complaints themselves, are found in Quick, chap. 15 (36–37). The fourth national synod (Lyon, 1563) also added an article to the Discipline stating that magistrates could be members of the consistory as long as the one office did not interfere with the other, Quick, chap. 4, art. 7, and chap. 8, art. 24 (32, 34). This article remained in the Discipline throughout the early modern period. The *assemblée extraordinaire des ministres et anciens de la province de Languedoc* (Nîmes, December 1573) addressed the issue of whether ministers could be compelled to reveal to the civil magistrate things that had been confessed to them; in general, the assembly answered no, though with some caveats (Auzière, fols. 76v–77r).

[16]"Plus se plaignent lesdits magistrats qu'ils ne sont assez obeis des ministres, d'autant qu'iceux ministres ne veulent pas aller par tout ou le magistrat les veut envoyer." ANS, 4–Lyon–1563, "faits particuliers," 32.2.

beyond writing to the ministers to do everything they could to advance the Kingdom of God wherever possible without neglecting their own church. Instead, the synod wrote to the Estates and attempted to delineate carefully between the areas of competence of the magistrate and the minister:

> [T]he office of ministers is to govern their flock according to the Word of God and the *Discipline ecclésiastique,* and it is the magistrate's task to see that all estates, even the ministers, walk roundly and rightly in their callings. And in those areas where the ministers fail, they are to have them admonished according to the order of the *Discipline ecclésiastique* by *classes* and synods, not intending this in any way to include faults punishable by the laws which are the jurisdiction of the magistrate.[17]

The synod thus affirmed the rights of the ministers under the *droits des corps:* they were to perform the legitimate work of the *corps* under the supervision of the magistrate and were in all ways subject to the civil laws; at the same time, the magistrate must not trespass on the right of the *corps* to regulate its legitimate activities and to discipline its members.

Turning to the complaints about the consistories, the synod agreed to write to the churches of Languedoc admonishing them to handle "light" faults privately rather than summon people to the consistory; in fact, there is a separate article in the acts of the synod which indicated that no one was to be called before the consistory without sufficient cause.[18] At the same time, it reminded the magistrate that the consistory could take legitimate action about some types of faults that legally might be considered trivial: "even though a crime is legally 'public' when it merits exemplary punishment, nonetheless we call 'public' those [offenses] which cause scandal or set a bad example, being known to all or to many. However, in public faults this does not prevent the circumstances from being considered when proceeding to censures and corrections."[19] Thus here again, the synod maintains

---

[17][L]'office des ministres est de regler leurs troupeaux selon la parole de Dieu et Discipline ecclesiastique, et aux magistrats appartient de veiller que tous Estats et mesme les ministres cheminent rondement et droitement en leur vocation, et la ou les ministres defaudront, ils les facent admonester selon l'ordre de la Discipline ecclesiastique par les classes et synodes, n'entendans toutefois en ce comprendre les fautes punissables par les loix desquelles la connaissance appartient au magistrat. ANS, 4–Lyon–1563, "faits particuliers," 32.2.

[18]ANS, 4–Lyon–1563, "faits généraux," 6.

[19][C]ombien que par la disposition de droit un crime sera apellé public qui merite punition exemplaire, toutefois nous apellons public ce qui engendre scandale ou mauvais exemple pour estre parvenu a la notice de tous ou plusieurs. Cependant, cela n'empesche qu'es fautes publiques ne soient

the right of the consistory to pursue its legitimate interests by "censuring" and "correcting" faults that have become public knowledge even if before the law they are insignificant.

The national synod also recognized that the consistory must not overstep its bounds, particularly by deciding lawsuits. The synod indicated that it would instruct the churches not to get involved in deciding such disputes unless a public scandal was involved, in which case the consistory should act on the scandal rather than on the suit itself; the consistory was permitted to encourage the parties in the suit to settle their differences outside of court, however.[20] It is not clear if this article deals with involvement in lawsuits per se: it may be concerned primarily with arbitration, a common substitute for litigation in the Midi, traditionally performed by *seigneurs,* curates, or notaries. The same national synod that addressed the concerns of the Estates of Languedoc also added an article to the Discipline to prohibit *les corps des consistoires* from selecting or acting as arbitrators, though its members could do so as private individuals.[21] This provision seems to have been intended to prevent the consistory from becoming involved in matters which were not strictly part of the "legitimate interests" of the *corps,* but which properly belonged to the civil courts; it also addressed the issue raised by the Estates of the consistories' usurpation of the rights of the magistrate. Whatever the intention, this may well have been the single most-ignored article in the Discipline. Existing records from Poitou, Guyenne, and Languedoc indicate that consistories did become involved in civil suits, in some cases even imposing such sanctions as fines and excommunication on those who would not come to terms without recourse to the civil courts. In fact, such arbitration seems to have been highly successful; Garrisson notes that arbitration was rarely refused and was considerably less expensive and troublesome than going to court. This explains the popularity of arbitration over litigation, at least in the Midi. In this cultural system, the consistory could and did quite naturally

---

considerees les circonstances pour proceder es censures et corrections. ANS, 4–Lyon–1563, "faits particuliers," 32.3.

[20]ANS, 4–Lyon–1563, "faits particuliers," 32.4.

[21]Quick, 4–Lyon–1563, chap. 11, art. 10 (35), cf. 4–Lyon–1563, 16. Although the acts indicate that this was to be added to the Discipline, it is missing in both manuscripts of DE 1563; it does appear in DE 1565, "Des consistoires," 13. According to Quick, chap. 3, art. 10 (32), the fourth national synod particularly prohibited arbitration in disputes over worldly goods, Quick, 6–Vertueil–1567, chap. 10, art. 10 (85), also indicates that the sixth national synod (Vertueil, 1567) decided that the consistory could mediate in disputes between husband and wife to try to reconcile marital conflicts. Neither of these passages from Quick are supported by the currently available manuscripts, however.

take on the function of mediator within the Protestant community, whatever the Discipline had to say about the practice.[22]

The national synods continued to try to prevent consistories from even appearing to usurp the functions of the civil magistrate, though at the same time they were anxious to preserve the legitimate prerogatives of consistories. For example, the national synods permitted consistories to administer oaths before accepting testimony since this did not seem to "abrogate" the prerogatives of the magistrate. When a crime was committed, the magistrate was to investigate it before the consistory took any action, unless delay was impossible. In general, the church was to cooperate with the magistrate, even to the point of informing the civil authorities of an impenitent "brother" guilty of a serious crime; ministers who had crimes confessed to them were to be guided by their conscience to determine whether to report them.[23]

Concerning the requests of the Estates, the synod and ministers agreed without question that the magistrate would be invited to attend meetings of "consistories, classes, and synods." The national synod thought that even Catholic magistrates could not legitimately be prevented from attending consistory meetings; synods were a considerably more complex issue, however. Properly speaking, the only national corps in France was the Roman Catholic clergy, and the French Reformed churches never claimed to be another such corps. All other corps were local, and thus it was the individual church, not the synod, which had rights under the droit des corps. This dovetailed nicely with the French Protestant emphasis on the local church as the foundation of their ecclesiastical system, but it did pose some problems for justifying the collective government of the churches.[24] To make matters worse, synods were illegal according to the monarchy, the Edict of January, and most of the edicts of pacification. Of course, the Eglises Réformées held synods anyway. The churches were nonetheless sensitive to the illegality of their actions, and so the fourth national synod (Lyon, 1563)

---

[22]See the list of cases settled by arbitration compiled by Janine Garrisson, *Protestants du Midi*, 107–8. Garrisson notes that consistories performed this function in the Palatinate as well (ibid., 107).

[23]Quick, 7–La Rochelle–1571, chap. 12, art. 2, par. 1 (101); 2–Poitiers–1561, chap. 6, art. 16 (18–19), cf. ANS, 2–Poitiers–1561, "faits particuliers," 19; Quick, 4–Lyon–1563, chap. 16, art. 13 (38), cf. ANS, 4–Lyon–1563, "faits particuliers," 32.

[24]Morély's synods, which had no authority but were simply consultative bodies, could be justified much more easily under the *droit des corps* than the Discipline's synods. Given Morély's background, it is possible that this aspect of French law contributed to his thinking at this point, particularly since it could be integrated so well into the other more readily identified influences on his thought.

decided to petition the monarchy to permit the Protestants to hold synods, though they agreed not to present this petition without the consent of the principal Protestant nobles at court.[25] Under these circumstances, the request from the Estates of Languedoc must have seemed reasonable: not only was it a logical parallel to the magistrate's position vis-à-vis the consistory, but it was politically expedient and provided a certain amount of cover to the otherwise illegal synodical meetings.

The political leaders of Languedoc did become involved in meetings of the *classes* and synods of the province. For example, the *classe* meeting at Nîmes on 29 August 1570, assembled "in the presence of M. de Saulzet, Counselor Magistrate at the Presidial Seat of that city"; similarly, the provincial synod of Sauve, 4 October 1570, met "on the authority of Monseigneur de Damville, Marshal of France and Governor and Lieutenant General for the king in the country of Languedoc, with M. de Lafarelle, Royal Judge of Vigan, in attendance," and the provincial synod of Nîmes, 7 June 1571, met "in the presence of M. de Chate, Criminal Judge, M. de Saulzet Roques, Seigneur de Clauzonne, Counselor of the King."[26] Not surprisingly, after the St. Bartholomew's Day massacres, the magisterial presence at synods dropped off considerably.

The final issue raised by the Estates of Languedoc in 1563 was their desire to place ministers as they saw fit. The synod replied that though magistrates had rights in all civil matters, they did not have parallel rights within the churches; ministerial placement was thus for ministers and synods to decide, not the magistrate.[27] In matters where both civil and ecclesiastical issues were involved, such as the number of ministers in a particular church, the two sides were to decide jointly.[28] Placement of ministers was clearly an issue within the legitimate interests of the churches, and since the churches had mutually decided to delegate

[25]ANS, 4–Lyon–1563, "faits particuliers," 15.

[26]"[À] la presence de M. de Saulzet conseiller magistrat au siege presidial de ladite ville"; "de l'autorite de Monsigneur de Dampville Mareschal de France et gouverneur et lieutenant general pour le Roy au pais de Languedoc. Y assistant M. de Lafarelle juge royal du Vigan"; "à la presence de M. de Chate juge criminel, M. de Saulzet Roques Seigneur de Clauzonne conseiller du Roy." Auzière, fols. 15, 23, 42r.

[27]Since the term "minister" generally means "minister of the Word" or "pastor," elders and deacons seem to have been omitted here. This may reflect a growing clericalization of the national synod.

[28]In Languedoc, payment of ministers was an area of mutual interest: at the provincial synod of Nîmes (June 1588), a church whose minister had been unpaid for a time and who had died was threatened with the loss of its pastor and with civil action if it did not pay his heirs what they owed him; see Auzière, fol. 199r; a similar case appears in the provincial synod of Nîmes, May 1590; Auzière, fol. 219r.

that matter to the provincial synods, it was to remain there without magisterial interference.[29]

In the national synod's response to the Estates of Languedoc, the underlying principle of the *droit des corps*—that legal bodies have the right to regulate their internal affairs under the watchful eye of the magistrate, who was to see that they did not overstep the bounds of their "legitimate interests"—provided guidelines for relations between the church and the magistracy, though with a certain amount of difficulty when it came to synods. The national synods were careful not to overstep these bounds, with surprising results at times. For example, Protestant nobles could not prohibit Roman Catholic Mass in their own castles if it was established by "public authority." Further, births were to be registered with Roman Catholic priests and tithes paid to them, since the king commanded these things and they did not violate any law of God.[30]

This does not mean that everything worked smoothly: the acts of the provincial synods of Bas Languedoc record a number of instances in which the magistrate interfered with the work of the consistory. These mostly occurred in cases of mixed jurisdiction, where both church and magistrate had a legitimate interest. Marital law in particular was a "mixed matter" in which the civil authorities had a legitimate concern: since Protestants argued that marriage was not a sacrament, the law of the land generally determined marital practice, even overruling biblical law in the case of levirate marriages.[31] The church also had a legitimate interest in regulating marriage as part of its mandate to oversee morality, and a significant percentage of the Discipline and of the "faits particuliers" in the acts of the national synods was devoted to marital questions.[32] The general trend was for the

---

[29]Quick, chap. 15 (36-37), cf. ANS, 4-Lyon-1563, "faits particuliers," 32.6, 7. In some cases, it was politic to allow the authorities to have their way; for example, when Louis of Nassau requested that M. de Chambrun be sent to him as a minister, the church at Calvisson to which de Chambrun had been assigned by the local colloquy objected. After some discussion, including a proposal that the matter be sent to the national synod, the provincial synod overrode the objections and granted Louis's request; see provincial synod of Nîmes, June 1571; Auzière, fol. 60r. Similarly, M. Baldran was loaned to M. de Chastillon for three months, after which he was to return to his church; see provincial synod of Nîmes, May 1590, Auzière, fols. 226v–227r.

[30]ANS, 6–Vertueil–1567, "Resolution d'aucuns articles de la Religion par M. Calvin," 7, cf. Quick, chap. 9, art. 7 (78); ANS, 1–Paris–1559, "faits particuliers," 10, 18, cf. Quick, chap. 3, art. 8, 16 (8, 9).

[31]Reulos, "L'histoire de la Discipline," 543; ANS, 4–Lyon–1563, "faits particuliers," 50; cf. Quick, chap. 4, art. 16 (40). For a thorough discussion of French Protestant views of marriage, see Pierre Bels, *Le Mariage des Protestants Français jusqu'en 1685; Fondements doctrinaux et pratique juridique*, Librairie Générale de Droit et de Jurisprudence (Paris: R. Pichon et R. Durand-Auzias, 1968).

[32]See Roussel, "Discipline," 183–84. In a case of dual competency over marital issues, the provincial synod of Nîmes, June 1571, dealt with a man who had proposed marriage to a woman before

churches and the magistrate to cooperate. In marital issues, magistrates played an important role in a range of areas, particularly in deciding the validity of marriage proposals and in investigating charges of adultery; and were also encouraged to be involved in defending the sanctity of marriage in other ways as well. Marital issues were not the only area of cooperation. The synods often called on the local authorities to enforce civil law in conjunction with action by the churches. In some cases, these involved regulation of businesses. For example, the synod of Nîmes (February 1572) asked the magistrate to take action with the consistories to monitor activities in taverns in conformity with the ordinances of the king and his lieutenants.[33]

The relationship between secular authorities and the French Reformed churches goes beyond the local magistrates, to the connections between higher-level political authorities and various church bodies. In general in the sixteenth century, confessional standards were as much a political as a religious issue; although moral reform was a major concern across the religious spectrum and Calvinism had made community discipline more central to piety and religious practice than nearly any other magisterial church, the Huguenot political leadership was almost as concerned as the churches with enforcing Calvinist moral and doctrinal standards. For example, *L'assemblee de la noblesse et commun estat du pais de Dauphine, teneue a Valence le xxviie jour de janvier 1563 a Noel*[34] passed an extensive set of regulations to govern behavior and support the activities of the consistories: all persons were to attend church services whatever their station in society; a number of activities were prohibited on Sunday; all infants were to be baptized publicly; gambling was prohibited, as were oaths and profanity. Violations of these regulations were punishable by both the civil magistrate and ecclesiastical censures. Magistrates were to come before the consistory to sign the Confession of Faith. Sedition was banned(!) and the civil magistrate was given authority to punish Libertines and Anabaptists (who were both defined as seditious), along with *coureurs* (itinerant preachers without a "legitimate calling").[35]

---

the consistory; some opposition arose, so he took the case to court. Before the matter was decided, however, he married the woman. The synod publicly suspended him from the Lord's Supper because he had caused great scandal by cohabiting with the woman before the case had been resolved. Auzière, fol. 50.

[33] Auzière, fol. 287r–v.

[34] *Documents protestants inédits*, 46–71.

[35] The provincial synod of Languedoc held at Nîmes in May 1590 also recognized the magistrate's competence in the latter areas: it called for action "even by the magistrate" against a self-appointed minister and rebel against the Discipline; see Auzière, fol. 223. The synod was more hesitant to do so

All persons were subject to the authority of the consistory, which also had the authority to approve representatives to both ecclesiastical and civil assemblies. The consistory also had a hand in trying civil offenses, notably those involving sexual immorality: those found guilty of immorality were to be exiled unless they confessed their sin and repented publicly. The assembly also regulated poor relief and ministerial salaries and stated that with the advice of the consistories, future political assemblies could transfer surplus ministers to other areas.[36] The Estates of Dauphiné called for a high degree of cooperation between the magistrate and the consistory in enforcing Calvinist piety and practice in the communities.

In addition to working with the consistories, secular leaders also cooperated with the operations of the provincial synods. For example, M. de Lafarelle, a royal judge attending the provincial synod of Sauve, October 1570, threatened civil penalties against a suspended pastor if he did not obey the synod. The judge also intervened in an examination of the writings of Decolans, a pastor accused of heresy and schism. The judge asked for copies of all of the books Decolans had written to forward to the governor; the provincial synod, which had remanded the case to the national synod, agreed to send the books to the governor as long as it was understood that the synod did not approve of them. The next year, after Decolans had been condemned, a criminal judge attending the provincial synod of Nîmes ordered him not to write, say, or preach anything that had been censured on pain of his life. Evidently, this did not dissuade him: he continued acting as a pastor even though suspended. The provincial synod of Mauguir (February 1572) excommunicated him as a rebel and a schismatic, and informed the magistrates in Nîmes of this.[37]

Liaison with the Royal Court
Along with their efforts to establish working relationships with local (Protestant) magistrates and provincial estates, the French Reformed churches also sent deputies to represent their interests at the royal courts of France and Navarre. Selecting, sending, and paying these representatives was usually the responsibility of the

---

in the case of a number of presumed Anabaptists, however: it censured not only the families involved, but also the pastors and churches for not supporting the censures sufficiently and for deferring to the magistrate in pursuing the case, fol. 225r–v.

[36] *Documents protestants inédits*, 47–53.

[37] Auzière, fols. 40v, 33v–34r, 57v, 66v. Decolans continued to be active even after this, however: the provincial synod meeting in Montpellier in May 1581 requested the magistrate to prevent "Coulans" from troubling the church, and the following year the synod of Uzès had to deal with infants baptized by Decolans and alerted the magistrate of his activities; see Auzière, fols. 159r, 164r–v.

provincial synods; although the national synods established the legislative frame-work for these liaisons, they did not initially send representatives themselves.[38] The process began with the second national synod (Poitiers, 1561), which called on each province to send a "solicitor" to the royal court; these deputies were to work together to look after the interests of the churches. The deputies were also to look for an opportunity to present the Confession to the king with the assistance of the Protestant nobles at court to show the king they were not dangerous sectar-ians.[39] The consistory records of the church of Le Mans shed some additional light on these deputies. This consistory sent M. Le Barbier, sieur de Francourt, an elder of the church, to the court "for the affairs of our church." As the Le Mans church understood it, the national synod of Poitiers had authorized them to do this in the event that a general deputy for the provinces of Anjou, Touraine, and Maine could not be sent.[40] Other churches also became directly involved with the court. For example, in the wake of the Edict of January (1562), the church at Paris sent a memorandum entitled *Avis et conseil des ministres et députés des Églises de France étant en Cour,* which advised that the provisions of the edict—including particu-larly the prohibition of armed Protestant meetings—be kept scrupulously.[41]

The description of the activities of the deputies passed by the 1561 synod was modified slightly at the next national synod (Orléans, 1562), which added that there was to be no primacy among these deputies and that they were not to depart from their provincial synod's instructions in important matters without prior approval or, in cases of emergency, without consulting the nearest church; further, the deputies were to consult together concerning the best means to present the Confession to the king.[42] The fourth national synod (Lyon, 1563) further stipulated

---

[38]This was particularly the case for deputies at the royal court or liaisons with provincial gover-nors; on a local level, the contact between the church and the magistrate was, not surprisingly, the responsibility of the individual consistory.

[39]Quick, chap. 6, art. 25, 29 (19–20), cf. ANS, 2–Poitiers–1561, "faits particuliers," 30, 35.

[40]"[P]our les affaires de nostre eglise," 23 August 1561; "nous avons depputé monsieur de Fran-court pour aller à la cour solliciter les affairs de nostre église, suyvant ce qui fut décidé au synode de Poictiers au cas que on ne peust en depputer un général pour les troys provinces d'Anjou, Touraine et le Maine." 4 September 1561, Le Mans, 21, 24. In some cases, these deputies were sent promptly. For example, the acts of the provincial synods of Dauphiné and Lyonnois include several early references to provincial deputies to the court, e.g., provincial synod of Dye (1561), *Documents protestants inédits,* 23; provincial synod at Château de Peraut (1561), ibid., 27.

[41]*Histoire ecclésiastique,* 1:369–71.

[42]ANS, 3–Orléans–1562, "faits généraux," 9; the article was omitted in Quick, though its basic provisions are included in his version of the acts of the second national synod (Poitiers, 1561), chap. 6, art. 29 (20). Evidently, the deputies continued to act without prior approval from the provincial syn-ods, however: the sixth national synod (Vertueil, 1567) was compelled to call on the deputies at court

that the deputies' activities at court were to be restricted to business approved by the provincial synod; any new business was to be sent to the province for approval, though they were still encouraged to act together with the other "ministers" at the court.[43]

In addition to their general charge of looking after the interests of the churches of their province, certain specific tasks were occasionally assigned to deputies at court by the national synod. For example, after the second national synod (Poitiers, 1561) called on the churches of Paris, Orléans, and Rouen to protest by all available means that the Council of Trent was null and void.[44] The third national synod (Orléans, 1562) asked these deputies to clarify whether under the Edict of January, the laws of consanguinity and affinity as applied to the Protestant community included spiritual kinship.[45] The fourth national synod (Lyon, 1563) asked Beza to write a formal protest of the Council of Trent in Latin and French and to send it to the royal court via the provincial deputies.[46] Although there are few subsequent references to these provincial deputies in the acts of the national synods, their activities continued through the rest of the century.[47]

---

to follow this canon more scrupulously; see Quick, chap. 5, art. 10 (73), cf. ANS, 6–Vertueil–1567, "faits particuliers/avertissements," 32.

[43]Quick, chap. 17, art. 6 (45), cf. ANS, 4–Lyon–1563, "faits particuliers," 17.

[44]ANS, 2–Poitiers–1561, "faits particuliers," 31; note that this article immediately follows one calling on the provinces to send deputies to court.

[45]Quick, chap. 2, art. 28 (24), cf. ANS, 3–Orléans–1562, "faits généraux," 11.

[46]Quick, chap. 17, art. 2 (45), cf. ANS, 4–Lyon–1563, "faits particuliers," 14.

[47]For example, the provincial synod of Saint-Jean-de-Gardonenquel (1592) made a roll of churches needing ministers and sent it to their deputies at court; see Auzière, fols. 255v–56r; Henri IV was king at this point and still a Protestant. An "extraordinary" provincial synod of Nîmes, meeting on 15 July 1593, just ten days before Henri IV's abjuration, answered a request from Henri that the synod send deputies to an assembly he was calling; Auzière, fol. 274r–v; the following year, the king sent a letter via the deputies to the provincial synod at Nîmes expressing his goodwill to the churches, after which the synod instructed the deputies to ask the king for the money he had promised for the support of the ministers; Auzière, fols. 283v–84r, 286v. Still later, the thirteenth national synod (Montauban, 1594) censured a colloquy, consistory, and minister for failing to pay the expenses of their deputy at court; Quick, chap. 6, art. 13 (171); that same year a provincial synod at Nîmes audited the accounts of theirs, Auzière, fol. 286v. There is also a record from the provincial synod of Anduze (1576) that the colloquies of the province were assessed for their share of the expenses for the deputy (fol. 103v). The provincial synods established liaisons with the *Assemblées politiques* in the years following the St. Bartholomew's Day massacres; given the conditions faced by the church at that time, the provincial level was the most effective place to establish such links. Even after the national synods resumed, the provincial synods still oversaw the relations between the churches and the Huguenots' political arm, though not necessarily by sending deputies themselves. For example, the provincial

In addition to the the provincial deputies, the national synod itself began to forge closer links directly with the royal courts, particularly that of Navarre. As early as 1561, the national synod had presented a *memoire* to the Estates of France, claiming that only the Estates General had the right to appoint royal councilors when the king was a minor, and that the councilors appointed by the regents were illegal.[48] The fourth national synod (1563) also acted on behalf of the churches as a whole, petitioning the king for permission to hold synods.[49] With the seventh national synod (La Rochelle, 1571), which was attended by many leading Protestant nobles, the ties between the national synod and the royal court of Navarre and the Protestant Princes of France were further strengthened. The eighth national synod (Nîmes, 1572) assigned Nicolas des Gallars to be the churches' liaison with the court at Navarre for another year, indicating that he had already been performing that function since at least the synod of la Rochelle (1571).[50] Even in the aftermath of St. Bartholomew's Day, liaisons with the royal courts continued to develop. At the next national synod (St. Foy, 1578), Henri de la Tour represented the king of Navarre, reprising on a smaller scale the royal participation in the synod of La Rochelle.[51] A further change occurred when the general assembly meeting at Saint-Jean-d'Angély named M. de Chassincourt, a member of Henri of Navarre's royal council, as the churches' deputy at court, an appointment confirmed by the twelfth national synod (Vitré, 1583).[52] This was the first time there was an agent for the *Eglises Réformées* as a whole at the royal court of France.[53]

---

synod of Languedoc (St. Ambrueys, 1579) called on each colloquy in the province to send one or two representatives to the province's *assemblée politique* (Auzière, fol. 142).

[48]Cf. Quick, 2–Poitiers–1561, chap. 2 (12–13). The Estates General would meet in August 1562, concurrently with an Assembly of the (Catholic) Clergy as part of the plans of Catherine de Médicis to try to maintain the power of the royal family against the Guises; see Léonard, *Histoire générale* 2:107–8. Ultimately, this meeting would not resolve the religious tensions in the society, as evidenced by the beginning of the Wars of Religion the next year.

[49]Quick, chap. 17, art. 3 (45), cf. ANS, 4–Lyon–1563, "faits particuliers," 15.

[50]Quick, chap. 7, art. 9 (112); this same article sent greetings to Geneva and requested the Genevan church's continued support of the churches of France, especially those of Béarn, indicating that the Béarnese churches were by this time considered in some sense part of the *Eglises Réformées* of France, even though they were not included in the division of provinces adopted at Nîmes.

[51]Quick, chap. 1, art. 2 (116).

[52]Quick, chap. 4, art. 29 (153). De Chassincourt's status as a member of the royal council of Navarre may have provided him with a degree of protection in the French royal court that other Protestants lacked.

[53]The synod also assigned de Chassincourt a specific responsibility: the king had agreed to dispense with the degrees of consanguinity and affinity demanded by the Catholic Church in marriages

The churches' representation at court thus changed over time. Early on, before the provinces were organized sufficiently to act themselves, individual churches such as Le Mans joined the more organized provincial synods in sending deputies to the court; these deputies from individual churches were superseded by provincial deputies; later still, deputies from the national synod joined the provincial deputies without replacing them. This is another indication of the growing role of the national synods, though again the provincial synods continued to maintain a large degree of autonomy in their activities at court.

International Relations

Along with its other responsibilities, the national synod also coordinated relations between the *Eglises Réformées* and foreign churches,[54] particularly after the pivotal seventh national synod of La Rochelle, 1571. Initially, involvement with foreign churches was largely limited to questions of heresy. The 1571 synod issued a warning to all the faithful of France to guard against anti-Trinitarian ideas from Poland and Transylvania;[55] it also condemned the writings of the well-known anti-Trinitarian Antonio del Corro and requested that the bishops of England suppress his work, since it had become somewhat in vogue among them.[56] The English bishops replied to the national synod almost immediately, apparently requesting clarification on the concerns expressed by the French churches about Corro's writings. As a result, the next national synod (Nîmes, 1572) asked Beza— who was attending the synod to help deal with Morély and company—to review

---

between Protestants; the national synod instructed those wishing to marry within those degrees of relationship to apply to the king via de Chassincourt, thereby avoiding the need for a papal dispensation; Quick, chap. 4, art. 20 (152).

[54]Geneva and Navarre are deliberately excluded from the list of "foreign" churches. Though not part of the kingdom of France, both of these regions maintained very free and open relations with the *Eglises Réformées*. In the case of Geneva, local churches, provincial synods, and national synods all contacted Calvin, Beza, the consistory, or the Company of Pastors directly with questions, requests for pastors, letters of attestation for students at the Academy, and a multitude of issues. Likewise, Henri of Navarre and other Béarnese leaders contacted both the national and provincial synods regularly to coordinate policy, to arrange for exchange of ministers, and generally to keep relations between Navarre and the French Reformed churches on an even keel.

[55]Quick, chap. 2, art. 3 (91).

[56]Quick, chap. 2, art. 4 (91). Aymon and Quick have "Cozain"; that the synod was actually referring to Corro is clear from a letter he wrote to Beza in 1568; see *Correspondance de Théodore de Bèze* 9 (1568), recueillie par Hippolyte Aubert, publiée par Henri Meylan, Alain Dufour, Claire Chimelli, et Béatrice Nicollier (Geneva: Droz, 1978), letter 635, pp. 156–61. The reference to Cozain may have come from mistakenly identifying Corro with Jean Cousin, one of Corro's leading opponents in London. A collection of documents related to this case can be found in Geneva, BPU MS fr. 407, fols. 27–137.

Corro's books and to advise the French churches on how to answer the letter from the English bishops; it also asked Nicolas des Gallars to prepare a response to Corro's book for the English church.[57] The French churches did not pursue the Corro case beyond this national synod; the Saint Bartholomew's Day massacres later that year gave French Protestants more immediate concerns than the influence of heterodox ideas in England.

While continuing to press the English bishops concerning Corro, the eighth national synod also had to try to calm a controversy with Zurich caused by the seventh national synod's condemnation of a group of Italian radicals in Lyon.[58] Among other things, this group denied Christ's physical presence in the Eucharist in terms that went well beyond Zwingli's; the synod of La Rochelle roundly condemned their view and specifically their rejection of the term "substance" in connection with Christ's presence in the Eucharist. This condemnation, together with the warning against the anti-Trinitarians mentioned in the previous paragraph and a strong statement of support for the Discipline designed to counter Morély, Ramus, and their associates, was circulated as an "Extract" from the acts of the synod of La Rochelle which is included with virtually all of the surviving copies of the Discipline of that synod.[59] Unfortunately for the national synod, its condemnation of those rejecting the term "substance" was written a bit too broadly; Ramus gleefully sent it off to Zurich together with an unflattering report about other decisions of the synod relating to the role of ecclesiastical officers and their relationship to the civil government. An alarmed Bullinger sent a very pointed letter to Beza complaining about these decisions; Beza immediately sent a very conciliatory response, explaining in detail the specific targets of the synod's actions and portraying Morély's reform program in the most negative terms possible.[60] This letter seems to have had the desired effect on Bullinger, but the national synod was still obliged to make clear that its condemnation of the Eucharistic views of the Italians of Lyon was not intended as an attack on Zurich and that the French churches did not in any way wish to condemn Bullinger's position. Accordingly, the eighth national synod (Nîmes, 1572) reaffirmed their use of the term "substance," while stating that this was "without any prejudice to foreign

---

[57]Quick, 7–Nîmes–1572, chap. 7, art. 2, 13 (111, 113).

[58]For a discussion of this group's views, see Henri Meylan, "Bèze et les Italiens de Lyon (1566)," *Bibliothèque d'Humanisme et Renaissance* 14 (1952): 235–49, esp. 244.

[59]Even after both the Discipline and the "Extract" were modified by the eighth national synod, they continued to be included together in their new forms in the surviving manuscripts.

[60]For a more complete summary of this entire affair focused particularly on the controversy surrounding the party of Morély, see Kingdon, *Geneva and the Consolidation,* 98–99; 102–5; the synod of Nîmes is discussed on 105–11; the text of Beza's letter to Bullinger is reproduced in app. 2, pp. 209–15.

churches who do not use the term"; they also softened the nearly Lutheran-sounding language in the original article to make it more acceptable to Zurich.[61] This left them in the curious position of condemning the rejection of the term "substance" within the kingdom without condemning it in foreign churches: should a minister move to France from an area such as the Pays de Vaud which held to a Zwinglian interpretation of the Supper, this article would condemn his views; should he then return home, his views would again become acceptable. Such was the nature of ecclesiastical politics among sixteenth-century Protestants.

The French Reformed churches developed their institutional structure in a complex and changing network of relationships with their local, regional, national, and international communities. French Protestantism was originally a highly local phenomenon. Even with the adoption of the Discipline, the French Reformed churches continued to support a significant degree of autonomy for the local church, in part out of their need to bring as many Protestant congregations into ecclesiastical fellowship with them as possible. One of their earliest challenges involved recruiting the many noble churches into their confessional and disciplinary fold; confessional agreement was fairly easy to achieve, but there were ongoing problems with nobles who refused to acknowledge the authority of the church, as well as noble churches which never integrated themselves into the colloquial and synodical structures of the Discipline. Given the surprising lack of references to noble house churches in the surviving records of the provincial and national synods, the extent that the Protestant nobility was involved with the "official" French Reformed churches needs to be reexamined carefully. With the de facto leadership of French Protestantism shifting in the early 1560s from the pastors to the nobility, the synodical church structures established by the more "clerical" national synods may have seemed largely irrelevant: the most important elements of policy were set elsewhere. To be sure, the churches did have their place in establishing doctrine and carrying out church discipline, two concerns which the Calvinist nobility shared with the church leaders. At the same time, in keeping with French Protestant traditions, discipline could generally be handled on a local level and, in the case of the noble churches, apparently without consistories. Synodical institutions thus had limited utility, a fact which may explain the lack of involvement of the noble churches in the collective government of the *Eglises Réformées.*

---

[61]Quick, chap. 2, art. 2 (104); cf. Kingdon, *Geneva and the Consolidation*, 110.

The emphasis on church discipline raised an issue familiar to Reformed churches elsewhere in Europe: the division of responsibilities between the consistory and the civil magistrate. The French churches attempted to deal with this issue by defining themselves in terms of the *droit des corps* of the kingdom, which gave corporations the right to regulate matters within their legitimate interests under magisterial supervision. Although this gave magistrates (even Catholic magistrates) the right to attend consistory meetings, identifying the churches as legal *corps* allowed the Huguenots to use established legal principles to define the authority of the consistory: it could regulate the "legitimate interests" of the churches, specifically including matters of faith and practice, as well as justify the churches' existence in terms of the kingdom's legal system. The national synod in particular was quite careful to protect the churches' prerogatives from encroachments by the magistrate. They were willing to be flexible on peripheral issues, but they would not surrender the legitimate interests of the churches to the magistrate under any circumstances. Like other magisterials, Catholic and Protestant alike, the Huguenots believed that both the churches and the (Protestant) magistrates should work together to promote a godly society, a principle endorsed by both political assemblies and synods. In general it seems to have worked reasonably well, judging from the surviving synodical records. There were tensions between church and magistrate to be sure, but they were relatively few compared to the frequent references to the magistrate and the consistories working together, particularly given the huge number of discipline cases which must have been handled by consistories in the decades for which we have synodical records. The fact that more were not challenged by the magistrate suggests that a successful modus vivendi was reached, at least in areas where both church and state were in the hands of Protestants. Later, with the coming of the Wars of Religion and the politicization of French Protestantism, the Huguenots created higher-level political assemblies and provincial Estates. Like the Protestant magistrates, these assemblies generally worked with the churches in enforcing discipline and promoting the growth of Protestantism in the kingdom.

The French Reformed churches also attempted to establish links with the French and Navarrese royal courts. Relations with the court of Navarre began quite early, and involved letters and representatives from all levels of the French Reformed churches' ecclesiastical government. In France, on the other hand, conditions in the royal court made such extensive contact and cooperation impossible. Nonetheless, soon after the founding of the *Eglises Réformées,* local churches had begun sending "solicitors" to the French court to represent their interests, as did the provincial synods as they became better organized. These provincial deputies eventually emerged as the primary representatives of the churches in the French royal court, though the high nobility and Princes of the Blood were the primary spokesmen for French Protestantism generally. The work of provincial deputies seems to have centered primarily on asking the king to enforce the edicts of pacification and to proclaim their loyalty to him. Given the general level of hostility of the monarchy toward Protestantism, anything beyond that would have been extremely difficult if not hazardous to attempt, unless the deputy was sufficiently highly connected to provide a shield against persecution. Toward the end of the century, the national synod began to send its own deputies to the French court, selecting for this task a member of the court of Navarre who by virtue of his position had this kind of protection against attack. That the national synod joined the provincial synods in sending a deputy to court suggests that the national synod was taking on more and more responsibility within the French Reformed Churches and that ecclesiastical government was growing more centralized.

The French Reformed churches worked not only to establish relations with political powers within the kingdom, but to build ties with foreign churches as well. The most important of these foreign churches was that of Geneva, which provided pastors, printed literature, and theological and, to some extent, political direction for the French churches. Aside from Geneva, however, the earliest official synodical actions dealing with foreign churches involved issues of doctrine: warnings about heresy, and fine-tuning doctrinal statements so as not to offend important political and military supporters within the international Protestant community.

Chapter 8
French Reformed Polity:
Local and National Influences

The institutional development of the French Reformed churches was far more complex than has generally been recognized. The Huguenot church was not simply a marriage of convenience between Calvinist theology and the ambitions of the nobility; rather, it developed out of a far wider range of influences both within France and internationally. Though working from an ecclesiastical base established by Bucer and Calvin, the French Reformed churches developed a number of important structural innovations of their own in response to the unique circumstances they faced; these innovations then spread to other national Reformed churches and so became an integral element of the Calvinist tradition in Western Europe.

The French Reformed Church order drew its inspiration from a number of sources. The Huguenots first looked to Martin Bucer for ecclesiastical advice, and later turned to his student John Calvin. Calvin's influence was particularly profound: Anthoine de la Roche Chandieu, the architect of the Discipline, was a protégé of Calvin, and the transformation of the church at Le Mans by Pierre Merlin, another of Calvin's students, speaks volumes for the impact of Genevan-trained missionary pastors. But the Discipline was influenced by churches in other areas beyond Strasbourg or Geneva. The most important of these was the Pays de Vaud, particularly as mediated by Pierre Viret. The Vaudois churches contributed the colloquy and, temporarily, the *classe* to the French church order, and may have pointed toward a solution to the problem of primacy in the office of synodical moderator. Along with Strasbourg, Geneva, and Berne, local Catholic traditions may have contributed to Huguenot church structure. For example, the French Reformed diaconate seems to have been influenced by Roman Catholicism, though whether directly or through a Protestant area such as Strasbourg or Zurich is unclear.

These external influences on French Protestantism are only a part of the story. The French Reformed churches adapted the ideas, principles, and models they found in other areas to suit the peculiar circumstances facing them in France. Their most important and influential innovation was the development of "presbyterian" or synodical polity. Although Calvin, Bucer, and other Protestant leaders advocated calling synods regularly to deal with doctrine and discipline (especially clerical discipline), these leaders all envisioned these synods operating within a modified episcopal context, that is, with a single pastor overseeing the meetings, acting as a spokesman for the synod, perhaps conducting visitations, and the like. Alternately, oversight responsibility might devolve to a church rather than a pastor, as it did within the canton of Berne. Further, Reformed theologians envisioned church and state working together cooperatively to establish their version of a Christian society. The state would see to external behavior and would support the church in its efforts to regulate doctrine and morality. Within France, this approach to church government was clearly impossible. Not only was Protestantism a minority religion subject to persecution rather than support by the state, but the organic growth of small cells of Protestants into churches meant that each community developed largely independently of the others. Under these circumstances, no individual pastor or local church could claim authority to act as an "overseer" of a synod. At the same time, institutional unity was increasingly becoming a desideratum: the Huguenots wanted to develop a common statement of faith and system of polity to unify the Protestants of the kingdom (particularly at a time when the nobility was increasingly converting to Protestantism) and to respond more effectively to a hostile monarchy bent on the extermination of Protestantism in the kingdom. The churches thus established a form of synodical polity to handle matters that concerned more than one church, but without permitting any church or pastor to have authority over other churches. Each synod elected a moderator to see that meetings ran smoothly, to answer correspondence, and generally to handle administrative matters for the synod; once the synod was over, the moderator's term expired. Similarly, each synod selected a new location for the next to prevent any hierarchy from emerging among the churches. This system was based on such fundamental principles of Protestant church government as the equality of pastors and churches and the need for collegiality in setting church policy, but adapted these principles to a context in which lack of magisterial support meant both great diversity within the churches and the absence of coercive and legal authority to enforce synodical decisions. In the process, the system ironically ended up embodying the principles of equality and collegiality far more consistently than other churches which had a freer hand in designing their church government.

The synodical system evolved considerably over the first few synods. Initially, only the provincial synod met regularly, though more local groups and the national synod were to meet on an ad hoc basis. The national synod quickly became a regular element of the church government, and in a little more than a decade the *colloque*—borrowed from the Pays de Vaud—followed suit. These units paralleled the basic levels of secular government: local/church, *bailliage*/colloquy, province/provincial synod, and kingdom/national synod. Also paralleling the de facto structure of the kingdom was the decentralized focus of Huguenot ecclesiology. All ecclesiastical affairs were to be handled on as local a level as possible, with as little outside interference as possible. Only matters of general interest were to be brought before a synod, plus appeals of disciplinary decisions and, to some extent, cases involving pastoral selection, oversight, and discipline. As in the kingdom, the province was effectively the most important level of church government, though the national synod claimed the right to overrule provincial decisions in the name of unity. Even legislation passed by the national synods originated in the provincial synods, whether as a result of an appeal, a question, or a straightforward proposal of a new article. These issues would be debated in the national synod or sent back to the provinces for discussion and recommendations; in the latter case, the issues would often be taken up at the next national synod as an item of legislation. The decision thus represented the collective opinion of the provinces, rather than the action of an autonomous, "higher" legislative body which could dictate policy to the provincial synods and local churches. Over time, the national synod passed more and more decisions which affected colloquies and local churches, partly as an inevitable result of the growing body of judicial and legislative action of the national synods, partly from a gradually increasing centralization of the administration of the churches. Nonetheless, these decisions never truly compromised the independence of the lower-level assemblies, since the vast majority of their work was unaffected by these actions.

Developing a unified system of collective government was a challenge due to lack of magisterial support and the fiercely defended independence of individual churches; attempting to develop a consistent form of local church government was even more of a challenge. The diaconate provides a good case study of the kinds of problems the churches faced. According to Bucer and Calvin, deacons were to be responsible for the charitable work of the churches; in Catholicism and in some Protestant areas, however, the diaconate was a stepping stone to the priesthood or the pastorate. In France, the two models of the diaconate blended together: in addition to their charitable responsibilities, deacons—particularly those planning on entering the pastoral ministry—were given liturgical and catechetical duties; in some places, the deacon was explicitly a *proposant,* a candidate for the pastoral ministry. Deacons were also given de facto disciplinary and administrative responsibilities as members of the consistory. Eventually, the inclusion of deacons on the consistory blurred the distinction between elders and deacons, leading to the eventual absorption of the diaconate by the elders. The neat Calvinist distinction of offices included in the Gallican Confession and the Discipline increasingly became a legal fiction as one or two of the elders in each church took over the charitable responsibilities of the deacons. The diaconate as defined in the Confession essentially disappeared from the French Reformed churches.

Although the Gallican Confession and the Discipline were written to provide a unifying doctrinal and organizational structure for French Protestants, they were not a complete success. In terms of doctrine, there was a sizeable minority of Protestants within the kingdom who were not happy with Calvinism. Many of these were the Nicodemites or Libertines condemned by Calvin and by the national synods. A still larger number of churches especially those located in noble households—accepted Calvinist doctrine but effectively opted out of the Discipline. The relationship between the older, primarily urban-based churches which formed the core of the *Eglises réformées* and the churches of the rural nobility has yet to be studied in detail, largely because scholars have often assumed either that the noble churches participated fully in the life of the French Reformed churches, or that the church simply followed the lead of the nobility who provided the political and military leadership for the Huguenots. These assumptions are not surprising: the Protestant nobility generally accepted Calvinism, or at the least had Calvinist pastors in their households; many prominent Protestant nobles participated in the Synod of La Rochelle in 1571; Beza had close contacts with both the nobility and the French Reformed churches and even moderated the eighth national synod (Nîmes, 1572); and the nobility and the churches generally shared a common concern about social discipline and control of morals. Yet the nobles steadfastly refused to establish consistories in their churches, and virtually never sent their pastors to synods; representatives of the churches were rarely invited to participate in Huguenot political assemblies or Estates except for pronouncing the invocations, public prayers, and benedictions; there were tensions over magisterial representation in synods, over use of financial resources, and over other issues of public policy. In general, it seems that the nobility needed the *Eglises réformées* to provide a clear de jure institutional structure in dealings with the monarchy, but adopted a de facto congregationalist polity for their churches and set their own political and military direction without giving the synods a second thought. For their part, the churches accepted the leading role of the nobility and tied their fortunes to those of the Huguenot Party, yet never succeeded either in co-opting the noble house churches into their institutional structures or in influencing Party policy to any great extent.

Given the hierarchical nature of sixteenth-century French society, it was perhaps inevitable that the nobility would refuse to establish consistories in which pastors in their employ and other commoners could sit in judgment over the morals of the nobles themselves. Similarly, they would be unlikely to support synodical authority: what right did these assemblies of their social inferiors have to tell them how to run churches in their own households? In addition to these objections, synodical government raised another important issue in the context of a monarchy. The type of synodical government that developed in France was based on representation: churches were governed by a council (the consistory), which sent representatives to other councils covering larger geographic areas (the colloquy and the provincial synod), and the provincial synod sent representatives to the national synod. In other words, in the Aristotelian political theory accepted during the period, the French Reformed Church had a republican form of government. This system may have developed of necessity out of the peculiar conditions from which the French Reformed churches emerged, particularly the lack of magisterial support and the independence of the local churches which followed from this, but this does not mean it was well suited to the political realities of the kingdom. From the perspective of the monarchy, the type of nonepiscopal synodical government adopted by the French Reformed churches was inherently subversive.

In the sixteenth century, church government and state government almost inevitably paralleled each other. Principalities, whether Catholic or Protestant, tended to have episcopal church structures since both were manifestations of Aristotle's monarchical form of government. Protestant city republics in South Germany and Switzerland tended to adopt a conciliar style of church government in keeping with the representative nature of their secular governments; although Catholic city republics had churches headed by bishops, the canons of the cathedral often functioned like a governing council and had a great deal of clout in the city, much like the members of the civil administration's small council. Problems arose when one attempted to mix a civil government based on one of Aristotle's forms of government with a church government based on another. Thus Berne rejected as tyranny and "episcopacy" any form of church government which placed ecclesiastical authority in the hands of a single person: Berne was a republic, and episcopacies were essentially monarchical. From the other direction,

James I of England responded to calls from some Puritan leaders to abolish bishops and to establish a Presbyterian Church of England with the words, "No bishops, no king." Eliminating episcopacy was seen as tantamount to eliminating the monarchy. It is thus not surprising that French Catholics accused the Huguenots of being republicans, a charge which the Huguenots vehemently denied. Indeed, after the Edict of Nantes, the Huguenots were often among the most ardent supporters of the crown in the mistaken hope that their loyalty would earn them the right to live in peace within the kingdom. Exploring this issue in detail is impossible here; suffice it to say that in the context of sixteenth-century France, the type of synodical government the Huguenots adopted may well have created irreconcilable differences between the French Reformed churches and both the nobility and the monarchy, including even the sympathetic Henri IV.

Though synodical government may have contributed to the problems the Huguenots faced in France, it had greater success elsewhere. It spread very quickly into the Low Countries, so that even in the midst of their rebellion against Spain the Dutch Reformed Church adopted a synodical form of government. Of course, the rebellion itself had to contend with highly independent provinces that actively resisted any type of central authority; as a result, the Dutch established a republic in the form of a confederation of largely autonomous provinces. Under these circumstances, the "republican" synodical government fit the political climate admirably. Later in the century, the kingdom of Scotland would adopt a form of church government based on the French model. The development of polity in the Scotskirk is a quite complex and contentious issue among historians. Some historians of the Scotskirk believe that the final Book of Discipline developed from purely indigenous factors and deny any connection with the French Reformed churches. Given the fact that the Discipline was in effect for decades before the Scotskirk developed its mature structure, and given the well-documented contacts between France and Scotland in the period, this seems unlikely. The key step in the process was the emergence of the presbytery, corresponding roughly to the colloquy in France. The presbyteries were dominated by the lairds, who were engaged in a never-ending struggle against any attempt by the monarchy to establish effective control of the kingdom. In this context, the presbytery seems to have been part of a deliberately decentralized approach to church government designed to weaken the monarchy by strengthening the position of the lairds. The effect of this was a more successful accommodation to the realities of the sixteenth century's hierarchical view of society than had occurred among the French Protestants: church government moved away from the republican principle and toward an aristocracy, a move which was essentially impossible in France given the division between the largely nonaristocratic Protestants of the French Reformed churches and the noble house churches.

The transmutation of synodical polity from an unacknowledged republicanism in France to a tool to reinforce the lairds in Scotland highlights the twin themes of this study. On the one hand, the French Reformed churches developed in the context of international Protestantism, and particularly Reformed Protestantism. Geneva was clearly the most important influence on the churches, but Strasbourg and Berne also made important contributions; the churches were concerned about keeping in the good graces of Zurich; they gave theological advice to the Church of England; they would even be involved later on with ecumenical dialogues with German Protestant states. But these contacts and influences were inevitably shaped by local experience. Legal and political factors, existing practices within the churches, the changing social composition of Protestantism, and a host of other elements all influenced the reception of ideas and institutions from outside of France. Local church structure, which could have been adopted in a fairly straightforward manner from Geneva, underwent important modifications as it interacted with conditions on the ground. Collective government was transformed even more, largely because of the antihierarchical focus of French Protestantism and the lack of magisterial support for the Huguenots. Although developed as an adaptation of Reformed principles and models from Berne and Geneva to the peculiar conditions in France, the system proved remarkably durable, providing a model that was itself accommodated to very different conditions in other Calvinist churches in Western Europe.

The adaptation of church structures to fit local needs was in keeping with Calvin's ecclesiology. Calvin, in his *Institutes of the Christian Religion* (IV. vii. 15), argued that the Bible provided principles for church government and fairly specific guidance for local church officers, but allowed the details of institutional structure to be accommodated to local circumstances. In other words, contrary to many discussions of the Reformation, Calvin's genuine organizational genius was not solely responsible for the development of the polities of the Reformed churches; rather, Calvin created a climate which encouraged institutionalization but left considerable freedom for the churches to organize themselves in the ways best suited to their particular circumstances. That the Huguenots created such a church order is not surprising. What is surprising is that this ecclesiastical structure, born amid persecution and war, should prove so useful to the other national Reformed churches of Western Europe.

Selected Bibliography

MANUSCRIPTS

Archive d'Etat de Genève
Registres du Consistoire, vol. 19. Microfilm copy in the H.H. Meeter Center for Calvin
Studies, Calvin College, Grand Rapids, Michigan.

Bibliothèque de l'Arsenal, Paris
Items are listed by number, folio, and description.

3847	13–76	"Fragments du quelques synodes." Mislabeled and incorrectly dated. The most relevant documents for this study include a fragment of the Discipline of 1571 (art. 1b of "Des Delinquents" to the end of the Discipline); extract from the national synod of La Rochelle (1571); "La manière de l'imposition des mains observée ordinairement es eglises de France en l'election des ministres"; synode national de La Rochelle, 1571, "faits particuliers" (dated).
	145–97	"Police et Discipline Ecclésiastique des Eglises Réformées ce Isles de Gerzé, Guernezé, Serk et Origui Arrestée et conclue celon commun accord par Messieurs les Gouverners desdittes Isles, et les Ministres et Anciens assemblés au Synode tenu à Guernezé au nom de toutes lesdittes Esglises le 28 jour du mois de Juin l'an 1576." Possibly an autograph copy.
	199–205	"Aphorismes touchant les charges ecclesiastique et l'exercise d'icelluy." Autograph copy.
4108		Articles of the first 22 synodes nationaux (i.e., to Charenton, 1623).
5411 t. 2		"Histoire des Assemblées generales, Consistoires, Colloques, Sinodes tant Provinciaux que Nationnaux et cercles de ceux de la Religion p.r. en France." Includes list of churches. Chap. 7: "forme en laquelle on assemble au Bas Languedoc, en Synode Provincial Qui est ordinairement au Mois de May."

Bibliothèque de la Société de l'Histoire du Protestantisme français, Paris
Items are listed by number and description.

23	Acts of the national synods copied by Pierre Ferry in the seventeenth century.
57	Acts of the national synods.
174	Discipline of 1571.

331	Acts of the national synods.
440	Pithou, Nicolas. *L'Histoire ecclésiastique de l'Eglise réformée de la ville de Troyes.*
566, vol.s 1–2	Provincial synods, *classes,* and colloquies of Bas Languedoc. Copied in the nineteenth century from manuscripts in the Bibliothèque Nationale, the Bibliothèque Publique et Universitaire de Genève, and from the archives of the consistory of the Reformed church of Nîmes by Auzière.
570, vol. 1	Provincial synods, *classes,* and colloquies of Haut Languedoc. Copied in the nineteenth century from manuscripts in the Archive Nationale and the Bibliothèque Publique et Universitaire de Genève by Auzière.
596	"Lettres B.P.U. Genève et pièces diverses concernant les E.R. Copies et extraits." Copied by Auzière in 1877.
765, vol. 4	MS Paul Ferry 26. Second dossier includes the *faits particuliers* of La Rochelle, 1571, the acts of the national synod of Nîmes, 1572, and "Question touchant la Discipline Ecclésiastique en troys points, scavoir la decision de la doctrine et discipline, collection et depposition des ministres, diacres, anciens, l'excommunication des freres et absolution, addressée au prof. Louis Capel" (autograph copy).

Bibliothèque Mazarine, Paris
Items are listed by number and description.

2601	Acts of the national synods.
2616	Acts of the national synods.

Bibliothèque Municipale, Grenoble

1949	*Discipline ecclésiastique* (1562). Best known copy. References are taken from a transcription by B. Roussel.

Bibliothèque Municipale, Le Mans

B66 ter.	*Discipline ecclésiastique* (1562).

Bibliothèque Nationale de France, Paris
Items are listed by font, number, and description.

Dupuy	698	Pithou, Nicolas. *L'Histoire ecclésiastique de l'Eglise réformée de la ville de Troyes.*
fr.	1926	Description in catalog says first 17 national synods; though it actually includes only 16. Also includes *Discipline Ecclésiastique* 1572 (dated 1571 on the MS).
	8669	"Synodes Provinciaux de Bas Languedoc 1572–1594" (autograph).
	13953	Catalog says XVIIe siècle; documents come from Paris, 1565. Includes *Discipline ecclésiastique* (1563); synode national de Poi-

tiers (1561), "faits particuliers"; "Memoires dresses en l'assemblee des ministres de Lion"; synode national de Lyon (1563), "faits particuliers"; "Articles arrestez en la conference generalle a Paris le vingt cinquiesme jour de decembre 1565."

| | 23331 | *Discipline ecclésiastique* of 1565. References to the text come from a transcription by G. Morinière, corrected by B. Roussel and Glenn S. Sunshine. |

na. fr. 1535   Catalog dated 1601, though it says 1603 at back.

       4026   BnF catalog dates this volume to XVIe siècle. Includes "Extract" from the national synod of La Rochelle (1571), including the complete text of the Discipline; "Extract" from the national synod of Nîmes (1572).

       7189   Acts of SN 1597–1601. Discipline of 1597 "corrected according to the synods of Montauban, Saumur, Montpellier and Gergeau." Dated 1601.

Bibliothèque Publique, Leyden

137   Contains copies of the acts of the first 22 national synods.

Bibliothèque Universitaire et Publique, Geneva

Items are listed by font, number, and description.

fr.   402   Extract of procès verbal of colloquy of Nîmes, 1561; acts of provincial synod of Montauban, 1561.

       405   *Discipline ecclésiastique* (1572).

       423   "Essai touchant les Anciens, Diacres et Conseils des Eglises de France, tiré des papiers de M. Antoine Vincent, libraire à Lyons" (1560).

Tronchin   10   *Discipline ecclésiastique* (1563). References are to a transcription by B. Roussel.

Bibliothèque Wallonne, The Hague

2324   Acts of the national synods. The 1559 synod includes two versions of the Discipline designated Wa and Wb in the notes.

Bodleian Library, Oxford

Rawlinson D638   Contains two series of the acts of the national synods, here designated Ra and Rb.

Cracow

MS Gall.   Acts of the national synods.

Library of the American Antiquarian Society, Worcester, Mass.

Unnumbered manuscripts relating to the organization of the Reformed churches in sixteenth-century France bound into a volume containing Douaren, *De sacris ecclesiae minis-*

teriis ac beneficiis (Paris, 1564), and du Pinet, *La conformité des églises réformées de France et l'église primitive en police et cérémonies* (Lyon, 1564).

Staats Archiv, Zurich

E II 437b   "Canones Synodales Gallicarum Ecclesiarum in Synodo Rupellana Conditi." Includes a copy of the 1571 Discipline.

Printed Sources

Album E. Lousse. Vol. 2. Louvain: Nauwelaerts, 1963; Paris: Béatrice-Nauwelaerts, 1963.

Armstrong, Brian G. *Calvinism and the Amyraut Heresy: Protestant Scholasticism and Humanism in Seventeenth-Century France.* Madison: University of Wisconsin Press, 1969.

———. *"Semper Reformanda:* The Case of the French Reformed Church, 1559–1620." In *Later Calvinism: International Perspectives.* Edited by W. Fred Graham. Sixteenth Century Essays & Studies 22. Kirksville, Mo.: Sixteenth Century Journal Publishers, 1994, 119–40.

Aymon, Jean. *Tous les synodes nationaux des Eglises Réformées de France.* 2 vols. The Hague: Chez Charles Delo, sur le Cingel, à l'Esperance, 1710.

Beza, Theodore. *Confession de la Foy Chrestienne, faite par Theodore de Besze, contenant la confirmation d'icelle, et la refutation des superstitions contraires: Reveue et augmentee de nouveau par luy, avec un abregé d'icelle.* [Geneva]: Conrad Badius, 1559.

———. *Correspondance de Théodore de Bèze.* Vol. 3: 1559–1561. Publiée par H. Meylan et A. Dufour. Travaux d'Humanisme et Renaissance 61. Geneva: Droz, 1963. Vol. 9: 1568. Recueillie par Hippolyte Aubert. Publiée par Henri Meylan, Alain Dufour, Claire Chimelli, et Béatrice Nicollier. Travaux d'Humanisme et Renaissance 164. Geneva: Droz, 1978.

Bossy, John. *Christianity in the West, 1400–1700.* Oxford: Oxford University Press, 1985.

Burnett, Amy Nelson. "Penance and Church Discipline in the Thought of Martin Bucer." Ph.D. diss., University of Wisconsin–Madison, 1989.

———. *The Yoke of Christ: Martin Bucer and Christian Discipline.* Sixteenth Century Essays & Studies 26. Kirksville, Mo.: Sixteenth Century Journal Publishers, 1994.

Calvin, John. *Ioannis Calvini Opera Quae Supersunt Omnia.* Edited by G. Baum, Ed. Cunitz, and E. Reuss. 59 vols. Brunswick: C. A. Schwetzke & Son, 1863–1900.

———. *Joannis Calvin Opera Selecta.* 5 vols. Edited by Petrus Barth and Guilelmus Niesel. Munich: Chr. Kaiser, 1928–1936.

———. *John Calvin: Selections from His Writings.* Edited with an introduction by John Dillenberger. Missoula, Mont.: Scholars Press, 1975.

Chrisman, Miriam Usher. *Strasbourg and the Reform: A Study in the Process of Change.* New Haven and London: Yale University Press, 1967.

Courvoisier, Jacques. *La notion d'église chez Bucer dans son développement historique.* Etudes d'histoire et de philosophie religieuses publiées par la Faculté de Théologie protestante de l'Université de Strasbourg 28. Paris: Librairie Félix Alcan, 1933.

Cramer, Frédéric Auguste. *Notes extraites des registres du Consistoire de l'Eglise de Genève, 1541–1814.* Geneva, 1853.

The Creeds of Christendom. Sixth edition. 3 vols. Edited by Philip Schaff. Revised by David S. Schaff. New York: Harper & Row, 1931. Reprint, Grand Rapids, Mich.: Baker, 1985.

Crouzet, Denis. *La Genèse de la Réforme française 1520–1560.* Regards sur l'Histoire: Histoire moderne 109. Sous la direction de Jean-Pierre Poussou. Paris: Sedes, 1996.

————. *Les Guerriers de Dieu: La Violence au Temps des Troubles de Religion (vers 1525–vers 1610).* 2 vols. Préface de Pierre Chaunu. Avant-propos de Denis Richet. Seyssel: Champ Vallon, 1990.

Davis, Natalie Zemon. *Society and Culture in Early Modern France.* Stanford: Stanford University Press, 1975.

Day, Daniel P. "Calvinism in Hungary: The theological and ecclesiastical transition to the Reformed Faith." In *Calvinism in Europe: 1540–1620.* Edited by Andrew W. Pettegrew, Alastair Duke, and Gillian Lewis. Cambridge: Cambridge University Press, 1994, 205–30.

————. "Hungary." In *The Early Reformation in Europe.* Edited by Andrew Pettegrew. Cambridge: Cambridge University Press, 1992, 49–69.

————. "Hungary"; "Synods: Synods in Eastern Europe." In *The Oxford Encyclopedia of the Reformation.* Edited by Hans J. Hillerbrand and others. New York and Oxford: Oxford University Press, 1996.

Denis, Philippe. "Viret et Morély: Les Raisons d'un Silence." *Bibliothèque d'Humanisme et Renaissance* 54 (1992): 395–409.

Denis, Philippe, and Jean Rott. *Jean Morély (ca. 1524–ca. 1594) et l'Utopie d'une Démocratie dans l'Église.* Travaux d'Humanisme et Renaissance 278. Geneva: Librairie Droz, 1993.

Diefendorf, Barbara B. *Beneath the Cross: Catholics and Huguenots in Sixteenth-Century Paris.* New York and Oxford: Oxford University Press, 1991.

Documents protestants inédits du XVIe siècle: Synode général de Poitiers 1557, synodes provinciaux de Lyon, Die, Peyraud, Montélimar et Nîmes en 1561 et 1562, assemblée des Etats du Dauphiné de 1563, etc. Edited by E. Arnaud. Paris: Grassart, 1872.

The Early Reformation in Europe. Edited by Andrew Pettegree. Cambridge and New York: Cambridge University Press, 1992.

Eberhard, Winfried. "Reformation and Counterreformation in East Central Europe." In *Handbook of European History, 1400–1600.* Edited by Thomas A. Brady, Jr., Heiko A. Obermann, and James D. Tracy. Vol. 2, *Visions, Programs, and Outcomes.* Leiden: E. J. Brill, 1995, 551–84.

Elwood, Christopher. *The Body Broken: The Calvinist Doctrine of the Eucharist and the Symbolization of Power in Sixteenth-Century France.* Oxford Studies in Historical Theology. New York and Oxford: Oxford University Press, 1999.

Febvre, Lucien. *Au coeur religieux du XVIe siècle.* Second edition. Paris: SEVPEN, 1968.

Félice, Guillaume de. *Histoire des synodes nationaux des Eglises Réformées de France.* Paris: Grassart, 1864.

————. *History of the Protestants of France from the Commencement of the Reformation to the Present Time.* Translated by Henry Lobdell. New York: Edward Walker, 1851.

Félice, Paul de. *Les Protestants d'autrefois: Vie intérieure des églises, moeurs et usages.* 3 vols. Paris: Librairie Fischbacher, 1896–1902.

Selected Bibliography

Ganoczy, Alexandre. *Calvin, théologien de l'église et du ministère.* Unam Sanctam 48. Paris: Les Editions du Cerf, 1964.

Garrisson, Janine. *Les Protestants au XVIe siècle.* Paris: Fayard, 1988.

——— [Janine Garrisson-Estèbe]. *Protestants du Midi 1559–1598.* Toulouse: Edouard Privat, Editeur, 1980.

Habent sua fata libelli, or, Books Have Their Own Destiny: Essays in Honor of Robert V. Schnucker. Edited by Robin B. Barnes, Robert A. Kolb, and Paula L. Presley. Sixteenth Century Essays & Studies 50. Kirksville, Mo.: Thomas Jefferson University Press, 1998.

Hammann, Gottfried. *Entre la secte et la cité: Le projet d'Eglise du réformateur Martin Bucer (1491–1551).* Histoire et Société 3. Geneva: Labor et Fides, 1984.

Handbook of European History, 1400–1600. 2 vols. Edited by Thomas A. Brady, Jr., Heiko A. Obermann, and James D. Tracy. Leiden: E. J. Brill, 1995.

Hauser, Henri. *Etudes sur la Réforme française.* Bibliothèque d'Histoire Religieuse. Paris: Alphonse Picard et Fils, 1909.

Heller, Henry. *The Conquest of Poverty: The Calvinist Revolt in Sixteenth Century France.* Studies in Late Medieval and Reformation Thought 35. Edited by Heiko A. Obermann. Leiden: E. J. Brill, 1986.

Higman, Francis M. *Censorship and the Sorbonne: A Bibliographical Study of Books in French Censured by the Faculty of Theology of the University of Paris, 1520–1551.* Travaux d'humanisme et Renaissance 172. Geneva: Droz, 1979.

Histoire ecclésiastique des Eglises Réformées au royaume de France. Edition nouvelle avec commentaire, notice bibliographique et table des faits et des noms propres par feu G. Baum et par Ed. Cunitz. 2 vols. Les Classiques du Protestantisme Français XVIe, XVIIe et XVIIIe Siècles. Paris: Librairie Fischbacher, 1883.

Holt, Mack P. *The French Wars of Religion, 1562–1629.* New Approaches to European History. Cambridge and New York: Cambridge University Press, 1995.

Jahr, Hannelore. *Studien zur Uberlieferungsgeschichte der Confession de foi von 1559.* Beiträge zur Geschichte und Lehre der Reformierten Kirche 16. Neukirchen-Vluyn: Neukirchener Verlag des Erziehungsvereins, 1964.

Kingdon, Robert M. "Calvin's Ideas about the Diaconate: Social or Theological in Origin?" In *Piety, Politics and Ethics: Reformation Studies in Honor of George Wolfgang Forell.* Edited by Carter Lindberg. Kirksville, Mo.: Sixteenth Century Journal Publishers, 1984, 167–80.

———. "The Deacons of the Reformed Church in Calvin's Geneva." In *Mélanges d'histoire du XVIe siècle offerts à Henri Meylan.* Travaux d'Humanisme et Renaissance 110. Geneva: Droz, 1970, 81–90.

———. *Geneva and the Coming of the Wars of Religion in France 1555–1563.* Geneva: Librairie E. Droz, 1956.

———. *Geneva and the Consolidation of French Protestantism 1564–1572: A Contribution to the History of Congregationalism, Presbyterianism, and Calvinist Resistance Theory.* Madison: University of Wisconsin Press, 1967.

———. "The Geneva Consistory as Established by John Calvin." *On the Way* 7.2 (Autumn, 1990): 30–44.

Knecht, R. J. *The French Wars of Religion 1559–1598.* Seminar Studies in History. London and New York: Longman, 1989.

Köhler, Walther. *Zürcher Ehegericht und Genfer Konsistorium.* 2 vols. Quellen und Abhandlungen zur Schweizerischen Reformationsgeschichte 7, 10. Leipzig: Heinsius, 1932–1942.

Labrousse, Elisabeth. "L'Eglise réformée du Carla en 1672–3." *Bulletin de la Société de l'Histoire du Protestantisme français* 106 (1960): 22–53, 191–231; 107 (1961): 223–72.

La Place, Pierre. *Commentaires de l'Estat de la religion et republique soubs les rois Henry et François seconds et Charles neufviesme* (1565). Edited by J. A. C. Buchon. Paris, 1836.

Lasco, John à. *Toute la forme et maniere du ministere ecclesiastique, en l'eglise des estrangers, dressée a Londres en Angleterre, par le prince tresfidele dudit pays, le Roy Edouard VI de ce nom: L'an apres l'incarnation de Christ 1550 avec le previlege de sa Majesté a lafin du livre.* Translated from Latin to French by Giles Ctematius [E. van der Erve]. [Emden]: Giles Ctematius [E. van der Erve], 1556.

[Lasco, John à, and Valerin Poullain]. *L'ordre des prieres et ministere ecclesiastique, avec la forme de penitence pub. et certaines prieres de l'Eglise de Londres et la confession de foy de l'Eglise de Glastonbury en Somerset.* London: [S. Mierdman?], 1552.

Later Calvinism: International Perspectives. Edited by W. Fred Graham. Sixteenth Century Essays & Studies 22. Kirksville, Mo.: Sixteenth Century Journal Publishers, 1994.

Lechler, G. V. *Geschichte der Presbyterial und Synodalverfassung seit der Reformation.* Leiden: D. Noothoven Van Goor, 1854.

Léonard, Emile G. *Histoire générale du Protestantisme.* Vol. 2: *L'Etablissement (1564–1700).* Paris: Presses Universitaires de France, 1961.

———. *A History of Protestantism.* Edited by H. H. Rowley. Translated by R. M. Bethell. Vol. 2, *The Establishment.* London: Nelson, 1967.

Le Noir, Philippe. *Histoire ecclésiastique de Bretagne depuis la Réformation jusqu'à l'Édit de Nantes.* Edited by B. Vaurigaud. Paris: Grassart; Nantes: Guéraud, 1851.

Le Roy Ladurie, Emmanuel. *Les paysans de Languedoc.* Paris: SEVPEN, 1966.

Major, J. Russell. *Representative Government in Early Modern France.* Studies presented to The International Commission for the History of Representative and Parliamentary Institutions 63. New Haven and London: Yale University Press, 1980.

McKee, Elsie Ann. *John Calvin on the Diaconate and Liturgical Almsgiving.* Travaux d'Humanisme et Renaissance 197. Geneva: Librairie Droz, 1984.

Méjan, François. *Discipline de l'Eglise réformée de France.* Paris: Société Commerciale d'Edition et de Librairie, 1947.

Mélanges d'histoire du XVIe siècle offerts à Henri Meylan. Travaux d'Humanisme et Renaissance 110. Geneva: Droz, 1970.

Mentzer, Raymond A., Jr. "Laity and Liturgy in the French Reformed Tradition." In *The Past Has Many Voices.* Edited by Lee Palmer Wandell. Kirksville, Mo.: Truman State University Press, 2003.

———. "Organizational Endeavour and Charitable Impulse in Sixteenth-Century France: The Case of Protestant Nîmes." *French History* 5 (1991): 1–29.

———. "The Printed Catechism and Religious Instruction in the French Reformed Church." In *Habent sua fata libelli, or, Books Have Their Own Destiny: Essays in Honor of Robert V. Schnucker.* Edited by Robin B. Barnes, Robert A. Kolb, and Paula L. Presley. Sixteenth Century Essays & Studies 50. Kirksville, Mo.: Thomas Jefferson University Press, 1998, 93–101.

Mentzer, Raymond A., Jr., Robert M. Kingdon, and Michel Reulos. "Police de l'Eglise réformée de Bayeux 1563." *Bulletin de la Société de l'Histoire du Protestantisme français* 130 (1984): 72–81.

Meylan, Henri. "Bèze et les Italiens de Lyon (1566)." *Bibliothèque d'Humanisme et Renaissance* 14 (1952): 235–49.

Monter, William. *Judging the French Reformation: Heresy Trials by Sixteenth-Century Parlements.* Cambridge, Mass., and London: Harvard University Press, 1999.

Morély, Jean. *Traicté de la discipline et police Chrestienne.* Lyon: Ian de Tournes, 1562; Geneva: Slatkine Reprints, 1968.

Mours, Samuel. *Les Eglises réformées en France: Tableaux et cartes.* Paris: Librairie Protestante; Strasbourg: Librairie Oberlin, 1958.

———. *Le Protestantisme en France au XVIe siècle.* Paris: Librairie Protestante, 1959.

Naphy, William G. *Calvin and the Consolidation of the Genevan Reformation.* Manchester and New York: Manchester University Press; distributed in the U.S. and Canada by St. Martin's Press, 1994.

Nicholls, David J. "France." In *The Early Reformation in Europe.* Edited by Andrew Pettegree. Cambridge and New York: Cambridge University Press, 1992, 120–41.

———. "Sectarianism and the French Reformation." *Bulletin of the John Rylands Library* 70 (1988): 35–44.

———. "Social Change and Early Protestantism in France: Normandy, 1560–62." *European Studies Review* 10 (1980): 279–308.

Olson, Jeannine E. *Calvin and Social Welfare: Deacons and the "Bourse française."* Selinsgrove: Susquehanna University Press; London and Toronto, Associated University Press, 1989.

———. *One Ministry, Many Roles: Deacons and Deaconesses through the Centuries.* St. Louis: Concordia, 1992.

Pannier, Jacques. *L'Eglise Réformée de Paris sous Louis XIII.* Paris: Librairie Ancienne Honoré Champion, 1931.

———. *Les Origines de la Confession de Foi et la Discipline des Eglises Réformées de France.* Etudes d'histoire et de philosophie religieuses publiées par la Faculté de Théologie protestante de l'Université de Strasbourg 32. Paris: Librairie Félix Alcan, 1936.

"Papier et registre du Consistoire de l'église du Mans réformées selon l'Evangile 1560–61 (1561–1562 *nouveau style*)." In *Recueil de pièces inédites pour servir à l'histoire de la Réforme et de la Ligue dans le Maine.* Publiées par MM. Anjubault et H. Chardon. Le Mans: Imprimerie Ed. Monnoyer, 1867.

The Past Has Many Voices. Edited by Lee Palmer Wandell. Kirksville, Mo.: Truman State University Press, 2003.

Piety, Politics and Ethics: Reformation Studies in Honor of George Wolfgang Forell. Edited by Carter Lindberg. Kirksville, Mo.: Sixteenth Century Journal Publishers, 1984.

"Police et Discipline de l'Eglise de Saint-Lô (1563)." Annexe to Michel Reulos, "Les débuts des Communautés réformées dans l'actuel département de la Manche (Cotentin et Avranchin)." "Réforme et Contre-Réforme en Normandie." *Revue du Département de la Manche* 24, *Numéro spécial*, fascs. 93, 94, 95 (1982): 31–57.

Post, Gaines. *Studies in Medieval Legal Thought: Public Law and the State, 1100–1322.* Princeton: Princeton University Press, 1964.

Potter, David. *A History of France, 1460–1560: The Emergence of a Nation State.* New York: St. Martin's Press, 1995.

Quick, John. *Synodicon in Gallia Reformata: Or, The Acts, Decisions, Decrees, and Canons of Those Famous National Councils of the Reformed Churches in France.* 2 Vols. London: Printed for T. Parkhurst and J. Robinson, at the Three Bibles and Crown in Cheapside, and the Golden Lion in St. Paul's Churchyard, 1692.

Recueil de pièces inédites pour servir à l'histoire de la Réforme et de la Ligue dans le Maine. Publiées par MM. Anjubault et H. Chardon. Le Mans: Imprimerie Ed. Monnoyer, 1867.

Registers of the Consistory of Geneva in the Time of Calvin. Vol. 1: 1542–1544. Edited by Robert M. Kingdon, Thomas A. Lambert, and Isabella Watt, with the assistance of Jeffrey R. Watt. Translated by M. Wallace McDonald. Grand Rapids, Mich.: The H. H. Meeter Center for Calvin Studies; Grand Rapids, Mich., and Cambridge, England: Eerdmans, 2000.

Registres de la Compagnie des Pasteurs de Genève au temps de Calvin. Vol. 1: 1546–1553. Published under the direction of the Archives d'Etat de Genève by Robert M. Kingdon and J.-F. Bergier. Travaux d'Humanisme et Renaissance 55. Geneva: Librairie Droz, 1964.

Registres du Consistoire de Genève au temps de Calvin. Vol. 1 (1542–1544). Published by Thomas A. Lambert and Isabella M. Watt, under the direction of Robert M. Kingdon, with the assistance of Jeffrey R. Watt. Travaux d'Humanisme et Renaissance 305. Geneva: Droz, 1996.

Registres du Consistoire de Genève au temps de Calvin. Vol. 2 (1545–1546). Published by Thomas A. Lambert, Isabella M. Watt, and Wallace McDonald, under the direction of Robert M. Kingdon. Geneva: Droz, 2002.

Reulos, Michel. "Les débuts des Communautés réformées dans l'actuel département de la Manche (Cotentin et Avranchin)." In "Réforme et Contre-Réforme en Normandie." *Revue du Département de la Manche* 24, *Numéro spécial,* fascs. 93, 94, 95 (1982), 31–39.

———. "L'histoire de la Discipline des Eglises Réformées françaises, élément de l'histoire de la réforme en France et de l'histoire du droit ecclésiastique réformé." In *La Storia de Diritto nel Quadro delle Scienze Storiche.* Atti del Primo Congresso Internationale della Società Italiana di Storia del Diritto. Florence: Leo S. Olschki, 1966, 533–44.

———. "L'organisation des Eglises réformées françaises et le Synode de 1559." *Bulletin de la Société de l'Histoire du Protestantisme français* 105 (1959): 9–24.

———. "Quelques remarques sur les documents découverts et signalés ci-dessus." *Bulletin de la Société de l'Histoire du Protestantisme français* 130 (1984): 82–86.

———. "Synodes, assemblées politiques des Réformés français et théories des Etats." In *Album E. Lousse.* Vol. 2. Louvain: Nauwelaerts, 1963; Paris: Béatrice-Nauwelaerts, 1963, 95–111.

Roelker, Nancy Lyman. *Queen of Navarre: Jeanne d'Albret, 1528–1572.* Cambridge, Mass.: Harvard University Press, 1968.

———. "The Role of Noblewomen in the French Reformation." *Archiv für Reformationsgeschichte* 63 (1972): 168–94.

Roussel, Bernard. "'Colonies' de Genève? Les premières années de vie commune des églises réformées du royaume de France (ca. 1559–ca. 1571). *Bulletin de la Société de l'Histoire et d'Archéologie de Genève* 1996–97: 1–13.

———. "La *Discipline* des Eglises réformées de France en 1559: Un royaume sans clergé?" In *De l'Humanisme aux Lumières, Bayle et le protestantisme.* Mélanges en l'honneur d'Elisabeth Labrousse. Textes recueillis par Michelle Magdelaine, Maria-Cristina Pitassi, Ruthe Whelan et Antony McKenna. Paris: Universitas; Oxford: Voltaire Foundation, 1996, 169–91.

———. "Pierre Viret en France." *Bulletin de la Société de l'Histoire du Protestantisme français* 144 (1998): 803–40.

Schickler, F. de. *Les églises du refuge en Angleterre.* 3 vols. Paris: Librairie Fischbacher, 1892.

Schilling, Heinz. *Civic Calvinism in Northwestern Germany and the Netherlands: Sixteenth to Nineteenth Centuries.* Sixteenth Century Essays & Studies 17. Kirksville, Mo.: Sixteenth Century Journal Publishers, 1991.

La Storia de Diritto nel Quadro delle Scienze Storiche. Atti del Primo Congresso Internazionale della Società Italiana di Storia del Diritto. Florence: Leo S. Olschki, 1966.

Sunshine, Glenn S. "Discipline as a Third Mark of the Church: Three Views." *Calvin Theological Journal* 32 (1998): 469–80.

———. "French Protestantism on the Eve of St.-Bartholomew: The Ecclesiastical Discipline of the French Reformed Churches, 1571–1572." *French History* 4 (1990): 340–77.

———. "Geneva Meets Rome: The Development of the French Reformed Diaconate." *Sixteenth Century Journal* 26 (1995): 329–46.

———. "Reformed Theology and the Origins of Synodical Polity: Calvin, Beza and the Gallican Confession." In *Later Calvinism: International Perspectives.* Edited by W. Fred Graham. Sixteenth Century Essays & Studies 22. Kirksville, Mo.: Sixteenth Century Journal Publishers, 1994, 141–58.

"Un synode dès 1557? Texte intégral des 'Articles Polytiques pour l'Eglise Réformée selon le S. Evangile, fait à Poitiers, 1557.'" *Bulletin d'information de l'Eglise Réformée de France* 18.3 (October 1956): 2–4.

Vuilleumier, Henri. *Histoire de l'Eglise Réformée du Pays de Vaud sous le régime Bernois.* Vol. 1: *L'Age de la Réforme.* Lausanne: Editions la Concorde, 1927.

Wanegffelen, Thierry. *Ni Rome ni Genève: Des fidèles entre deux chaires en France au XVIe siècle.* Bibliothèque Littéraire de la Renaissance, ser. 3, vol. 36. Paris: Honoré Champion, 1997.

Index

Index